Ladies' Home
JOURNAL ®

Quick & Easy
favorites

Meredith® Consumer Marketing
Des Moines, Iowa

Ladies' Home Journal® Quick & Easy Favorites Volume 2

Meredith Corporation Consumer Marketing
Vice President, Consumer Marketing: Janet Donnelly
Consumer Product Marketing Director: Heather Sorensen
Business Director: Ron Clingman
Consumer Marketing Product Manager: Wendy Merical
Senior Production Manager: Al Rodruck

Waterbury Publications, Inc.
Editorial Director: Lisa Kingsley
Creative Director: Ken Carlson
Associate Editors: Tricia Laning, Mary Williams
Associate Design Director: Doug Samuelson
Production Assistant: Mindy Samuelson
Cover Photographer: Jason Donnelly
Cover Food Stylist: Charles Worthington
Cover Prop Stylist: Sue Mitchell
Contributing Copy Editors: Terri Fredrickson, Gretchen Kauffman
Contributing Indexer: Elizabeth T. Parson

Ladies' Home Journal® **Magazine**
Editor-in-Chief: Sally Lee
Creative Director: Jeffrey Saks
Food and Entertaining Editor: Tara Bench

Meredith Publishing Group
President: Tom Harty

Meredith Corporation
Chairman and Chief Executive Officer: Stephen M. Lacy

In Memoriam: E.T. Meredith III (1933–2003)

Pictured on the front cover:
Chipotle Bean Enchiladas (recipe on page 65)

No matter the day and whatever the season, nothing is as satisfying as sitting down to a fresh, home-cooked meal. It's a far less expensive and a more healthful alternative to eating out or hitting the drive-through—and it just feels good to know that you've made something delicious and nourishing for your family.

The fast pace of life can leave little time or energy to cook—but there's a way around that. The recipes in *Quick & Easy Favorites* were created for busy cooks who want to feed their families well. With a handful of easy-to-find ingredients, simple preparation, and short start-to-finish times, most of them can be on the table in 30 minutes or less from the time you walk in the door.

And because health is paramount to our readers, look for the ♥ icon throughout the book. This "healthy" icon means that the recipe meets the following guidelines: 10 or fewer grams of fat per serving, less than 900 milligrams of sodium per serving, and 2 or more grams of fiber per serving.

The recipes in this book may be easy to make, but there are a few things you can do to make your meal planning as efficient as possible. Take a little time on the weekend to thumb through the book and select recipes for the upcoming week. Set a menu for each night, make a grocery list, and do the shopping.

When "What's for dinner?" is the question, you can answer with confidence—and get an enthusiastic "Yum!" in response.

Contents

CHAPTER 1

Soups & Sandwiches

Italian Meatball Soup

Stuffed Green Pepper Soup

Prep: 25 minutes **Cook:** 20 minutes

  8 ounces lean ground beef
  2 14.5-ounce cans diced tomatoes with
    green peppers and onions, undrained
  3 cups water
  1 14.5-ounce can beef broth
  1 5.7-ounce package tomato basil risotto mix
  ¾ cup chopped green sweet pepper
    (1 medium)

1. In a large saucepan cook beef over medium heat until browned. Drain off fat.
2. Stir undrained tomatoes, the water, beef broth, risotto mix and seasoning packet, and sweet pepper into beef in saucepan. Bring to boiling; reduce heat. Simmer, covered, about 20 minutes or until rice is tender.

MAKES 6 SERVINGS.

Per serving: 245 cal., 6 g total fat (2 g sat. fat), 23 mg chol., 990 mg sodium, 33 g carbo., 2 g fiber, 11 g pro.

Vegetable-Beef Soup

Prep: 5 minutes **Cook:** 1 hour 35 minutes

  1 tablespoon vegetable oil
  1 pound beef stew meat or boneless beef
    chuck roast, cut into ¾-inch cubes
  3 14.5-ounce cans beef broth
  1 14.5-ounce can diced tomatoes with basil,
    oregano, and garlic, undrained
  1 16-ounce package frozen broccoli, green
    beans, mushrooms, onions, and red sweet
    pepper

1. In a Dutch oven heat oil over medium-high heat. Add half of the beef; cook until browned. Remove beef; cook remaining beef (add additional oil if necessary).
2. Return all beef to Dutch oven. Stir in broth and undrained tomatoes. Bring to boiling; reduce heat. Simmer, covered, for 1½ to 1¾ hours or until beef is tender.
3. Stir in vegetables. Return to boiling; reduce heat. Simmer, covered, about 5 minutes more or just until vegetables are tender. **MAKES 6 SERVINGS.**

Per serving: 179 cal., 6 g total fat (2 g sat. fat), 45 mg chol., 1,095 mg sodium, 11 g carbo., 2 g fiber, 20 g pro.

Italian Meatball Soup

Prep: 15 minutes **Cook:** 10 minutes

  1 14.5-ounce can diced tomatoes with
    onion and garlic, undrained
  1 14.5-ounce can beef broth
 1½ cups water
  ½ teaspoon Italian seasoning, crushed
  ½ of a 16-ounce package frozen Italian-style
    cooked meatballs
  ½ cup small dried pasta (such as orzo,
    tripolini, ditalini, or stellini)
  1 cup frozen mixed vegetables
    Finely shredded Parmesan cheese

1. In a large saucepan stir together undrained tomatoes, beef broth, the water, and Italian seasoning. Bring mixture to boiling.
2. Add frozen meatballs, pasta, and frozen vegetables. Return to boiling; reduce heat. Simmer, covered, about 10 minutes or until pasta and vegetables are tender. Top each serving with cheese. **MAKES 4 SERVINGS.**

Per serving: 337 cal., 16 g total fat (7 g sat. fat), 42 mg chol., 1,419 mg sodium, 31 g carbo., 4 g fiber, 18 g pro.

Vegetable-Beef
Soup

Summer Stew

Start to Finish: 20 minutes

- 1 17-ounce package refrigerated cooked beef roast au jus
- 1 8-ounce package peeled fresh baby carrots, sliced
- ½ of a 16-ounce package refrigerated rosemary-and-roasted garlic-seasoned diced red-skin potatoes (about 2 cups)
- 1 14.5-ounce can diced fire-roasted tomatoes with garlic, undrained
- 2 tablespoons snipped fresh oregano

1. Pour juices from beef roast into a large saucepan; set meat aside. Add carrots and 1 cup water to pan. Bring to boiling; reduce heat. Simmer, covered, for 3 minutes. Add potatoes, undrained tomatoes, 1 tablespoon of the oregano, and 2½ cups water. Return to boiling. Simmer, covered, about 3 minutes or until vegetables are tender. Break beef into bite-size pieces. Add to stew; heat through. Season with salt.

2. Spoon stew into bowls; top with freshly ground black pepper and the remaining 1 tablespoon oregano. **MAKES 4 SERVINGS.**

Per serving: 253 cal., 9 g total fat (4 g sat. fat), 64 mg chol., 948 mg sodium, 20 g carbo., 3 g fiber, 25 g pro.

Hamburger-Vegetable Soup ♡

Prep: 20 minutes **Cook:** 10 minutes

- 1 pound lean ground beef or ground pork
- ½ cup chopped onion (1 medium)
- ½ cup chopped green sweet pepper
- 4 cups beef broth
- 1 14.5-ounce can diced tomatoes, undrained
- 1 10-ounce package frozen mixed vegetables
- ½ cup chopped, peeled potato
- ½ cup purchased shredded carrot
- 1 teaspoon dried basil, crushed
- 1 teaspoon Worcestershire sauce
- ⅛ teaspoon black pepper

1. In a large saucepan cook meat, onion, and sweet pepper over medium heat until meat is browned and onion is tender; drain off fat.

Hamburger-Vegetable Soup

2. Stir broth, undrained tomatoes, mixed vegetables, potato, carrot, basil, Worcestershire sauce, and black pepper into meat mixture. Bring to boiling; reduce heat. Simmer, covered, for 10 to 15 minutes or until vegetables are tender. **MAKES 6 SERVINGS.**

Per serving: 227 cal., 8 g total fat (3 g sat. fat), 48 mg chol., 613 mg sodium, 19 g carbo., 3 g fiber, 20 g pro.

Taco Soup

Prep: 10 minutes **Cook:** 10 minutes

- 1 pound lean ground beef
- 1 15-ounce can black beans, rinsed and drained
- 1 14.5-ounce can Mexican-style stewed tomatoes, undrained and cut up
- 1 10.75-ounce can condensed fiesta nacho cheese soup

1. In a large saucepan cook ground beef over medium heat until browned. Drain off fat.

2. Stir black beans, undrained tomatoes, cheese soup, and 2 cups water into the meat mixture in saucepan. If necessary, use a wire whisk to stir mixture until smooth. Bring to boiling; reduce heat. Simmer, covered, for 10 minutes. If desired, serve with broken *tortilla chips.* **MAKES 4 TO 6 SERVINGS.**

Per serving: 355 cal., 16 g total fat (7 g sat. fat), 78 mg chol., 1,148 mg sodium, 27 g carbo., 5 g fiber, 30 g pro.

Taco Bean Soup: Prepare as above, except omit ground beef. Stir in one 16-ounce can refried beans before cooking.

Per serving: 266 cal., 6 g total fat (2 g sat. fat), 6 mg chol., 1,646 mg sodium, 43 g carbo., 11 g fiber, 15 g pro.

Teriyaki
Beef Soup

Italian Wedding Soup

Prep: 20 minutes **Cook:** 12 minutes

1 tablespoon vegetable oil
1½ cups chopped red and/or yellow sweet
   peppers (2 medium)
½ chopped red onion or fennel
3 14.5-ounce cans chicken broth with
   roasted garlic
1 cup bottled marinara pasta sauce
1 16-ounce package frozen cooked Italian-
   style meatballs (32 bite-size meatballs)
1 cup dried mini penne pasta
3 cups packaged prewashed fresh baby
   spinach, chopped
   Shredded Italian-blend cheese

1. In a Dutch oven heat oil over medium heat. Add sweet peppers and onion; cook and stir about 5 minutes or until tender.
2. Add chicken broth and marinara sauce to sweet pepper mixture in Dutch oven; bring to boiling. Carefully stir in meatballs and pasta. Return to boiling; reduce heat. Simmer, uncovered, for 12 to 15 minutes or until pasta is tender. Stir in spinach. Sprinkle servings with shredded cheese. **MAKES 6 SERVINGS.**

Per serving: 387 cal., 23 g total fat (10 g sat. fat), 58 mg chol., 1,605 mg sodium, 25 g carbo., 5 g fiber, 19 g pro.

Quick Tip If you can't find mini penne for this soup, substitute any small pasta, such as elbow macaroni, mini shells, or ditalini—a short, fat tubular pasta.

Teriyaki Beef Soup ♡

Start to Finish: 30 minutes

8 ounces boneless beef top sirloin steak
2 teaspoons olive oil
1 large shallot, cut into thin rings
2 14.5-ounce cans lower-sodium beef broth
1 cup water
½ cup apple juice or apple cider
2 medium carrots, cut into thin bite-size
   strips (1 cup)
⅓ cup instant brown rice or quick-cooking
   barley
2 tablespoons light teriyaki sauce
1 tablespoon grated fresh ginger
3 cloves garlic, minced
¼ teaspoon crushed red pepper
2 cups coarsely chopped broccoli

1. Trim fat from steak. Cut steak into thin bite-size strips. In a large saucepan heat olive oil over medium-high heat. Add steak and shallot; cook and stir for 2 to 3 minutes or until meat is browned. Using a slotted spoon, remove beef and shallot from pan; set aside.
2. In the same saucepan combine beef broth, the water, apple juice, carrots, rice, teriyaki sauce, ginger, garlic, and crushed red pepper. Bring to boiling; reduce heat. Cover and simmer for 10 minutes.
3. Stir in broccoli and the beef mixture. Bring to boiling; reduce heat. Simmer, covered, for 3 to 5 minutes or until rice and vegetables are tender. **MAKES 5 SERVINGS.**

Per serving: 162 cal., 4 g total fat (1 g sat. fat), 28 mg chol., 481 mg sodium, 18 g carbo., 2 g fiber, 13 g pro.

Italian
Wedding
Soup

White Bean
Soup with
Sausage and
Kale

White Bean Soup with Sausage and Kale

Start to Finish: 30 minutes

- 12 ounces fresh mild Italian sausage links, sliced ½ inch thick
- ¼ cup water
- 1 tablespoon vegetable oil
- ½ cup chopped onion (1 medium)
- 1 teaspoon bottled minced garlic
- 2 15-ounce cans white kidney (cannellini) beans, rinsed and drained
- 2 14.5-ounce cans reduced-sodium chicken broth
- 1 14.5-ounce can diced tomatoes with basil, oregano, and garlic, undrained
- 4 cups coarsely chopped kale or spinach
  Black pepper

1. In a large skillet combine sausage and the water. Bring to boiling; reduce heat. Simmer, covered, about 10 minutes or until sausage is no longer pink. Uncover and cook about 5 minutes more or until sausage is browned, stirring frequently. Remove sausage with a slotted spoon; set aside.

2. Meanwhile, in a large saucepan heat oil over medium heat. Add onion and garlic; cook about 5 minutes or until tender. Stir in drained beans, broth, and undrained tomatoes. Bring to boiling; reduce heat. Simmer, covered, for 5 minutes.

3. Stir in cooked sausage and kale. Simmer, uncovered, about 3 minutes more or until kale is wilted. Season with pepper.

MAKES 5 SERVINGS.

Per serving: 394 cal., 19 g total fat (7 g sat. fat), 46 mg chol., 1,510 mg sodium, 38 g carbo., 10 g fiber, 25 g pro.

Quick Tip Look for kale with firm, deeply colored leaves and moist hardy stems. The leaves should appear fresh, unwilted, and have no signs of browning. Choose kale with smaller leaves because they will be more tender and have a milder flavor than those with large leaves.

Black Bean and Sausage Posole

Black Bean and Sausage Posole

Prep: 15 minutes **Cook:** 30 minutes

- 1 12-ounce package light bulk turkey-and-pork sausage
- 2 14.5-ounce cans reduced-sodium chicken broth
- 1 15-ounce can black beans, rinsed and drained
- 1 14.5-ounce can golden hominy, rinsed and drained
- 1 14.5-ounce can Mexican-style stewed tomatoes, undrained
- 1 cup frozen diced hash brown potatoes
- ½ cup chopped green sweet pepper
- ⅓ cup chopped onion (1 small)
- ½ teaspoon bottled minced garlic (1 clove)
- 1 teaspoon dried oregano, crushed
- ½ teaspoon chili powder

1. In a large saucepan cook the sausage until browned; drain off fat.

2. Stir in broth, drained beans, drained hominy, undrained tomatoes, hash brown potatoes, sweet pepper, onion, garlic, oregano, and chili powder. Bring to boiling; reduce heat. Simmer, covered for 30 minutes. **MAKES 6 SERVINGS.**

Per serving: 292 cal., 14 g total fat (1 g sat. fat), 45 mg chol., 1,295 mg sodium, 26 g carbo., 4 g fiber, 17 g pro.

Curried Chicken-Noodle Soup ♡

Start to Finish: 30 minutes

- 3 14.5-ounce cans reduced-sodium chicken broth
- 1 to 2 tablespoons green or red Thai curry paste
- 2 skinless, boneless chicken breast halves (about 10 ounces)
- 1 5-ounce package dried Japanese curly wheat-flour noodles or angel hair pasta
- 1½ cups chopped, peeled sweet potato (1 medium)
- ½ cup chopped tomato (1 medium)
- 1 cup unsweetened coconut milk
- ½ cup lightly packed fresh cilantro leaves

1. In a 4-quart Dutch oven combine broth and curry paste. Bring to boiling.
2. Meanwhile, slice chicken breasts crosswise into ¼-inch strips; sprinkle lightly with salt and set aside. Add noodles, sweet potato, and tomato to broth mixture. Return to boiling; reduce heat. Simmer, covered, for 2 minutes, stirring once to break up noodles. Add chicken; simmer, covered, for 2 to 3 minutes more or until chicken is tender and no longer pink. Stir in coconut milk. Remove soup from heat and sprinkle with cilantro.
MAKES 6 SERVINGS.

Per serving: 273 cal., 9 g total fat (7 g sat. fat), 27 mg chol., 690 mg sodium, 30 g carbo., 2 g fiber, 18 g pro.

Italian Chicken Orzo Soup

Start to Finish: 25 minutes

- 2 14.5-ounce cans reduced-sodium chicken broth
- 1 pound skinless, boneless chicken breast halves or thighs, cubed
- 1 14.5-ounce can diced tomatoes with basil, garlic, and oregano, undrained
- ½ cup dried orzo pasta
- 1 cup chopped zucchini
- 1 teaspoon finely shredded lemon peel
- 1 tablespoon lemon juice
   Salt and black pepper
- 4 to 6 tablespoons purchased basil pesto

1. In a large saucepan combine chicken broth, chicken, undrained tomatoes, and orzo. Bring to boiling; reduce heat. Simmer, uncovered, for 6 minutes.
2. Add zucchini, lemon peel, and lemon juice. Return to boiling; reduce heat. Simmer, uncovered, for 3 to 4 minutes or until orzo and zucchini are tender and chicken is no longer pink. Season with salt and pepper.
3. Ladle into bowls. Top with pesto.
MAKES 4 TO 6 SERVINGS.

Per serving: 371 cal., 12 g total fat (0 g sat. fat), 68 mg chol., 1,180 mg sodium, 30 g carbo., 1 g fiber, 35 g pro.

Chicken Soup with Spinach and Orzo ♡

Start to Finish: 20 minutes

- 4 14.5-ounce cans reduced-sodium chicken broth
- 1 cup dried orzo
- 12 ounces fresh asparagus spears, trimmed and bias-sliced into 1½-inch pieces
- 3 cups chopped fresh spinach, Swiss chard, or kale, or one 10-ounce package frozen chopped spinach, thawed
- 1½ cups chopped fresh tomatoes (3 medium)
- 1½ cups shredded cooked chicken (8 ounces)
- ⅓ cup cubed cooked ham
   Salt and black pepper
   Snipped fresh chives and/or parsley (optional)

1. In a covered 5- to 6-quart Dutch oven bring chicken broth to boiling. Add orzo. Return to boiling; reduce heat. Simmer, uncovered, for 6 minutes. Add asparagus; simmer about 2 minutes more or until orzo is tender and asparagus is crisp-tender.
2. Stir in spinach, tomatoes, chicken, and ham; heat through. Season with salt and pepper. If desired, sprinkle each serving with chives and/or parsley. **MAKES 6 SERVINGS.**

Per serving: 221 cal., 4 g total fat (1 g sat. fat), 35 mg chol., 837 mg sodium, 28 g carbo., 3 g fiber, 20 g pro.

All around the world, chicken soup—whether flavored with curry and coconut milk or tomatoes and pesto—is comfort in a bowl.

Tex-Mex
Cream of
Chicken
Soup

Tex-Mex Cream of Chicken Soup

Start to Finish: 30 minutes

  8 ounces uncooked ground chicken or turkey
  ¼ cup chopped onion (1 medium)
  2 cloves garlic, minced
  2 cups milk
  1 10.75-ounce can condensed cream of chicken soup
  ¾ cup chopped tomato (1 large)
  1 7-ounce can whole kernel corn with sweet peppers, drained
  1 4-ounce can diced green chiles, drained
  2 tablespoons snipped fresh cilantro or parsley
  ¼ teaspoon cayenne pepper
  1 cup shredded Monterey Jack cheese (4 ounces)
     Fresh cilantro or parsley (optional)

1. In a large saucepan or Dutch oven cook ground chicken, onion, and garlic over medium-high heat until chicken is browned and onion is tender. Drain off fat.

2. Stir in milk, soup, tomato, corn, chiles, the 2 tablespoons cilantro, and the cayenne pepper. Bring to boiling; reduce heat. Simmer, uncovered, for 5 minutes, stirring occasionally. Add cheese; cook and stir until cheese is melted. If desired, garnish servings with additional cilantro. **MAKES 4 SERVINGS.**

Per serving: 375 cal., 19 g total fat (9 g sat. fat), 68 mg chol., 1,481 mg sodium, 29 g carbo., 3 g fiber, 24 g pro.

Quick Tip If you're watching calories and fat grams, choose ground chicken or turkey made from breast meat only. If you can't find ground chicken or turkey breast in the meat department of your supermarket, ask a butcher to grind some for you. Most ground chicken or turkey is made from white and dark meat, as well as some skin. Ground turkey breast is about 3 percent fat, while regular ground turkey is about 10 percent fat.

Wild Rice-Chicken Soup

Wild Rice-Chicken Soup ♡

Start to Finish: 25 minutes

  1 6.2-ounce package quick-cooking long grain and wild rice mix
  2 14.5-ounce cans reduced-sodium chicken broth
  4 cloves garlic, minced
  1 tablespoon snipped fresh thyme or 1 teaspoon dried thyme, crushed
  4 cups chopped tomatoes (4 large)
  2 cups chopped cooked chicken (10 ounces)
  1 cup finely chopped zucchini (1 small)
  ¼ teaspoon freshly ground black pepper
  1 tablespoon Madeira or dry sherry (optional)

1. Prepare rice mix following package directions, except omit the seasoning packet and the butter.

2. Meanwhile, in a Dutch oven combine chicken broth, garlic, and dried thyme (if using); bring to boiling. Stir in tomato, chicken, zucchini, fresh thyme (if using), and pepper. Return to boiling; reduce heat. Simmer, covered, for 5 minutes. Stir in cooked rice and, if desired, Madeira. Heat through. **MAKES 8 SERVINGS.**

Per serving: 174 cal., 3 g total fat (1 g sat. fat), 31 mg chol., 311 mg sodium, 22 g carbo., 2 g fiber, 15 g pro.

Turkey Ravioli Soup

1. In a large bowl combine turkey and curry powder; toss to coat. In a large saucepan heat oil over medium-high heat; add turkey. Cook and stir about 2 minutes or until browned. Carefully stir in the water, seasoning packet from the ramen noodles, broccoli, and carrots. Cook, covered, on high heat just until boiling.

2. Break up noodles; add to soup. Cook, uncovered, for 3 minutes, stirring once or twice. Season with salt and pepper. If desired, top servings with cilantro. **MAKES 4 SERVINGS.**

Per serving: 241 cal., 8 g total fat (2 g sat. fat), 53 mg chol., 520 mg sodium, 19 g carbo., 2 g fiber, 24 g pro.

Quick Tip Curry powder is a blend of up to 20 spices that most often includes cardamom, chiles, cumin, fennel, fenugreek, cinnamon, cloves, coriander, and turmeric (which gives it the distinctive yellow color). It comes in both mild and hot varieties—choose according to your taste.

Turkey Tortilla Soup

Start to Finish: 20 minutes

    3   6-inch corn tortillas, cut into strips
    2   tablespoons vegetable oil
    1   cup purchased red or green salsa
    2   14.5-ounce cans reduced-sodium chicken
        broth
    2   cups cubed cooked turkey (10 ounces)
    1   large zucchini, coarsely chopped
        Sour cream (optional)
        Fresh cilantro leaves (optional)
        Lime wedges (optional)

1. In a large skillet cook tortilla strips in hot oil until crisp; remove with slotted spoon and drain on paper towels.

2. In a large saucepan combine salsa and broth; bring to boiling over medium-high heat. Add turkey and zucchini; heat through.

3. Ladle soup into 4 bowls; sprinkle with tortilla strips. If desired, serve with sour cream, cilantro, and lime wedges. **MAKES 4 SERVINGS.**

Per serving: 262 cal., 11 g total fat (2 g sat. fat), 53 mg chol., 920 mg sodium, 16 g carbo., 3 g fiber, 26 g pro.

Turkey Ravioli Soup ♡

Start to Finish: 25 minutes

    6   cups reduced-sodium chicken broth
    ¾   cup chopped red sweet pepper (1 medium)
    ½   cup chopped onion (1 medium)
    1½ teaspoons dried Italian seasoning,
        crushed
    1½ cups cooked turkey cut into bite-size
        pieces (about 8 ounces)
    1   9-ounce package refrigerated light cheese
        ravioli
    2   cups shredded fresh spinach
        Finely shredded Parmesan cheese
        (optional)

1. In a 6-quart Dutch oven combine chicken broth, sweet pepper, onion, and Italian seasoning. Bring to boiling; reduce heat. Simmer, covered, for 5 minutes.

2. Add turkey and ravioli to Dutch oven. Return to boiling; reduce heat. Simmer, uncovered, about 6 minutes or just until ravioli is tender. Stir in spinach. Ladle soup into 4 bowls. If desired, sprinkle each serving with Parmesan cheese. **MAKES 6 SERVINGS.**

Per serving: 246 cal., 7 g total fat (3 g sat. fat), 48 mg chol., 879 mg sodium, 24 g carbo., 2 g fiber, 22 g pro.

Curried Turkey Soup ♡

Start to Finish: 20 minutes

    12 ounces turkey breast tenderloin, cut into
        ½-inch cubes
    2   teaspoons curry powder
    1   tablespoon vegetable oil
    5   cups water
    1   3-ounce package chicken-flavor ramen
        noodles
    1   cup broccoli florets
    1   cup packaged shredded fresh carrots
        Salt and black pepper
        Fresh cilantro leaves (optional)

Turkey Tortilla
Soup

Veggie Fish
Chowder

Veggie Fish Chowder

Prep: 20 minutes **Cook:** 10 minutes

- 1 pound fresh or frozen cod, salmon, or other firm-textured fish
- 1 32-ounce carton reduced-sodium chicken broth
- 1 cup water
- 1 cup thinly sliced carrots (2 medium)
- 1 cup sugar snap peas, halved diagonally
- 1 4-ounce package (or half of a 7.2-ounce package) butter-and-herb-flavor instant mashed potatoes
- ¼ cup finely shredded Parmesan cheese

1. Thaw fish, if frozen. Rinse fish; pat dry. Cut fish into 4 pieces. Sprinkle fish lightly with black pepper; set aside. In a 4-quart saucepan bring broth and the water to boiling. Add carrots; cook, covered, for 5 minutes. Add fish and peas. Return to boiling. Reduce heat. Simmer, covered, about 3 minutes or until fish flakes easily when tested with a fork. Stir in potatoes; simmer for 2 minutes.
2. Break fish into bite-size pieces. Ladle chowder into 4 bowls. Sprinkle with Parmesan cheese. **MAKES 4 SERVINGS.**

Per serving: 269 cal., 5 g total fat (2 g sat. fat), 52 mg chol., 1,269 mg sodium, 28 g carbo., 3 g fiber, 28 g pro.

Quick Tip Flavored instant mashed potatoes act as a tasty thickener for this chowder. They're a handy item to have in your pantry because they have a long shelf life and many uses. Try them as a breading for fried foods or use them in place of bread crumbs in your favorite meat loaf recipe.

Tuna Tortellini Soup

Start to Finish: 20 minutes **Makes:** 6 servings

- 3 cups milk
- 2 10.75-ounce cans condensed cream of potato soup
- 1 cup frozen peas
- 1 teaspoon dried basil, crushed
- 1 9-ounce package refrigerated cheese tortellini
- 1 12-ounce can tuna, drained and flaked
- ⅓ cup dry white wine

Spiced Pumpkin and Shrimp Soup

1. In a large saucepan combine milk, soup, peas, and basil; bring just to boiling. Add tortellini. Simmer, uncovered, for 6 to 8 minutes or until tortellini is tender, stirring frequently to prevent sticking. Stir in tuna and wine. Heat through. **MAKES 6 SERVINGS.**

Per serving: 351 cal., 9 g total fat (4 g sat. fat), 59 mg chol., 1,267 mg sodium, 38 g carbo., 2 g fiber, 27 g pro.

Quick Tip If you're watching fat and calories, water-pack tuna is the better choice. However, tuna packed in oil has the better flavor. Either works well in this recipe.

Spiced Pumpkin and Shrimp Soup ♡

Start to Finish: 30 minutes

- 2 tablespoons butter
- 2 medium onions, sliced
- 1 cup sliced carrots (2 medium)
- 1 tablespoon snipped fresh cilantro
- 2 teaspoons grated fresh ginger
- ½ teaspoon ground allspice
- 2 cloves garlic, minced
- 1 14.5-ounce can chicken broth
- 1 15-ounce can pumpkin
- 1 cup milk
- 1 8-ounce package frozen, peeled and deveined cooked shrimp, thawed
  Plain yogurt or dairy sour cream (optional)
  Snipped fresh chives (optional)

1. In a large saucepan melt butter over medium heat. Add onions, carrots, cilantro, ginger, allspice, and garlic to hot butter. Cook, covered, for 10 to 12 minutes or until vegetables are tender, stirring once or twice.
2. Transfer vegetable mixture to a blender or food processor. Add ½ cup of the broth. Cover and blend or process until nearly smooth.
3. In the same saucepan combine pumpkin, milk, and the remaining 1¼ cups broth. Stir in vegetable mixture and shrimp; heat through. If desired, serve topped with yogurt and chives. **MAKES 4 SERVINGS.**

Per serving: 247 cal., 10 g total fat (5 g sat. fat), 134 mg chol., 537 mg sodium, 20 g carbo., 5 g fiber, 21 g pro.

Crab and Corn Chowder

Start to Finish: 15 minutes

- 1 14.75-ounce can cream-style corn
- 1 4- to 6-ounce container semisoft cheese with garlic and herbs, cut up
- 1½ cups milk
- 1 8-ounce package flake-style imitation crabmeat
- 1 cup grape tomatoes, halved
- 2 tablespoons snipped fresh parsley

1. In a large saucepan combine corn and cheese; heat and stir until cheese melts. Gradually stir in milk; cook and stir until heated through.
2. Stir in crabmeat and tomatoes. Sprinkle with parsley. **MAKES 4 SERVINGS.**

Per serving: 289 cal., 12 g total fat (8 g sat. fat), 45 mg chol., 816 mg sodium, 35 g carbo., 2 g fiber, 12 g pro.

Pepper and Basil Tortellini Soup ♡

Start to Finish: 20 minutes

- 1 14.5-ounce can Italian-style stewed tomatoes, undrained
- 1 14.5-ounce can reduced-sodium chicken broth
- 1¼ cups water
- 1 9-ounce package refrigerated three-cheese tortellini
- 1 cup chopped red and/or yellow sweet pepper (1 large)
- ⅓ cup snipped fresh basil
   Grated Parmesan cheese (optional)

1. In a large saucepan combine undrained tomatoes, chicken broth, and the water; bring to boiling. Add tortellini and sweet pepper. Return to boiling; reduce heat. Simmer, covered, about 7 minutes or until tortellini is tender. Stir in basil. If desired, serve with Parmesan cheese. **MAKES 4 SERVINGS.**

Per serving: 245 cal., 5 g total fat (2 g sat. fat), 30 mg chol., 816 mg sodium, 40 g carbo., 3 g fiber, 13 g pro.

Chilled Cucumber-Chickpea Soup

Start to Finish: 25 minutes

- 1 recipe Coriander-Paprika Spice Rub
- 8 ounces peeled and deveined cooked cocktail shrimp, chopped
- 2 medium cucumbers
- 1 15-ounce can chickpeas (garbanzo beans), rinsed and drained
- ¼ cup tahini (sesame seed paste)
- ¼ cup packed fresh mint leaves
- 2 tablespoons lemon juice
- 1 tablespoon olive oil
- 1 tablespoon honey
- 2 cloves garlic, smashed
- 1½ teaspoons ground coriander
- ¼ teaspoon cayenne pepper
- ¼ teaspoon salt
- ¼ teaspoon black pepper
- 3 cups ice cubes
- ⅓ cup cherry tomatoes, quartered
- 2 green onions, cut into 1-inch slivers

1. Prepare Coriander-Paprika Spice Rub. In a medium bowl toss shrimp with spice rub; set aside. Thinly slice enough cucumber to measure ⅓ cup; set aside. Peel, seed, and cut up remaining cucumbers.
2. In a blender combine cut-up cucumbers, chickpeas, tahini, mint, lemon juice, olive oil, honey, garlic, coriander, cayenne, salt, and black pepper. Cover; blend until smooth, scraping sides as needed.
3. Just before serving, with motor running, add ice cubes, a few at a time, through lid opening until smooth and thickened (blender will be full). Pour into 4 bowls. Top each serving with shrimp, sliced cucumber, tomatoes, and green onions. **MAKES 4 SERVINGS.**

Coriander-Paprika Spice Rub: In a small bowl combine 1 teaspoon ground coriander, ½ teaspoon paprika, ¼ teaspoon salt, and ¼ teaspoon black pepper.

Per serving: 357 cal., 14 g total fat (2 g sat. fat), 111 mg chol., 752 mg sodium, 41 g carbo., 7 g fiber, 22 g pro.

When the weather is cool, a bowl of hot soup warms the body and soul.
When the weather is hot, chilled soup keeps you cool.

Chilled Cucumber-Chickpea Soup

Tuscan Bean
Soup

Tuscan Bean Soup

Start to Finish: 20 minutes

 3 tablespoons olive oil
 1 cup packaged peeled baby carrots,
    coarsely chopped
 ⅓ cup chopped onion (1 small)
 2 15-ounce cans white kidney (cannellini)
    beans, rinsed and drained
 1 32-ounce carton reduced-sodium chicken
    broth
 2 to 3 teaspoons dried Italian seasoning,
    crushed
 1 5-ounce package fresh baby spinach
    Freshly cracked black pepper
    Cracker bread (optional)

1. In a 4-quart Dutch oven heat 1 tablespoon
of the olive oil over medium-high heat. Add
carrots and onion; cook and stir for
3 minutes. Add beans, chicken broth, and
Italian seasoning. Bring to boiling; slightly
mash beans. Reduce heat. Simmer,
uncovered, for 8 minutes, stirring occasionally.
2. Meanwhile, in a large skillet heat the
remaining 2 tablespoons olive oil over
medium-high heat. Add spinach; toss with
tongs for 1 to 2 minutes or just until wilted.
Remove from heat. Ladle soup into bowls;
top with spinach and sprinkle with pepper. If
desired, serve with cracker bread.
MAKES 4 SERVINGS.

Per serving: 254 cal., 11 g total fat (2 g sat. fat), 0 mg
chol., 919 mg sodium, 36 g carbo., 12 g fiber, 16 g pro.

Curried
Vegetable
Soup

Curried Vegetable Soup ♥

Start to Finish: 20 minutes

 3 cups cauliflower florets
 1 14-ounce can unsweetened coconut milk
 1 14.5-ounce can vegetable or chicken
    broth
 1 tablespoon curry powder
 ¼ cup chopped fresh cilantro
 2 cups frozen baby peas-vegetable blend
 ¼ teaspoon salt
    Fresh cilantro leaves (optional)
    Crushed red pepper (optional)
    Curry Pita Crisps (optional)

1. In a 6-quart Dutch oven combine
cauliflower, coconut milk, broth, curry
powder, and the ¼ cup cilantro. Bring to
boiling over high heat. Reduce heat to
medium-low. Simmer, covered, about

10 minutes or until cauliflower is tender. Stir
in frozen vegetables. Cook, uncovered, until
heated through. Stir in salt.
2. If desired, sprinkle servings with cilantro
and crushed red pepper and serve with
Curry Pita Crisps. **MAKES 4 SERVINGS.**

Curry Pita Crisps: Preheat broiler. Place
pita wedges on baking sheet. Brush with
1 tablespoon olive oil. Sprinkle with
¼ teaspoon curry powder. Broil 3 to 4 inches
from heat about 4 minutes or until golden,
turning once.

Per serving: 138 cal., 6 g total fat (4 g sat. fat), 0 mg
chol., 620 mg sodium, 19 g carbo., 4 g fiber, 3 g pro.

Quick Tip If you make this curried soup with
vegetable broth, it is not only a vegetarian but
also a vegan soup, meaning no animal
products at all.

Deli Roast
Beef
Sandwiches

Beef and Mushroom Calzones ♡

Prep: 30 minutes **Bake:** 8 minutes
Oven: 425°F

    8 ounces lean ground beef
    ½ cup sliced fresh mushrooms
    ¼ cup chopped green and/or red sweet
       pepper
    ½ cup shredded mozzarella cheese
       (2 ounces)
    ⅓ cup pizza sauce
    1 13.8-ounce package refrigerated pizza
       dough
    1 tablespoon milk
       Shredded mozzarella cheese (optional)
       Warmed pizza sauce (optional)

1. Preheat oven to 425°F.

2. In a medium skillet cook beef, mushrooms, and sweet pepper until beef is browned; drain off fat. Stir in the ½ cup mozzarella cheese and the ⅓ cup pizza sauce.

3. Unroll pizza dough. Roll or stretch dough into a 10×15-inch rectangle. Cut dough into six 5-inch squares. Divide the beef mixture evenly over one half of each square. Brush dough edges with water. Lift a corner and stretch dough over beef mixture to opposite corner. Seal the edges by pressing with the tines of a fork.

4. Place calzones on a greased baking sheet. Prick tops with a fork to allow steam to escape. Brush with milk. If desired, sprinkle with mozzarella cheese. Bake for 8 to 10 minutes or until golden brown. Let stand for 5 minutes before serving. If desired, serve with warmed pizza sauce. **MAKES 6 SERVINGS.**

Per serving: 235 cal., 8 g total fat (3 g sat. fat), 31 mg chol., 358 mg sodium, 26 g carbo., 1 g fiber, 13 g pro.

Deli Roast Beef Sandwiches ♡

Start to Finish: 10 minutes

    8 ounces thinly sliced deli roast beef
    4 slices pumpernickel, rye, or whole wheat
       bread
    ½ cup purchased coleslaw
       Herb pepper seasoning

1. Arrange roast beef on 2 of the bread slices. Spread coleslaw over roast beef; sprinkle with herb pepper seasoning. Top with the remaining 2 bread slices. . **MAKES 2 SANDWICHES.**

Per sandwich: 369 cal., 8 g total fat (2 g sat. fat), 80 mg chol., 507 mg sodium, 34 g carbo., 5 g fiber, 39 g pro.

Beef and Mushroom Calzones

Chipotle
Brisket
Sandwiches

Chipotle Brisket Sandwiches

Start to Finish: 15 minutes

1   17-ounce package refrigerated cooked, seasoned, and sliced beef brisket with barbecue sauce
1   to 2 canned chipotle chile peppers in adobo sauce, chopped*
½   of a 16-ounce package shredded cabbage with carrot (coleslaw mix) (about 4 cups)
⅓   cup bottled coleslaw dressing
6   kaiser rolls, split and toasted

1. In a large saucepan combine the beef brisket with barbecue sauce and the chipotle peppers. Cook and stir about 5 minutes or until heated through.
2. Meanwhile, in a large bowl combine shredded cabbage mixture and coleslaw dressing; toss to coat.
3. To serve, spoon beef mixture onto roll bottoms. Top with coleslaw mixture. Add roll tops. **MAKES 6 SERVINGS.**

Per serving: 414 cal., 18 g total fat (5 g sat. fat), 39 mg chol., 1,085 mg sodium, 47 g carbo., 2 g fiber, 16 g pro.

*Note: Because chile peppers contain volatile oils that can burn your skin and eyes, avoid direct contact with them as much as possible. When working with chile peppers, wear plastic or rubber gloves. If your bare hands touch the chile peppers, wash your hands and nails well with soap and water.

Roast Beef Sandwiches with Horseradish Slaw

Roast Beef Sandwiches with Horseradish Slaw

Start to Finish: 15 minutes

⅓   cup light sour cream
2   tablespoons snipped fresh chives
2   tablespoons spicy brown mustard
1   teaspoon prepared horseradish
½   teaspoon sugar
¼   teaspoon salt
1   cup packaged shredded broccoli with carrots (broccoli slaw mix)
8   ounces thinly sliced cooked roast beef
8   ½-inch slices sourdough bread, toasted

1. In a medium bowl combine sour cream, chives, mustard, horseradish, sugar, and salt. Add shredded broccoli; toss to coat.
2. To assemble, divide roast beef among 4 of the bread slices. Top with broccoli mixture. Top with remaining bread slices. If desired, secure sandwiches with wooden toothpicks. **MAKES 4 SANDWICHES.**

Per sandwich: 315 cal., 11 g total fat (4 g sat. fat), 53 mg chol., 630 mg sodium, 30 g carbo., 2 g fiber, 23 g pro.

Garlic-Mustard
Steak
Sandwiches

Beef and Red Onion Sandwiches

Start to Finish: 20 minutes

    8 sliced dried tomatoes or dried tomato
       halves (not oil packed)
    2 tablespoons olive oil
   12 ounces beef sirloin steak, ¾ inch thick
    1 small red onion, thinly sliced
       Salt and black pepper
    4 square bagels or ciabatta rolls, split
    ¼ cup mayonnaise or salad dressing
    1 cup mixed salad greens

1. Preheat broiler. Place dried tomatoes in a small bowl; cover with water. Microwave on high for 1 minute. Meanwhile, brush olive oil on steak and onion; arrange on the unheated rack of a broiler pan. Broil 3 to 4 inches from heat for 12 to 16 minutes or until desired doneness, turning once halfway through broiling. Thinly slice steak across the grain into bite-size pieces.
2. Meanwhile, drain tomatoes. Lightly spread split sides of rolls with mayonnaise. Layer rolls with steak, onion, drained tomatoes, and salad greens. **MAKES 4 SANDWICHES.**

Per sandwich: 451 cal., 22 g total fat (4 g sat. fat), 51 mg chol., 681 mg sodium, 40 g carbo., 3 g fiber, 26 g pro.

Garlic-Mustard Steak Sandwiches

Prep: 15 minutes **Broil:** 16 minutes

    4 to 6 hoagie rolls, split
    2 tablespoons honey mustard
    ½ teaspoon dried marjoram or thyme, crushed
    1 clove garlic, minced
    ¼ teaspoon coarsely ground black pepper
    1 1- to 1½-pound beef flank steak
    1 large red onion, sliced ½ inch thick
    4 to 6 slices Swiss cheese
       Honey mustard (optional)

1. Preheat broiler. Place rolls, cut sides up, on the unheated rack of a broiler pan. Broil 4 to 5 inches from heat for 1 to 2 minutes or until toasted. Set aside.
2. In a bowl stir together the 2 tablespoons mustard, marjoram, garlic, and pepper. Trim fat from the steak. Score steak on both sides by making shallow diagonal cuts at 1-inch intervals in a diamond pattern. Brush both sides of steak with mustard mixture.
3. Place steak on the unheated rack of a broiler pan. Place onion slices beside steak. Broil 4 to 5 inches from heat for 15 to 18 minutes or until steak is medium (160°F) and onion is tender, turning steak and onion slices once halfway through broiling.
4. Thinly slice steak at an angle across the grain. Separate onion slices into rings. Arrange steak strips, onion rings, and cheese on roll bottoms. Broil about 1 minute or until cheese begins to melt. Add roll tops. If desired, pass additional mustard.
MAKES 4 TO 6 SANDWICHES.

Per sandwich: 685 cal., 22 g total fat (9 g sat. fat), 65 mg chol., 844 mg sodium, 78 g carbo., 4 g fiber, 43 g pro.

Beef and Tapenade Open-Face Sandwiches

Start to Finish: 10 minutes

    ⅓ cup light mayonnaise or salad dressing
    1 teaspoon Dijon or yellow mustard
    4 slices crusty Italian country or sourdough
       bread
    ¼ cup purchased olive tapenade
   12 ounces thinly sliced deli roast beef
    2 small tomatoes, thinly sliced
    1 cup fresh baby spinach

1. In small bowl combine mayonnaise and mustard. Lightly spread on 1 side of each bread slice. Spread with tapenade. Top with roast beef, tomato slices, and spinach.
MAKES 4 SANDWICHES.

Per sandwich: 362 cal., 19 g total fat (4 g sat. fat), 46 mg chol., 1,681 mg sodium, 21 g carbo., 2 g fiber, 21 g pro.

Beef and Red Onion Sandwiches

Meatballs and Greens on Ciabatta

Meatballs and Greens on Ciabatta

Start to Finish: 15 minutes

⅓ cup olive oil
¼ cup fresh lemon juice
1 bunch Italian (flat-leaf) parsley, large stems removed
2 cloves garlic
   Salt and black pepper
1 16- to 18-ounce package frozen cooked Italian-style meatballs, thawed
6 ciabatta rolls, split and toasted
½ of a small head romaine, cut up or torn

1. In a food processor or blender combine olive oil, lemon juice, parsley, and garlic. Cover and process or blend until finely chopped. Season with salt and pepper.
2. Transfer parsley mixture to a large skillet; add meatballs. Cook, covered, over medium heat, until heated through, stirring and spooning sauce over meatballs occasionally.
3. Place 1 ciabatta roll, toasted side up, on each plate. Top with romaine. Remove meatballs from skillet with a slotted spoon; place on romaine. Drizzle with warm parsley mixture. **MAKES 6 SANDWICHES.**

Per sandwich: 534 cal., 31 g total fat (10 g sat. fat), 49 mg chol., 1,002 mg sodium, 43 g carbo., 6 g fiber, 20 g pro.

Meatball and Pineapple Hoagie

Meatball and Pineapple Hoagies

Start to Finish: 20 minutes

2 tablespoons olive oil
1 large sweet onion, halved and sliced
1 16-ounce package frozen cooked meatballs, thawed
1 cup peeled, cored pineapple, chopped (about ¼ of a pineapple)
1 cup desired chutney
¼ teaspoon crushed red pepper
4 hoagie buns, split and toasted

1. In a large skillet heat olive oil over medium heat. Add onion; cook about 8 minutes or until tender, stirring frequently. Stir in meatballs, pineapple, chutney, and crushed red pepper. Cover skillet; cook about 3 minutes more or until heated through, stirring once. Serve in buns. **MAKES 4 SANDWICHES.**

Per sandwich: 878 cal., 40 g total fat (13 g sat. fat), 40 mg chol., 1,403 mg sodium, 109 g carbo., 6 g fiber, 24 g pro.

Bacon and Egg
Salad
Sandwiches

Pecan-Crusted Sliders

Start to Finish: 25 minutes

12 ounces pork tenderloin, sliced crosswise
    into 8 pieces
 1 egg
 2 tablespoons honey
 1 cup finely chopped pecans
 1 teaspoon salt
 ½ teaspoon black pepper
 2 tablespoons vegetable oil
 1 small green apple
1½ cups packaged shredded broccoli
    (broccoli slaw mix)
 ¼ cup mayonnaise or salad dressing
 8 small buns or dinner rolls, split
    Dijon mustard (optional)

1. With the palm of your hand, flatten pork slices into ¼-inch thickness. In a shallow dish whisk together egg and 1 tablespoon of the honey. In another shallow dish combine pecans, salt, and pepper. Dip pork into egg mixture, then into nut mixture, pressing to coat.

2. In an extra-large skillet heat oil over medium-high heat. Cook pork in hot oil for 2 to 3 minutes per side or until golden and slightly pink in center.

3. Meanwhile, for slaw, quarter apple; remove core and seeds. Thinly slice apple. In a medium bowl combine apple, shredded broccoli, mayonnaise, and the remaining 1 tablespoon honey. Season with salt and pepper. For sliders, place pork in buns; top with slaw. If desired, pass mustard.

MAKES 4 SERVINGS (2 SLIDERS EACH).

Per serving (2 sliders): 694 cal., 44 g total fat (6 g sat. fat), 115 mg chol., 1,029 mg sodium, 49 g carbo., 5 g fiber, 29 g pro.

Bacon and Egg Salad Sandwiches

Start to Finish: 20 minutes

 6 eggs
 8 slices applewood-smoked bacon
 8 slices challah bread
 ½ cup mayonnaise or salad dressing
 2 teaspoons yellow mustard
12 to 16 basil leaves
 ½ of an English cucumber, chopped

1. Place eggs in a medium saucepan; cover with water. Bring to boiling over high heat; cover and remove from heat. After 6 minutes, remove 2 eggs. Rinse with cold water; peel and set aside. Let remaining eggs stand in hot water for 4 minutes more. Drain; rinse with cold water. Peel and coarsely chop the 10-minute eggs.

2. Meanwhile, in an extra-large skillet cook bacon until crisp; drain. Discard drippings; wipe skillet with a paper towel. Lightly toast both sides of bread slices in skillet. In a small bowl combine mayonnaise and mustard.

3. Top 4 of the bread slices with basil leaves, chopped egg, and cucumber. Halve the remaining 2 eggs and place one half on each sandwich. Top with mayonnaise mixture, bacon, and remaining bread slices.

MAKES 4 SANDWICHES.

Per sandwich: 614 cal., 40 g total fat (10 g sat. fat), 391 mg chol., 765 mg sodium, 38 g carbo., 2 g fiber, 22 g pro.

Pecan-Crusted
Sliders

Ham Calzones ♡

Prep: 20 minutes **Bake:** 20 minutes
Oven: 375°F

- 4 cups torn fresh spinach with stems removed
- 1 16-ounce loaf frozen white bread dough, thawed
- 3 cloves garlic, minced
- 1 teaspoon dried Italian seasoning, crushed
- 1 cup ricotta cheese or cottage cheese, drained
- 4 ounces thinly sliced ham, chopped (1 cup)
- 4 ounces thinly sliced Swiss cheese
- 1 cup tomato and herb pasta sauce, heated

1. Preheat oven to 375°F. In a large bowl pour enough boiling water over spinach to cover. Let stand for 5 minutes. Drain well, squeezing out liquid; set aside.

2. Divide bread dough into 4 equal portions. On lightly floured surface roll each portion of dough into 7-inch circle. Brush circles with garlic and Italian seasoning. Divide ricotta cheese evenly among circles, spreading only on half of each circle and to within ½ inch of edges. Layer spinach, ham, and Swiss cheese over ricotta cheese.

3. Moisten edges of dough with water. Fold dough in half over filling. Seal edges with tines of fork. Prick tops three or four times with fork. Place calzones on lightly greased baking sheet.

4. Bake about 20 minutes or until golden. Serve with warm pasta sauce. **MAKES 4 CALZONES.**

Per calzone: 484 cal., 6 g total fat (2 g sat. fat), 32 mg chol., 802 mg sodium, 64 g carbo., 2 g fiber, 32 g pro.

Make-Ahead Directions: Prepare calzones as above. Cool. Cover and chill the calzones overnight. To reheat, place calzones on a baking sheet. Bake calzones, uncovered, in a 375°F oven for 12 to 15 minutes or until heated through.

Provolone and Ham Melt

Provolone and Ham Melt

Prep: 15 minutes **Cook:** 8 minutes

- 8 slices multigrain or whole wheat bread Butter, softened
- 4 teaspoons mayonnaise or salad dressing
- 4 ounces provolone cheese, thinly sliced
- ⅓ cup bottled roasted red sweet peppers, well drained and cut into strips
- 1 pear or apple, cored and thinly sliced
- 4 ounces thinly sliced cooked ham and/or prosciutto
- 2 tablespoons mango chutney

1. Spread 1 side of each bread slice with butter. Place 4 of the bread slices, buttered sides down, on griddle. Spread with mayonnaise. Top with cheese, red peppers, pear slices, and ham.

2. Cut up any large pieces of chutney; spread the unbuttered sides of the 4 remaining bread slices with chutney. Place over bread slices on griddle, buttered sides up.

3. Cook sandwiches over medium heat about 8 minutes or until bread is toasted and cheese is melted, turning once halfway through cooking. **MAKES 4 SANDWICHES.**

Per sandwich: 466 cal., 22 g total fat (11 g sat. fat), 53 mg chol., 1,085 mg sodium, 48 g carbo., 7 g fiber, 20 g pro.

Ham and Pear Melt

Start to Finish: 10 minutes

- 2 7- to 8-inch whole wheat flour tortillas
- 6 ounces very thinly sliced ham
- 2 small ripe pears, cored and thinly sliced
- 1 cup finely shredded Swiss, Colby-Monterey Jack, or mozzarella cheese (4 ounces)

1. Place tortillas on a baking sheet or broiler pan. Broil tortillas 4 to 5 inches from the heat just until warm. Layer half the ham, half the sliced pears, and half the shredded cheese on each warm tortilla.

2. Broil layered tortillas about 2 minutes or until cheese is melted and bubbly. Fold tortillas in half or roll up into a spiral. Cut each in half. **MAKES 2 SERVINGS.**

Per serving: 474 cal., 25 g total fat (13 g sat. fat), 100 mg chol., 1,446 mg sodium, 29 g carbo., 11 g fiber, 33 g pro.

Chicken and Hummus Pitas

Asparagus- and Mushroom-Topped Chicken Sandwiches

Start to Finish: 20 minutes

- 8 ounces asparagus spears, trimmed
- 2 tablespoons olive oil
  Salt and coarsely ground black pepper
- 4 4-inch portobello mushroom caps
- 4 skinless, boneless chicken breast halves (1 pound)
- 8 ½-inch slices country Italian bread
- 1 8-ounce tub cream cheese spread with chive and onion

1. Tear off a 36×18-inch piece of heavy foil; fold in half to make an 18-inch square. Place asparagus in center of foil; drizzle with 1 teaspoon of the olive oil and sprinkle lightly with salt and pepper. Bring up opposite edges of foil and seal with a double fold. Fold remaining edges to completely enclose asparagus, leaving space for steam to escape. Set aside. Remove stems from mushrooms. Brush chicken and mushrooms with the remaining olive oil; sprinkle lightly with salt and pepper.

2. For a charcoal grill, place chicken, mushrooms, and foil packet with asparagus on the rack of an uncovered grill directly over medium coals. Grill for 12 to 15 minutes or until chicken is no longer pink (170°F) and mushrooms are tender, turning chicken and mushrooms once halfway through grilling. (For a gas grill, preheat grill. Reduce heat to medium. Place chicken, mushrooms, and foil packet on grill rack over heat. Cover; grill as above.) Remove chicken, mushrooms, and foil packet from grill; slice mushrooms.

3. Toast bread slices on grill rack for 1 to 2 minutes, turning once. Spread 1 side of each bread slice with cream cheese. On serving plates stack half of the bread slices, spread sides up, chicken, remaining bread slices, mushrooms, and asparagus.

MAKES 4 SANDWICHES.

Per sandwich: 583 cal., 29 g total fat (15 g sat. fat), 121 mg chol., 751 mg sodium, 40 g carbo., 4 g fiber, 37 g pro.

Chicken and Hummus Pitas ♡

Start to Finish: 25 minutes

- 1 tablespoon olive oil
- 1 teaspoon lemon juice
- ¼ teaspoon paprika
  Dash salt
  Dash black pepper
- 2 skinless, boneless chicken breast halves (about 12 ounces total)
- 2 large whole wheat pita bread rounds, halved
- ½ of a 7-ounce carton hummus
- ¾ cup coarsely chopped roma tomatoes
- ½ cup thinly sliced cucumber
- ⅓ cup plain low-fat yogurt

1. In a small bowl combine oil, lemon juice, paprika, salt, and pepper. Place chicken on the unheated rack of a broiler pan. Brush both sides of chicken with the oil mixture. Broil 4 to 5 inches from heat for 7 minutes. Turn chicken; broil for 5 to 8 minutes more or until chicken is no longer pink. Cool slightly; cut into strips.

2. To serve, carefully open pita halves and spread hummus inside; stuff with chicken, tomatoes, cucumber, and yogurt.

MAKES 4 SERVINGS.

Per serving: 279 cal., 8 g total fat (1 g sat. fat), 51 mg chol., 328 mg sodium, 26 g carbo., 4 g fiber, 26 g pro.

Fajita-Ranch
Chicken
Wraps

Fajita-Ranch Chicken Wraps ♡

Start to Finish: 30 minutes

- 12 ounces chicken breast strips for stir-fry
- ½ teaspoon chili powder
- ¼ teaspoon garlic powder
  Nonstick cooking spray
- 2 small red, yellow, and/or green sweet peppers, seeded and cut into thin strips
- 2 tablespoons bottled reduced-calorie ranch salad dressing
- 2 10-inch whole wheat, tomato, or jalapeño flour tortillas, warmed
- ½ cup purchased deli-style fresh salsa
- ⅓ cup reduced-fat shredded cheddar cheese

1. Sprinkle chicken with chili powder and garlic powder. Coat a large unheated nonstick skillet with cooking spray. Preheat skillet over medium heat. Cook chicken in skillet over medium heat for 4 to 6 minutes or until no longer pink. Remove chicken from skillet. Add sweet peppers to skillet; cook about 5 minutes or until tender. Return chicken to skillet. Add dressing; toss to coat.
2. Divide chicken mixture among warmed tortillas, placing it to 1 side of each tortilla. Top with salsa and cheese. Fold tortillas over; cut each into 2 pieces. **MAKES 4 SERVINGS (½ WRAP EACH).**

Per serving (½ wrap): 267 cal., 7 g total fat (2 g sat. fat), 57 mg chol., 706 mg sodium, 24 g carbo., 5 g fiber, 26 g pro.

Chicken-Artichoke Sandwiches

Start to Finish: 20 minutes **Bake:** 12 minutes
Oven: 450°F

- ⅓ cup refrigerated basil pesto
- 6 ½-inch bias slices of Italian bread
- 3 ounces thinly sliced prosciutto
- 1 14-ounce can artichoke hearts, drained and thinly sliced
- 1 7-ounce jar roasted red peppers, drained and cut into strips
- 12 ounces cooked chicken or turkey, cut into bite-size strips (about 2¼ cups)
- 4 to 6 ounces shredded provolone cheese (1 to 1½ cups)

Chicken-Artichoke Sandwiches

1. Preheat oven to 450°F.
2. Lightly spread pesto on 1 side of each bread slice. Top slices with prosciutto, artichoke slices, red pepper strips, and chicken strips.
3. Place sandwiches on a large foil-lined baking sheet. Cover loosely with foil. Bake about 8 minutes or until nearly heated through. Uncover sandwiches and sprinkle with cheese. Bake 4 to 5 minutes more or until cheese melts. **MAKES 6 SANDWICHES.**

Per sandwich: 387 cal., 20 g total fat (6 g sat. fat), 67 mg chol., 855 mg sodium, 20 g carbo., 1 g fiber, 31 g pro.

Caprese Chicken Sandwiches

Start to Finish: 20 minutes

- 4 skinless, boneless chicken breast halves
- 1 tablespoon vegetable oil
  Salt and black pepper
- 4 French rolls, split
- ¼ cup mayonnaise or salad dressing
- 4 ounces fresh mozzarella cheese, sliced
- 1 large tomato, sliced
- 8 fresh basil leaves

1. Brush chicken breasts with oil; sprinkle with salt and pepper.
2. For a charcoal grill, grill chicken on the rack of an uncovered grill directly over medium coals for 12 to 15 minutes or until chicken is no longer pink (170°F), turning once halfway through grilling. (For a gas grill, preheat grill. Reduce heat to medium. Place chicken on grill rack over heat. Cover; grill as above.) If desired, grill rolls for 1 to 2 minutes to toast.
3. Cut chicken breast halves diagonally in half to fit rolls. Spread rolls with mayonnaise. Layer chicken on roll bottoms. Top with mozzarella cheese, tomato slices, and basil leaves. Add roll tops. **MAKES 4 SANDWICHES.**

Per sandwich: 478 cal., 24 g total fat (7 g sat. fat), 107 mg chol., 634 mg sodium, 21 g carbo., 2 g fiber, 42 g pro.

Turkey Burgers and Home Fries

Quick Tip Greek pita bread comes in two types—pocket bread and flatbread. The pocket bread is great when it's fresh, soft, and pliable, and you fill it with something fairly light, such as chicken salad. But it can crack or tear easily stuffed with a burger and fixings. This recipes calls for Greek pita flatbread, which is pocketless. Wrap the bread around the fillings and tuck in.

Peppered Turkey Panini

Start to Finish: 20 minutes

⅓ cup broken walnuts (optional)
8 ½-inch slices country Italian bread
½ cup refrigerated classic bruschetta topper
2 tablespoons mayonnaise or salad dressing
12 ounces sliced cooked peppered or smoked turkey breast
1 cup large spinach leaves
Olive oil

1. Preheat an extra-large skillet over medium heat. Add walnuts (if using) to skillet; cook and stir for 2 minutes or until toasted. Remove nuts from skillet and set aside.
2. To assemble sandwiches, spread 1 side of 4 bread slices with bruschetta topper; spread the slices with mayonnaise. Layer walnuts, turkey, and spinach on top of the bruschetta-spread slices. Top with mayonnaise-spread slices, mayonnaise sides down. Brush sandwiches lightly with olive oil.
3. Place the sandwiches in panini maker or heated skillet. Weight sandwiches down by placing a large skillet on top of sandwiches and a few cans of food in skillet. Grill about 2 minutes; turn. Replace weight and cook about 2 minutes more or until golden and heated through. **MAKES 4 SANDWICHES.**

Per sandwich: 448 cal., 23 g total fat (4 g sat. fat), 43 mg chol., 1,522 mg sodium, 35 g carbo., 2 g fiber, 26 g pro.

Turkey Burgers and Home Fries

Prep: 10 minutes **Cook:** 12 minutes
Broil: 11 minutes

½ cup mayonnaise or salad dressing
2 teaspoons curry powder
2 tablespoons olive oil
2 cups refrigerated sliced potatoes
Salt and black pepper
1 pound uncooked ground turkey breast
2 ounces feta cheese with basil and tomato, crumbled
¼ teaspoon salt
4 Greek pita flatbreads
Red onion slices (optional)
Fresh spinach (optional)
Feta cheese, crumbled (optional)

1. Preheat broiler. In a small bowl stir together mayonnaise and curry powder; set aside. In an extra-large skillet heat olive oil over medium-high heat. Add potatoes; sprinkle with salt and pepper. Cook for 6 minutes; turn potatoes. Cook about 6 minutes more or until crisp.
2. Meanwhile, in a medium bowl combine turkey, 2 tablespoons of the curry-mayonnaise, the 2 ounces feta cheese, and ¼ teaspoon salt. Shape turkey mixture in four ½-inch-thick patties. Place patties on the unheated rack of a broiler pan. Broil 4 inches from heat for 11 to 13 minutes or until done (165°F), turning once halfway through broiling.
3. Spread the remaining curry-mayonnaise on bread; place patties on bread. If desired, layer with onion, spinach, and feta. Serve with potatoes. **MAKES 4 BURGERS.**

Per burger: 658 cal., 33 g total fat (6 g sat. fat), 91 mg chol., 1,033 mg sodium, 51 g carbo., 3 g fiber, 38 g pro.

Peppered
Turkey Panini

Shrimp
Quesadillas

Shrimp Quesadillas

Start to Finish: 20 minutes

Nonstick cooking spray
4 8-inch vegetable tortillas
½ of a 7-ounce carton garlic or spicy three-pepper hummus (⅓ cup)
6 ounces peeled, deveined cooked medium shrimp
1 6-ounce jar marinated artichoke hearts, drained and coarsely chopped
1 4-ounce package crumbled feta cheese

1. Coat 1 side of each tortilla with cooking spray. Place tortillas, sprayed sides down, on work surface; spread with hummus. Top half of each tortilla with shrimp, artichokes, and cheese. Fold tortillas in half, pressing gently.
2. Preheat a large nonstick skillet over medium heat for 1 minute. Cook quesadillas in hot skillet, two at a time, for 4 to 6 minutes or until golden and heated through, turning once. **MAKES 4 QUESADILLAS.**

Per quesadilla: 430 cal., 20 g total fat (7 g sat. fat), 108 mg chol., 1,098 mg sodium, 42 g carbo., 4 g fiber, 21 g pro.

Quick Tip Hummus is a handy ingredient to have around as a sandwich spread or dip to serve with veggies or crackers. Purchased hummus is convenient but not inexpensive. The basic ingredients for hummus—canned chickpeas, lemon juice, olive oil, garlic, and tahini—are relatively inexpensive. Make a big batch of hummus from your favorite recipe and freeze it in small containers. Thaw in the refrigerator. The consistency may get a little grainy, but after stirring, it will be as smooth as when you first made it.

Tuna Bruschetta Sandwiches

Start to Finish: 20 minutes

8 1-inch slices country Italian bread
1 8-ounce package frozen spinach-artichoke dip, thawed
2 5-ounce pouches lemon-pepper marinated chunk light tuna
2 small red and/or yellow sweet peppers, cut into thin strips
1 cup shredded Italian cheese blend

Open-Face Portobello Sandwiches

1. Preheat broiler. Place bread on a baking sheet. Broil 4 inches from heat about 2 minutes or until toasted. Remove from oven.
2. Turn bread slices over; spread with dip. Top with tuna, pepper strips, and cheese. Broil for 3 to 4 minutes or until cheese melts and mixture is heated through.
MAKES 4 SANDWICHES.

Per sandwich: 488 cal., 15 g total fat (6 g sat. fat), 60 mg chol., 1,132 mg sodium, 47 g carbo., 3 g fiber, 40 g pro.

Open-Face Portobello Sandwiches ♡

Start to Finish: 25 minutes

⅔ cup chopped tomato (1 medium)
2 teaspoons snipped fresh basil or thyme
⅛ teaspoon salt
2 medium fresh portobello mushrooms (about 4 inches in diameter)
1 teaspoon balsamic vinegar or red wine vinegar
½ teaspoon olive oil
½ of a 12-inch Italian flatbread (focaccia), quartered, or half of a 12-inch thin-crust Italian bread shell
Finely shredded Parmesan cheese (optional)

1. Preheat broiler. In a small bowl combine tomato, basil, and salt; set aside.
2. Clean mushrooms; cut off stems even with caps. Discard stems. Combine vinegar and oil; gently brush mixture over the mushrooms. Place mushrooms on the unheated rack of the broiler pan.
3. Broil mushrooms 4 to 5 inches from the heat for 6 to 8 minutes or just until tender, turning once. Drain mushrooms on paper towels. Thinly slice mushrooms.
4. Place bread on a baking sheet. Place under broiler for 2 to 3 minutes or until heated through.
5. To serve, top toasted bread with mushroom slices and tomato mixture. If desired, top with Parmesan cheese. **MAKES 4 SANDWICHES.**

Per sandwich: 161 cal., 3 g total fat (1 g sat. fat), 2 mg chol., 71 mg sodium, 29 g carbo., 3 g fiber, 7 g pro.

CHAPTER 2

Meatless

Orzo Pasta
with
Mushrooms
and Leeks

Ziti with Eggplant and Dried Tomato Pesto

Start to Finish: 35 minutes **Oven:** 425°F

- 1 medium onion, cut into 8 wedges
- 2 tablespoons olive oil
- 1 medium eggplant (about 1 pound), halved lengthwise
- 6 ounces dried ziti, rigatoni, or penne pasta
- ⅓ cup Dried Tomato Pesto or ⅓ cup purchased dried tomato pesto
- ¼ teaspoon coarsely ground black pepper
  Salt
- 2 tablespoons crumbled goat cheese (chèvre) or feta cheese (optional)
  Snipped fresh basil (optional)

1. Preheat oven to 425°F. Place onion in a large shallow baking pan; brush with 1 tablespoon of the oil. Roast for 10 minutes; stir. Brush eggplant with remaining oil. Place eggplant in pan, cut sides down. Roast about 15 minutes more or until onion is golden brown and eggplant is tender.
2. Meanwhile, cook pasta following package directions; drain. Add Dried Tomato Pesto and black pepper to pasta; toss gently to coat. Transfer pasta to a warm serving dish; keep warm.
3. Cut eggplant into ½-inch slices. Toss eggplant and onion with pasta. Season with salt. If desired, top with cheese and basil.
MAKES 4 SERVINGS.

Dried Tomato Pesto Drain ¾ cup oil-pack dried tomatoes, reserving oil. Add enough olive oil to the reserved oil to make ½ cup; set aside. Place tomatoes, ¼ cup pine nuts or slivered almonds, ¼ cup snipped fresh basil, ½ teaspoon salt, and 4 teaspoons bottled minced garlic in a food processor. Cover; process until finely chopped. With machine running, gradually add the oil, processing until almost smooth. Divide pesto into thirds. Refrigerate or freeze unused portions. Makes three ⅓-cup portions.

Per serving: 370 cal., 19 g total fat (3 g sat. fat), 0 mg chol., 112 mg sodium, 43 g carbo., 4 g fiber, 8 g pro.

Orzo Pasta with Mushrooms and Leeks ♡

Start to Finish: 25 minutes

- ¾ cup dried orzo pasta
- 1 tablespoon butter
- 4 ounces assorted fresh mushrooms (such as porcini, cremini, chanterelle, shiitake, or button), sliced or quartered (1½ cups)
- ⅓ cup chopped leek or green onions
- ¼ teaspoon black pepper
- ⅛ teaspoon salt
- 1 clove garlic, minced
- ¼ cup water
- ½ to 1 teaspoon snipped fresh marjoram or ¼ teaspoon dried marjoram, crushed
- ½ teaspoon instant beef or chicken bouillon granules
  Grated Romano cheese (optional)

1. Cook orzo following package directions; drain well.
2. Meanwhile, in a large skillet heat butter over medium-high heat; stir in the mushrooms, leek, pepper, salt, and garlic.
3. Cook, uncovered, for 5 minutes. Add the water, dried marjoram (if using), and bouillon granules. Reduce heat; cook about 5 minutes or until liquid is almost absorbed. Stir in fresh marjoram (if using).
4. Toss mushroom mixture with pasta. If desired, sprinkle with Romano cheese.
MAKES 4 SERVINGS.

Per serving: 167 cal., 4 g total fat (2 g sat. fat), 8 mg chol., 209 mg sodium, 29 g carbo., 2 g fiber, 5 g pro.

Ziti with Eggplant and Dried Tomato Pesto

Pasta and Sweet Pepper Primavera

Start to Finish: 20 minutes

- 14 ounces asparagus spears
- 8 ounces dried cavatappi (corkscrews) or rotini pasta (about 2½ cups)
- 1 large red or yellow sweet pepper, cut into 1-inch pieces
- 4 baby sunburst squash, halved (½ cup)
- ½ of a medium yellow summer squash or zucchini, sliced (½ cup)
- 1 10-ounce container refrigerated light Alfredo sauce
- 2 tablespoons snipped fresh tarragon or thyme
- ¼ teaspoon crushed red pepper

1. Snap off and discard woody bases from asparagus. Bias-slice asparagus into 1-inch pieces (you should have about 1½ cups).
2. Cook pasta following package directions, adding asparagus, sweet pepper, and squash to pasta during the last 3 minutes of cooking; drain. Return pasta and vegetables to hot saucepan.
3. Meanwhile, in a small saucepan combine Alfredo sauce, tarragon, and crushed red pepper. Cook and stir over medium heat about 5 minutes or until mixture is heated through. Pour over pasta and vegetables; toss gently to coat. **MAKES 4 SERVINGS.**

Per serving: 421 cal., 12 g total fat (6 g sat. fat), 31 mg chol., 622 mg sodium, 66 g carbo., 2 g fiber, 15 g pro.

Quick Tip Purchase sweet peppers that have richly colored, shiny skin and are firm and heavy for their size. Avoid those that are limp, shriveled, or have soft or bruised spots.

Angel Hair Pasta with Asparagus, Tomatoes, and Basil

Start to Finish: 20 minutes

- 16 fresh asparagus spears
- 1 9-ounce package refrigerated angel hair pasta
- 1 tablespoon olive oil
- 4 cloves garlic, minced
- ¼ teaspoon black pepper

Tortellini Stir-Fry

- 6 medium roma tomatoes, seeded and chopped (2¼ cups)
- ¼ cup dry white wine
- ¼ teaspoon salt
- 1 tablespoon butter
- ¼ cup shredded fresh basil

1. Snap off and discard woody bases from asparagus. Remove tips; set tips aside. Bias-slice remaining asparagus stalks into 1- to 1½-inch pieces; set aside.
2. Cook pasta following package directions; drain. Return pasta to saucepan.
3. Meanwhile, in a large skillet heat oil over medium heat. Add garlic and pepper; cook for 1 minute, stirring constantly. Add tomatoes and cook about 2 minutes, stirring often.
4. Add asparagus stalks, wine, and salt. Cook, uncovered, for 3 minutes. Add asparagus tips; cook, uncovered, for 1 minute more. Add butter; stirring until melted. Add asparagus mixture and basil to pasta; toss gently to coat. Transfer to a warm serving dish.
MAKES 3 SERVINGS.

Per serving: 484 cal., 11 g total fat (3 g sat. fat), 10 mg chol., 185 mg sodium, 81 g carbo., 15 g fiber, 15 g pro.

Tortellini Stir-Fry

Start to Finish: 20 minutes

- 1 9-ounce package refrigerated cheese-filled tortellini
- 1 tablespoon vegetable oil
- 1 16-ounce package fresh cut or frozen stir-fry vegetables (such as broccoli, snow peas, carrots, and celery)
- ¾ cup peanut stir-fry sauce
- ¼ cup chopped dry-roasted cashews

1. Cook tortellini following package directions. Drain and set aside.
2. In a wok or large skillet heat oil over medium-high heat. Add fresh cut vegetables; cook and stir for 3 to 5 minutes (7 to 8 minutes for frozen vegetables) or until crisp-tender. Add tortellini and stir-fry sauce; toss gently to coat. Heat through. Sprinkle with cashews; serve immediately. **MAKES 4 SERVINGS.**

Per serving: 400 cal., 16 g total fat (3 g sat. fat), 30 mg chol., 1,256 mg sodium, 48 g carbo., 4 g fiber, 18 g pro.

Linguine with Gorgonzola Sauce

Trattoria-Style Spinach Fettuccine

Start to Finish: 18 minutes

1 9-ounce package refrigerated spinach fettuccine
1 medium carrot
1 tablespoon olive oil
1 medium shallot or 2 green onions, chopped (2 tablespoons)
4 red and/or yellow tomatoes, chopped (2 cups)
¼ cup oil-packed dried tomatoes, drained and snipped
½ cup crumbled garlic and herb or peppercorn feta cheese (2 ounces)

1. Cut pasta strands in half with kitchen shears. Cook pasta following package directions; drain. Return pasta to hot pan.
2. Meanwhile, peel carrot. Using a sharp vegetable peeler, slice carrot lengthwise into wide, flat "ribbons." Set ribbons aside.
3. In a large skillet heat oil over medium heat. Cook shallot for 30 seconds. Stir in fresh tomatoes, carrot ribbons, and dried tomatoes. Cook, covered, for 5 minutes, stirring once.
4. Spoon tomato mixture over cooked pasta; toss gently. Sprinkle with cheese.

MAKES 4 SERVINGS.

Per serving: 311 cal., 11 g total fat (4 g sat. fat), 73 mg chol., 250 mg sodium, 44 g carbo., 2 g fiber, 13 g pro.

Quick Tip For the best flavor, look for fresh tomatoes that are marked "vine-ripened." Many of the tomatoes that supermarkets carry have been picked green and ripened with ethylene gas and never have the flavor of tomatoes that are allowed to ripen on the vine. If the tomatoes you purchase are not quite ripe yet, place them with an apple in a paper bag poked with a few holes. Let them stand at room temperature for 2 to 3 days.

Linguine with Gorgonzola Sauce

Start to Finish: 20 minutes

1 9-ounce package refrigerated linguine pasta
1 pound fresh asparagus, trimmed and cut into 1-inch pieces, or one 10-ounce package frozen cut asparagus
1 cup half-and-half or light cream
1 cup crumbled Gorgonzola or other blue cheese (4 ounces)
¼ teaspoon salt
2 tablespoons chopped walnuts, toasted*

1. Cook linguine and asparagus following package directions for the linguine; drain. Return pasta mixture to pan.

2. Meanwhile, in a medium saucepan combine half-and-half, ¾ cup of the Gorgonzola cheese, and the salt. Bring to boiling over medium heat; reduce heat. Simmer for 3 minutes, stirring frequently.
3. Pour sauce over linguine mixture; toss gently to coat. Transfer to a warm serving dish. Sprinkle with the remaining ¼ cup Gorgonzola cheese and the walnuts.

MAKES 4 SERVINGS.

Per serving: 399 cal., 20 g total fat (11 g sat. fat), 111 mg chol., 590 mg sodium, 39 g carbo., 3 g fiber, 18 g pro.

*Note To toast nuts and seeds, spread them in a single layer in a shallow baking pan. Bake in a 350°F oven for 5 to 10 minutes or until light golden brown, watching carefully and stirring once or twice.

Trattoria-Style
Spinach
Fettuccine

Smoky Mushroom Stroganoff

Start to Finish: 25 minutes

- 1 8.8-ounce package dried pappardelle (wide egg noodles)
- 1 tablespoon olive oil
- 1½ pounds sliced mushrooms (such as button, cremini, and/or shiitake)
- 2 cloves garlic, minced
- 1 8-ounce carton light sour cream
- 2 tablespoons all-purpose flour
- 1½ teaspoons smoked paprika
- ¼ teaspoon black pepper
- 1 cup vegetable broth
  Snipped fresh parsley (optional)

1. Cook noodles following package directions. Drain; keep warm.
2. In an extra-large skillet heat olive oil over medium-high heat. Add mushrooms and garlic to hot oil in skillet; cook for 5 to 8 minutes or until tender, stirring occasionally. Remove mushrooms with a slotted spoon; cover to keep warm.
3. For sauce, in a medium bowl combine sour cream, flour, paprika, and pepper. Add broth, stirring until smooth. Add sour cream mixture to skillet. Cook and stir until thickened and bubbly; cook and stir for 1 minute more. Serve mushroom mixture and sauce over noodles. If desired, sprinkle with parsley.
MAKES 4 SERVINGS.

Per serving: 407 cal., 13 g total fat (5 g sat. fat), 72 mg chol., 443 mg sodium, 59 g carbo., 4 g fiber, 17 g pro.

Italian Pasta Primavera ♡

Start to Finish: 30 minutes

- 1 16-ounce package dried fusilli
- 8 ounces broccoli, rinsed, trimmed, and cut into florets (about 2 cups)
- 8 ounces cauliflower, rinsed, trimmed, and cut into florets (about 2 cups)
- 1½ cups milk
- 3 tablespoons all-purpose flour
- 1 teaspoon salt
- ¼ teaspoon black pepper
- 1 cup grated Parmesan cheese
- ¼ cup oil-packed dried tomatoes, well drained and chopped

1. In a 4- to 6-quart Dutch oven cook pasta following package directions, adding broccoli and cauliflower for the last 4 to 5 minutes of cooking time. Drain and return pasta and vegetables to Dutch oven.
2. Meanwhile, in a medium microwave-safe mixing bowl whisk together milk, flour, salt, and pepper. Microwave, covered, on high for 3 to 4 minutes, stirring every 30 seconds or until thickened. Add milk mixture, Parmesan cheese, and dried tomatoes to cooked pasta in Dutch oven. Stir gently to combine.
MAKES 6 SERVINGS.

Per serving: 415 cal., 7 g total fat (3 g sat. fat), 17 mg chol., 657 mg sodium, 68 g carbo., 5 g fiber, 19 g pro.

Quick Tip Reserve the oil from oil-packed dried tomatoes and use it to flavor a homemade salad dressing—or to liven up hot cooked pasta.

Pasta with Broccoli and Asiago

Start to Finish: 25 minutes

- 4 ounces dried spaghetti, linguine, fettuccine, or angel hair pasta
- 1 cup chopped broccoli
- ½ of a 5.2-ounce container semisoft cheese with garlic and herbs
- ¼ cup milk
  Finely shredded Asiago or Parmesan cheese

1. Cook pasta following package directions, adding the broccoli for the last 4 minutes of cooking time. Drain and return pasta and broccoli to pan.
2. For sauce, in a small saucepan combine semisoft cheese and milk. Cook and stir over medium-low heat until smooth. Pour sauce over pasta; toss to coat. Sprinkle with Asiago cheese. **MAKES 2 SERVINGS.**

Per serving: 411 cal., 20 g total fat (13 g sat. fat), 11 mg chol., 316 mg sodium, 47 g carbo., 3 g fiber, 14 g pro.

Even the most dedicated meat eaters won't miss the meat in these savory dishes loaded with veggies and pumped up with seasonings.

Tomatoes and Ravioli with Escarole

Macaroni and Cheese with Caramelized Onions

Prep: 25 minutes **Bake:** 30 minutes
Stand: 10 minutes **Oven:** 350°F

- 4 strips bacon
- 1 large sweet onion, halved and thinly sliced
- 1½ cups regular or multigrain dried elbow macaroni (6 ounces)
- 2 cups shredded mozzarella cheese (8 ounces)
- 4 ounces processed Gruyère cheese, shredded
- 1 cup half-and-half or light cream
- ⅛ teaspoon black pepper

1. Preheat oven to 350°F. In a large skillet cook bacon over medium heat until crisp, turning once. Drain bacon on paper towels; crumble. Reserve bacon drippings in skillet.
2. Cook onion in reserved bacon drippings over medium heat for 5 to 8 minutes or until onion is tender and golden brown. Set aside.
3. In a large saucepan cook macaroni following package directions. Drain and return to saucepan. Stir in the crumbled bacon, onion, 1½ cups of the mozzarella cheese, the Gruyère cheese, half-and half, and pepper. Toss gently to combine. Spoon into a 1½-quart casserole.
4. Bake, uncovered, for 20 minutes. Stir gently. Top with the remaining mozzarella cheese. Bake for 10 minutes more or until top of casserole is brown and bubbly. Let stand for 10 minutes. **MAKES 4 SERVINGS.**

Per serving: 632 cal., 39 g total fat (21 g sat. fat), 110 mg chol., 617 mg sodium, 37 g carbo., 4 g fiber, 33 g pro.

Tomatoes and Ravioli with Escarole

Start to Finish: 30 minutes

- 1 tablespoon olive oil or vegetable oil
- ½ cup chopped onion (1 medium)
- 2 cloves garlic, minced
- 3 cups sliced fresh mushrooms (8 ounces)
- 2 cups chopped roma tomatoes (6 medium)
- ¾ cup chicken broth
- 4 cups coarsely chopped escarole
- 1 tablespoon snipped fresh basil
- 1 teaspoon snipped fresh rosemary
- 1 9-ounce package refrigerated cheese-filled ravioli
- ¼ cup pine nuts, toasted (see note, page 54)

1. For the sauce, in a large skillet heat oil over medium heat. Add onion and garlic; cook for 2 minutes. Add mushrooms, tomatoes, and broth. Bring to boiling. Reduce heat; simmer, uncovered, about 7 minutes or until mushrooms are tender and sauce is slightly reduced (you should have about 3 cups). Add escarole, basil, and rosemary, stirring just until escarole is wilted.
2. Meanwhile, cook pasta following package directions; drain. Return pasta to saucepan. Pour sauce over pasta; toss to coat. Transfer to a warm serving dish. Sprinkle with pine nuts. **MAKES 4 SERVINGS.**

Per serving: 339 cal., 14 g total fat (3 g sat. fat), 34 mg chol., 454 mg sodium, 43 g carbo., 4 g fiber, 16 g pro.

Spinach Tortellini with Beans and Feta

Spinach Tortellini with Beans and Feta

Start to Finish: 20 minutes

1 9-ounce package refrigerated cheese-filled spinach tortellini
1 15-ounce can white kidney (cannellini) beans, rinsed and drained
¾ cup crumbled garlic-and-herb-flavor feta cheese (3 ounces)
2 tablespoons olive oil
1 cup chopped tomato (1 large)
  Black pepper
4 cups baby spinach

1. Cook tortellini following package directions. Drain and return to pan.

2. Add drained beans, feta cheese, and olive oil to tortellini in saucepan. Cook over medium heat until beans are hot and cheese begins to melt; gently stir occasionally. Add tomato; cook for 1 minute more. Sprinkle with pepper.

3. Divide spinach among 4 plates or shallow salad bowls. Top with tortellini mixture.

MAKES 4 SERVINGS.

Per serving: 448 cal., 18 g total fat (7 g sat. fat), 61 mg chol., 858 mg sodium, 55 g carbo., 9 g fiber, 24 g pro.

Quick Tip Although cannellini beans are nice for this recipe because of their big, buttery bite, most canned white beans are interchangeable in many recipes. Canned Great Northern beans or tiny navy beans are good options.

Caramelized Onions and Garlic with Cavatelli

Caramelized Onions and Garlic with Cavatelli ♡

Start to Finish: 30 minutes

10 ounces dried cavatelli or other medium-size pasta (3½ cups)
1 tablespoon olive oil
2 medium onions, sliced
1 teaspoon sugar
1 medium zucchini, halved lengthwise and sliced
4 cloves garlic, minced
2 tablespoons water
1 to 2 tablespoons balsamic vinegar
¼ cup pine nuts or chopped walnuts, toasted (see note, page 54)
1 tablespoon snipped fresh thyme
  Salt and black pepper

1. Cook pasta following package directions; drain and keep warm.

2. Meanwhile, in a large heavy skillet heat olive oil over medium-low heat. Add onions; cook, covered, for 13 to 15 minutes or until onions are tender. Uncover; add sugar. Cook and stir over medium-high heat for 4 to 5 minutes more or until onions are golden.

3. Add zucchini and garlic. Cook and stir for 2 minutes. Stir in the water and vinegar; cook for 2 to 3 minutes more or until zucchini is crisp-tender.

4. To serve, in a large bowl toss together warm pasta, onion mixture, nuts, and thyme. Season with salt and pepper.

MAKES 4 SERVINGS.

Per serving: 386 cal., 10 g total fat (1 g sat. fat), 0 mg chol., 97 mg sodium, 64 g carbo., 3 g fiber, 12 g pro.

Polenta with Fresh Tomato Sauce

Mediterranean Frittata

Start to Finish: 30 minutes

- 3 tablespoons olive oil
- 1 cup chopped onion (1 large)
- 1 teaspoon bottled minced garlic
- 8 eggs
- ¼ cup half-and-half, light cream, or milk
- ½ cup crumbled feta cheese (2 ounces)
- ½ of a 7-ounce jar (½ cup) roasted red sweet peppers, drained and chopped
- ½ cup sliced kalamata or pitted ripe olives
- ¼ cup slivered fresh basil
- ⅛ teaspoon black pepper
- ½ cup onion-and-garlic croutons, coarsely crushed
- 2 tablespoons finely shredded Parmesan cheese
  Fresh basil leaves (optional)

1. Preheat broiler. In a large broilerproof skillet heat 2 tablespoons of the oil over medium heat. Add onion and garlic; cook just until onion is tender.

2. Meanwhile, in a large bowl beat together eggs and half-and-half. Stir in feta cheese, roasted sweet peppers, olives, basil, and black pepper. Pour egg mixture over onion mixture in skillet. Cook over medium heat. As mixture sets, run a spatula around the edge of the skillet, lifting egg mixture to allow the uncooked portion to flow underneath. Continue cooking and lifting edges until egg mixture is almost set (surface will be moist). Reduce heat as necessary to prevent overcooking.

3. Combine crushed croutons, Parmesan cheese, and the remaining 1 tablespoon of oil; sprinkle mixture over frittata.

4. Broil 4 to 5 inches from heat for 1 to 2 minutes or until top is set. Cut frittata into wedges to serve. If desired, garnish with fresh basil leaves. **MAKES 6 SERVINGS.**

Per serving: 242 cal., 19 g total fat (6 g sat. fat), 297 mg chol., 339 mg sodium, 7 g carbo., 1 g fiber, 12 g pro.

Polenta with Fresh Tomato Sauce ♡

Start to Finish: 20 minutes

- 4 teaspoons olive oil
- ½ teaspoon bottled minced garlic
- 2 cups coarsely chopped roma tomatoes (6 medium)
- ¼ cup pitted halved kalamata olives or sliced pitted ripe olives
- 2 teaspoons snipped fresh rosemary or 2 tablespoons snipped fresh thyme
- 1 16-ounce package prepared polenta
- ½ cup shredded smoked Gouda or Swiss cheese (2 ounces)

1. For the sauce, in a medium saucepan heat 2 teaspoons of the oil and the garlic over medium heat. Add tomatoes; cook for 2 minutes. Stir in olives and rosemary. Bring to boiling; reduce heat. Simmer, uncovered,

for 8 minutes, stirring occasionally. Season with salt and pepper.

2. Meanwhile, cut polenta into 8 slices. In a large nonstick skillet or on a griddle heat the remaining 2 teaspoons oil over medium heat. Add polenta; cook about 6 minutes or until golden brown, turning once. Sprinkle with cheese. Serve on top of tomato sauce.

MAKES 4 SERVINGS.

Per serving: 226 cal., 10 g total fat (3 g sat. fat), 16 mg chol., 608 mg sodium, 27 g carbo., 5 g fiber, 8 g pro.

Quick Tip Purchase fresh tomatoes that are firm, richly colored, and noticeably fragrant. They should be free of any blemishes, heavy for their size, and give slightly when lightly pressed. Store ripe tomatoes at room temperature away from direct sunlight and use within a few days. Never refrigerate fresh tomatoes; it will damage the texture and the flavor.

Mediterranean Frittata

Chipotle Bean Enchiladas

Spring Peas
Risotto

Chipotle Bean Enchiladas

Prep: 25 minutes **Bake:** 40 minutes
Oven: 350°F

10 6-inch corn tortillas
 1 15-ounce can pinto beans or black beans,
    rinsed and drained
 1 tablespoon chopped chipotle pepper in
    adobo sauce (see note, page 31)
 1 8-ounce package shredded Mexican
    cheese blend (2 cups)
 2 10-ounce cans enchilada sauce

1. Preheat oven to 350°F. Grease a 2-quart
rectangular baking dish; set aside. Stack the
tortillas and wrap tightly in foil. Warm tortillas
in the preheated oven for 10 minutes.
2. Meanwhile, for the filling, in a medium bowl
combine beans, chipotle pepper, 1 cup of the
cheese, and ½ cup of the enchilada sauce.
Spoon about ¼ cup of the filling onto 1 edge
of each tortilla. Starting at the edge with the
filling, roll up each tortilla.
3. Arrange tortillas, seam sides down, in the
prepared baking dish. Top with the remaining
enchilada sauce. Cover with foil.
4. Bake about 25 minutes or until heated
through. Remove foil. Sprinkle with the
remaining 1 cup cheese. Bake about
5 minutes more or until cheese melts.
MAKES 5 SERVINGS.

Per serving: 487 cal., 19 g total fat (8 g sat. fat), 40 mg
chol., 1,091 mg sodium, 63 g carbo., 14 g fiber, 23 g pro.

Spring Peas Risotto

Start to Finish: 30 minutes

 2 tablespoons olive oil
 ½ cup chopped onion (1 medium)
 2 cloves garlic, minced
 1 cup arborio rice
 2 14.5-ounce cans vegetable broth
 1 cup frozen tiny or regular-size peas
 ¼ cup coarsely shredded carrot
 2 cups fresh spinach, shredded
 ¼ cup grated Parmesan cheese
 1 tablespoon snipped fresh thyme

1. In a large saucepan heat oil over medium
heat. Cook onion and garlic until onion is
tender. Add the rice. Cook and stir about
5 minutes or until rice is golden.
2. Meanwhile, in a medium saucepan bring
broth to boiling; reduce heat. Add 1 cup of
the broth to the rice mixture, stirring
constantly. Continue to cook and stir over
medium heat until liquid is absorbed.
3. Add another 1 cup of the broth to the rice
mixture, stirring constantly. Continue to cook
and stir until liquid is absorbed. Add another
1 cup broth, ½ cup at a time, stirring
constantly until the broth has been absorbed.
4. Stir in remaining ½ cup broth, the peas,
and carrot. Cook and stir until the rice is
slightly creamy and just tender.
5. Stir in spinach, cheese, and thyme.
MAKES 4 SERVINGS.

Per serving: 263 cal., 10 g total fat (2 g sat. fat), 5 mg
chol., 1,047 mg sodium, 388 g carbo., 3 g fiber, 9 g pro.

Chili Corn Pie

Prep: 20 minutes **Bake:** 20 minutes
Stand: 5 minutes **Oven:** 375°F

 2 11-ounce packages frozen bean chili
 1 11.5-ounce package refrigerated corn
    bread twists
 ⅓ cup shredded cheddar cheese
 1 tablespoon snipped fresh cilantro
 ¼ cup sour cream

1. Preheat oven to 375°F. Heat the chili
following microwave package directions.
2. On a lightly floured surface unroll corn
bread twist dough. Press at perforations to
seal. Roll to an 11×7-inch rectangle.
3. Spoon chili into a 2-quart rectangular
baking dish. Place corn bread dough on top
of chili. Using a sharp knife, cut slits in corn
bread dough to allow steam to escape.
4. Bake about 20 minutes or until corn bread
is lightly browned. Sprinkle with cheese and
cilantro. Let stand for 5 minutes before
serving. Top servings with sour cream.
MAKES 4 SERVINGS.

Per serving: 512 cal., 24 g total fat (9 g sat. fat), 44 mg
chol., 1,429 mg sodium, 50 g carbo., 3 g fiber, 22 g pro.

Black Bean and Corn Quesadillas

Black Bean and Corn Quesadillas

Start to Finish: 20 minutes **Oven:** 300°F

- 1 8-ounce package shredded Mexican-style four-cheese blend (2 cups)
- 8 8-inch whole wheat or flour tortillas
- 1½ cups bottled black bean and corn salsa
- 1 medium avocado, seeded, peeled, and chopped
  Sour cream

1. Preheat oven to 300°F. Divide cheese evenly among tortillas, sprinkling cheese over half of each tortilla. Top each tortilla with 1 tablespoon of the salsa and the avocado. Fold tortillas in half, pressing gently.
2. Heat a large skillet over medium-high heat for 2 minutes; reduce heat to medium. Cook 2 of the quesadillas for 2 to 3 minutes or until lightly browned and cheese is melted, turning once. Remove quesadillas from skillet; place on a baking sheet. Keep warm in the preheated oven. Repeat with remaining quesadillas, cooking 2 at a time.

3. Cut quesadillas into wedges. Serve with sour cream and the remaining salsa.
MAKES 4 SERVINGS.

Per serving: 647 cal., 35 g total fat (16 g sat. fat), 61 mg chol., 1,405 mg sodium, 48 g carbo., 23 g fiber, 31 g pro.

Saucy Beans and Eggplant

Start to Finish: 20 minutes

- 1 small eggplant (about 10 to 12 ounces), cut into 8 slices
- 3 tablespoons olive oil
- ¼ cup seasoned fine dry bread crumbs
- 1 cup instant brown rice
- ¼ sliced green onions (optional)
- 1 15-ounce can navy or Great Northern beans, rinsed and drained
- 1 26-ounce jar roasted garlic pasta sauce

1. Lightly brush eggplant slices with oil; sprinkle with salt and freshly ground black pepper. Place bread crumbs in a shallow dish. Dip eggplant slices into bread crumbs to coat both sides. In an extra-large skillet heat the remaining oil over medium-high heat. Add eggplant in a single layer. Cook about

5 minutes on each side or until browned and tender, turning often for even browning.
2. Meanwhile, in a saucepan cook the rice following package directions. If desired, stir in green onions. In another saucepan combine beans and pasta sauce; heat through. Serve eggplant with rice and beans. If desired, top with crumbled *feta cheese* and additional black pepper. **MAKES 4 SERVINGS.**

Per serving: 511 cal., 14 g total fat (2 g sat. fat), 0 mg chol., 1,099 mg sodium, 82 g carbo., 13 g fiber, 17 g pro.

Cauliflower and Chickpea Gratin

Prep: 30 minutes **Cook:** 15 minutes

- 3 tablespoons olive oil
- 2 cups chopped onions (2 large)
- 2 14.5-ounce cans diced tomatoes, drained
- 1 15-ounce can garbanzo beans (chickpeas), rinsed and drained
- 6 cloves garlic, minced (1 tablespoon)
- ¼ cup snipped fresh parsley
- 2 tablespoons capers, rinsed and drained
- 1 tablespoon snipped fresh oregano
- 1 tablespoon lemon juice
- 1 teaspoon snipped fresh thyme
- 1¾ pounds cauliflower, cut into florets
- 4 ounces feta cheese, crumbled

1. In a large saucepan heat oil over medium heat. Add onion; cook about 5 minutes or until tender, stirring occasionally. Add drained tomatoes, garbanzo beans, and garlic. Bring to boiling; reduce heat. Simmer, covered, for 15 minutes. Stir in parsley, capers, oregano, lemon juice, thyme, ½ teaspoon salt, and ¼ teaspoon black pepper.
2. In a covered large saucepan cook cauliflower in a small amount of boiling water about 5 minutes or just until tender; drain.
3. Transfer cauliflower to a 2- to 2½-quart broilerproof baking dish. Top with hot tomato mixture. Sprinkle with feta cheese. Broil 3 to 4 inches from the heat for 1 to 2 minutes or just until cheese begins to brown. Serve immediately. **MAKES 6 SERVINGS.**

Per serving: 271 cal., 12 g total fat (4 g sat. fat), 17 mg chol., 951 mg sodium, 35 g carbo., 9 g fiber, 10 g pro.

Saucy Beans
and Eggplant

Skillet Vegetables on Cheese Toast

Start to Finish: 20 minutes

- 8 slices rustic wheat bread
- 2 tablespoons olive oil
- ½ of an 8-ounce package peeled fresh whole baby carrots, halved lengthwise
- 1 8-ounce package button mushrooms, halved
- 1 small red onion, cut into thin wedges
- 4 cloves garlic, peeled and coarsely chopped
- 2 tablespoons water
  Salt and black pepper
- 4 ounces soft goat cheese (chèvre)
  Fresh basil (optional)

1. Preheat broiler. Place bread on baking sheet; set aside.

2. In a large skillet heat olive oil over medium-high heat. Add carrots, mushrooms, onion, and garlic; cook for 2 to 3 minutes or until vegetables begin to brown. Add the water. Cook, covered, over medium heat about 5 minutes or until vegetables are crisp-tender, stirring once. Sprinkle with salt and pepper.

3. Meanwhile, for cheese toast, lightly toast bread 3 inches from broiler heat for 1 to 2 minutes. Spread goat cheese on 1 side of each slice. Broil 3 inches from heat for 1 to 2 minutes or until cheese is softened. Place cheese toasts on 4 plates; top with vegetables. If desired, drizzle additional olive oil and sprinkle basil. **MAKES 4 SERVINGS.**

Per serving: 461 cal., 21 g total fat (6 g sat. fat), 13 mg chol., 596 mg sodium, 56 g carbo., 8 g fiber, 15 g pro.

Red Beans and Couscous

Start to Finish: 20 minutes **Oven:** 350°F

- ¾ cup walnuts, coarsely chopped
- 2 cups packaged shredded fresh carrots
- 2 cups water
- 1 15- to 16-ounce can red beans, rinsed and drained
- 1½ cups couscous
- 1½ cups refrigerated salsa
  Salt

Vegetarian Chili with Rice

1. Preheat oven to 350°F. Place walnuts in a shallow baking pan. Bake about 8 minutes or until toasted.

2. Meanwhile, in a large saucepan combine carrots, water, and drained beans; bring to boiling. Stir in couscous. Remove from heat and let stand for 5 minutes. Stir in salsa and walnuts. Season with salt.
MAKES 4 SERVINGS.

Per serving: 796 cal., 16 g total fat (2 g sat. fat), 0 mg chol., 955 mg sodium, 139 g carbo., 17 g fiber, 30 g pro.

Vegetarian Chili with Rice ♡

Prep: 15 minutes **Cook:** 15 minutes

- 1 15.5-ounce can red kidney beans, rinsed and drained
- 1 15-ounce can Great Northern beans, rinsed and drained
- 1 14.5-ounce can diced tomatoes, undrained
- 1 8-ounce can tomato sauce
- 1 cup water
- ¾ cup chopped green sweet pepper (1 medium)
- ½ cup chopped onion (1 medium)
- 1 tablespoon chili powder
- 1 teaspoon sugar
- 2 cloves garlic, minced
- ½ teaspoon dried basil, crushed
- ½ teaspoon ground cumin
- ¼ teaspoon salt
  Dash cayenne pepper
- 2 cups hot cooked rice

1. In a large saucepan combine kidney beans, Great Northern beans, undrained tomatoes, tomato sauce, the water, green pepper, onion, chili powder, sugar, garlic, basil, cumin, salt, and cayenne pepper. Bring to boiling; reduce heat. Simmer, covered, for 15 minutes, stirring occasionally.

2. Serve chili in bowls. Top with hot cooked rice. **MAKES 4 SERVINGS.**

Per serving: 386 cal., 1 g total fat (0 g sat. fat), 0 mg chol., 777 mg sodium, 78 g carbo., 14 g fiber, 20 g pro.

Tex-Mex
Beans with
Dumplings

5. Simmer, covered, for 10 to 12 minutes or until a toothpick inserted into the center of a dumpling comes out clean. If desired, sprinkle with shredded *cheddar cheese.*

MAKES 5 SERVINGS.

Per serving: 351 cal., 7 g total fat (1 g sat. fat), 0 mg chol., 695 mg sodium, 61 g carbo., 12 g fiber, 15 g pro.

Spicy Black Beans and Rice ♡

Start to Finish: 30 minutes

  2 tablespoons olive oil or vegetable oil
½ cup chopped onion (1 medium)
  4 cloves garlic, minced
  1 15-ounce can black beans, rinsed and drained
  1 14.5-ounce can Mexican-style stewed tomatoes
⅛ to ¼ teaspoon cayenne pepper
  2 cups hot cooked brown or long grain rice
    Chopped onion (optional)

1. In a medium saucepan heat oil over medium heat. Add the ½ cup onion and garlic; cook until onion is tender. Carefully stir in beans, undrained tomatoes, and cayenne pepper. Bring to boiling; reduce heat. Simmer, uncovered, for 15 minutes.

2. To serve, mound rice on 4 dinner plates; make a well in the center of each. Spoon bean mixture into centers. If desired, sprinkle with additional chopped onion.

MAKES 4 SERVINGS.

Per serving: 279 cal., 8 g total fat (1 g sat. fat), 0 mg chol., 631 mg sodium, 47 g carbo., 7 g fiber, 11 g pro.

Quick Tip Brown rice differs from white rice in that it is less processed. The outer husk and bran—which contains fiber and nutrients—are removed from white rice. Only the husk is removed from brown rice, while the bran is left intact. For most recipes, you can substitute one for the other. Brown rice adds distinct, nutty flavor to dishes.

Tex-Mex Beans with Dumplings ♡

Start to Finish: 35 minutes

⅓ cup all-purpose flour
⅓ cup yellow cornmeal
  1 teaspoon baking powder
¼ teaspoon salt
  1 egg white, lightly beaten
¼ cup fat-free milk
  2 tablespoons vegetable oil
  1 cup chopped onion (1 large)
  1 clove garlic, minced
  1 15-ounce can garbanzo beans (chickpeas), rinsed and drained
  1 15-ounce can red kidney beans, rinsed and drained
  2 8-ounce cans tomato sauce
  1 4.5-ounce can diced green chiles, drained
  2 teaspoons chili powder
1½ teaspoons cornstarch
    Shredded cheddar cheese (optional)

1. In a medium bowl stir together flour, cornmeal, baking powder, and salt. In a small bowl combine egg white, milk, and vegetable oil; set aside.

2. In a large skillet combine onion, garlic, and ¾ cup water. Bring to boiling; reduce heat. Simmer, covered, about 5 minutes or until tender. Stir in garbanzo beans, kidney beans, tomato sauce, chiles, and chili powder.

3. In a small bowl stir together cornstarch and 1 tablespoon water. Stir into bean mixture. Cook and stir until slightly thickened and bubbly. Reduce heat.

4. Add milk mixture to cornmeal mixture; stir just until combined. Drop from a tablespoon onto the hot bean mixture to make 5 mounds.

Spicy Black
Beans and Rice

Saffron Pilaf
with Grilled
Vegetables

Saffron Pilaf with Grilled Vegetables ♡

Prep: 20 minutes **Grill:** 10 minutes

- 1 14.5-ounce can vegetable broth
- 1 cup jasmine, basmati, or wild-pecan long grain rice
- ⅛ teaspoon saffron threads or ¼ teaspoon ground turmeric
- 2 tablespoons olive oil
- 1 clove garlic, minced
- 1 red sweet pepper, seeded and quartered
- 1 large zucchini, halved lengthwise
- 1 eggplant, sliced ½ inch thick
- 1 ounce herbed semisoft goat cheese (chèvre), crumbled
- 2 tablespoons coarsely chopped hazelnuts or pecans, toasted (see note, page 54)

1. In a saucepan combine broth, rice, saffron, and ¼ cup water. Heat to boiling; reduce heat. Simmer, covered, about 15 minutes or until rice is tender and liquid is absorbed.
2. Meanwhile, in a small bowl combine olive oil and garlic; brush over sweet pepper, zucchini, and eggplant.
3. For a charcoal grill, grill vegetables on the lightly greased rack of an uncovered grill directly over medium coals about 10 minutes or until tender, turning once. (For a gas grill, preheat grill; reduce heat to medium. Place vegetables on grill rack. Cover and grill as above.) Sprinkle vegetables with salt and black pepper.
3. Transfer vegetables to a cutting board; Sprinkle with salt and pepper. Cut vegetables into bite-size pieces; stir into rice. Top with cheese and nuts. **MAKES 4 SERVINGS.**

Per serving: 333 cal., 12 g total fat (2 g sat. fat), 7 mg chol., 443 mg sodium, 48 g carbo., 5 g fiber, 9 g pro.

Polenta with Portobello Sauce

Start to Finish: 25 minutes

- 1 tablespoon olive oil
- 1 8-ounce fresh portobello mushroom, stem removed, quartered, and sliced (2½ cups)
- ½ cup finely chopped onion (1 medium)
- 3 cloves garlic, minced

Polenta with Portobello Sauce

- 2 tablespoons dry red wine
- 2 teaspoons snipped fresh oregano or ½ teaspoon dried oregano, crushed
- 3 roma tomatoes, chopped
  Salt and freshly ground black pepper
- 1 cup water
- ⅓ cup cornmeal
- 1 tablespoon butter
- ⅛ teaspoon salt
- ⅓ cup shredded Havarti or brick cheese
  Fresh oregano (optional)

1. In a large skillet heat olive oil over medium-high heat. Add mushroom slices, onion, and garlic. Cook and stir for 4 to 5 minutes or until mushroom slices are tender. Add the wine and the ½ teaspoon dried oregano (if using). Bring to boiling; reduce heat. Simmer, covered, for 5 minutes. Stir in tomatoes and the 2 teaspoons fresh oregano (if using); heat through. Remove from heat. Season with salt and pepper. Cover and keep warm.
2. Meanwhile, for polenta, in a small bowl stir together ½ cup of the water and the cornmeal; set aside. In a small saucepan bring the remaining ½ cup water, the butter, and the ⅛ teaspoon salt just to boiling. Slowly add the cornmeal mixture, stirring constantly. Reduce heat to low. Cook and stir about 10 minutes or until polenta is thick. Remove from heat. Stir in cheese.
3. To serve, divide the polenta between 2 shallow pasta bowls or soup bowls. Top with mushroom mixture. If desired, garnish with additional fresh oregano. **MAKES 2 SERVINGS.**

Per serving: 373 cal., 22 g total fat (5 g sat. fat), 42 mg chol., 455 mg sodium, 35 g carbo., 6 g fiber, 11 g pro.

Three-Grain Risotto

Prep: 30 minutes **Cook:** 28 minutes

    2   medium fennel bulbs with tops
    1   tablespoon olive oil
  1/3   cup finely chopped onion (1 small)
    3   cloves garlic, minced
  1/2   teaspoon ground white pepper
  1/2   cup arborio or short grain rice
  1/2   cup quick-cooking barley
  1/4   cup quinoa or instant brown rice
    1   14.5-ounce can reduced-sodium
        vegetable broth
    1   cup water
  1/4   cup dry white wine or water
    1   tablespoon snipped fresh rosemary or
        1 teaspoon dried rosemary, crushed
    1   teaspoon snipped fresh marjoram or
        1/2 teaspoon dried marjoram, crushed
    1   cup shredded Caciotta with sage,
        provolone, or mozzarella cheese (4 ounces)
  1/2   cup half-and-half or light cream
        Fresh rosemary sprigs (optional)

1. Remove any tough or brown outer layers of fennel bulbs. Rinse whole fennel with cold water; gently shake dry. Remove and discard the top 2 inches of fennel stalks, reserving green fronds. Snip fronds; set aside. Remove and finely chop remaining fennel stalks.
2. Cut 1 fennel bulb into six 1/4-inch slices; set aside. Pull apart leaf and stalk sections of the remaining bulb. Chop and set aside (about 1 cup).
3. In a covered small saucepan cook fennel slices in a small amount of lightly salted water about 5 minutes or just until tender. Drain; set aside. In a large saucepan heat olive oil over medium heat. Add chopped fennel, onion, garlic, and pepper; cook for 4 to 5 minutes or until tender, stirring often. Add rice, barley, and quinoa; cook and stir for 3 minutes more.
4. Stir in vegetable broth, the water, white wine, snipped or dried rosemary, and marjoram. Return to boiling; reduce heat. Simmer, covered, about 20 minutes or until grains are tender, stirring often.
5. Remove saucepan from heat. Add cheese and half-and-half, stirring until cheese is melted. To serve, sprinkle with fennel leaves.

Garnish with reserved cooked fennel slices and, if desired, fresh rosemary sprigs.
MAKES 6 SERVINGS.

Per serving: 283 cal., 11 g total fat (5 g sat. fat), 21 mg chol., 386 mg sodium, 35 g carbo., 9 g fiber, 10 g pro

Quick Tip Fennel is an anise-flavor bulb commonly used in Italian cooking. The bulb itself, the stalks, and feathery fronds, or leaves, all can be used. The bulb and stalks are eaten raw or cooked—the fronds are most often used as a fresh garnish. Choose fennel that is bright white, with no bruises or scuff marks, and that feels heavy for its size. Fronds should be bright green and fresh—not wilted or wet.

Corn and Bean Quesadillas

Start to Finish: 20 minutes

  1/2   cup drained canned corn
  1/4   teaspoon chili powder
    1   cup fat-free refried beans
    4   7- to 8-inch fat-free flour tortillas
    1   cup chopped, peeled papaya, mango, or
        peaches
    1   4-ounce can green chiles, drained and cut
        in strips (see note, page 31)
  3/4   to 1 cup shredded Chihuahua or
        Monterey Jack cheese (3 to 4 ounces)
        Nonstick cooking spray
        Fat-free sour cream (optional)
        Guacamole (optional)
        Fresh cilantro leaves (optional)

1. In a small bowl combine corn and chili powder; set aside. Spread about 1/4 cup of the refried beans on half of each tortilla. Layer papaya, the corn mixture, and green chiles. Sprinkle with cheese. Fold tortillas in half, pressing gently.
2. Lightly coat a large nonstick skillet with cooking spray. Cook quesadillas over medium heat for 2 to 3 minutes or until lightly browned, turning once. Cut each quesadilla in wedges. If desired, serve with sour cream, guacamole, and/or cilantro leaves.
MAKES 3 TO 4 SERVINGS.

Per serving: 382 cal., 10 g total fat (6 g sat. fat), 34 mg chol., 1,260 mg sodium, 58 g carbo., 6 g fiber, 18 g pro.

Quick Tip Mexican cheeses are categorized as fresh, soft, semisoft, semifirm, and firm. Chihuahua—also called asadero—is a semifirm cheese that is a terrific melting cheese. Monterey Jack is a good replacement if you can't find it. The most familiar firm cheese—perfect for crumbling over refried beans—is called Cotija (co-TEE-ah). Dry feta is a good stand-in—though Cotija is widely available.

Zucchini Cakes with Mushroom Ragoût

Prep: 10 minutes **Bake:** 11 minutes
Oven: 400°F

        Nonstick cooking spray
    1   cup shredded zucchini (1/2 of a medium)
    1   8.5-ounce package corn muffin mix
    1   cup shredded cheddar cheese (4 ounces)
  1/4   cup milk
    1   egg, lightly beaten
  1/4   teaspoon cayenne pepper
    1   tablespoon olive oil
   12   ounces assorted mushrooms, quartered
        (4 1/2 cups)
        Salt and black pepper
    1   cup drained bottled roasted red sweet
        peppers

1. Preheat oven to 400°F. Lightly coat twelve 2 1/2-inch muffin cups with cooking spray; set aside.
2. In a large bowl combine zucchini, muffin mix, cheese, milk, egg, and cayenne pepper; mix well. Spoon evenly into prepared muffin cups. Bake for 11 to 14 minutes or until golden.
3. Meanwhile, in a large skillet heat olive oil over medium-high heat. Add mushrooms; cook for 3 to 4 minutes or until tender, stirring occasionally. Season with salt and black pepper. Place roasted peppers in blender. Cover; blend until nearly smooth.
4. For each serving, arrange 3 cakes on a plate with some of the mushrooms and pureed peppers. **MAKES 4 SERVINGS.**

Per serving: 443 cal., 21 g total fat (7 g sat. fat), 84 mg chol., 701 mg sodium, 49 g carbo., 2 g fiber, 16 g pro.

Zucchini
Cakes with
Mushroom
Ragout

Garden Sliders ♡

Start to Finish: 30 minutes

1 15- to 16-ounce can Great Northern or cannellini (white kidney) beans, rinsed and drained
2 tablespoons olive oil
2 cloves garlic, minced
½ teaspoon Italian seasoning, crushed
  Salt and black pepper
1 medium yellow summer squash, cut into ¼-inch slices
24 ¼-inch slices baguette-style French bread
2 medium roma tomatoes, cut into ¼-inch slices
1 small cucumber, cut into ¼-inch slices
  Celery leaves, small tomato wedges, and/or pickle slices (optional)

1. For bean spread, in a blender or food processor combine drained beans, 1 tablespoon of the oil, garlic, and Italian seasoning. Cover; blend or process until smooth. Season with salt and pepper.
2. Toss squash slices with the remaining 1 tablespoon oil. Place squash in a grill basket. For a charcoal grill, place basket on grill rack directly over medium coals. Grill about 5 minutes or just until squash is tender, turning once. (For a gas grill, preheat grill; reduce heat to medium. Place basket on grill rack. Cover and grill as above.)
3. Spread 1 side of each bread slice with bean spread. Top half of the bread slices with tomato, squash, and cucumber. Top with remaining bread slices, spread sides down. Secure sandwiches with wooden picks. If desired, top with celery leaves.
MAKES 6 SERVINGS.

Per serving: 240 cal., 4 g total fat (0 g sat. fat), 0 mg chol., 578 mg sodium, 46 g carbo., 6 g fiber, 12 g pro.

Zucchini-Carrot Burgers

Zucchini-Carrot Burgers ♡

Start to Finish: 25 minutes

¼ cup refrigerated or frozen egg product, thawed
1 tablespoon olive oil
1 teaspoon dried oregano, crushed
1 cup crushed stone-ground wheat crackers (about 22)
1 cup finely shredded zucchini
1 cup finely shredded carrot
¼ cup chopped green onions
½ cup plain low-fat yogurt
2 small cloves garlic, minced
1 teaspoon finely shredded lemon peel
4 slices country-style bread
  Leaf lettuce
½ of a small cucumber, thinly sliced
1 small tomato, thinly sliced

1. In a medium bowl combine egg product, 1 teaspoon of the oil, and the oregano. Add the crushed crackers, zucchini, carrot, and green onions; mix well. Form the vegetable mixture into four 3½-inch-diameter patties.
2. In a large nonstick skillet heat the remaining 2 teaspoons oil over medium heat. Cook patties in hot oil for 5 to 7 minutes or until golden brown, turning once. Meanwhile, for sauce, in a small bowl combine the yogurt, garlic, and lemon peel.
3. To serve, top bread slices with lettuce, cucumber, sauce, patties, and tomato. Serve immediately. **MAKES 4 SERVINGS.**

Per serving: 253 cal., 8 g total fat (2 g sat. fat), 2 mg chol., 364 mg sodium, 38 g carbo., 5 g fiber, 9 g pro.

White Bean and Goat Cheese Wraps ♡

Start to Finish: 20 minutes

1 19-ounce can cannellini (white kidney) beans, rinsed and drained
1 4-ounce package soft goat cheese (chèvre)
1 tablespoon snipped fresh oregano
1 tablespoon snipped fresh parsley
6 8-inch whole wheat flour tortillas, warmed if desired
6 cups fresh baby spinach leaves
1 12-ounce jar roasted red sweet peppers, drained and thinly sliced

1. In a medium bowl mash beans lightly with a fork. Add goat cheese, oregano, and parsley; stir until well mixed.

2. Divide bean mixture among tortillas, spreading evenly. Top bean mixture with spinach and roasted peppers. Roll up tortillas; cut in half to serve. **MAKES 6 SERVINGS.**

Per serving: 248 cal., 8 g total fat (4 g sat. fat), 9 mg chol., 552 mg sodium, 31 g carbo., 16 g fiber, 18 g pro.

White Bean and Sweet Potato Chili

Start to Finish: 30 minutes

1 tablespoon vegetable oil
1 cup chopped onion (1 large)
3 cloves garlic, minced
2 15- to 19-ounce cans cannellini (white kidney) beans, rinsed and drained
2 14.5-ounce cans Mexican-style stewed tomatoes, cut up and undrained
1 14.5-ounce can vegetable or chicken broth
1 4-ounce can diced green chile peppers, undrained
1 15-ounce can cut sweet potatoes, drained and cut into bite-size pieces

1. In a 4-quart Dutch oven heat oil over medium heat. Add onion and garlic; cook until tender. Stir in beans, undrained tomatoes, broth, and green chiles. Bring to boiling, reduce heat.

2. Stir in sweet potatoes. Simmer, uncovered, for 15 minutes. **MAKES 6 SERVINGS.**

Per serving: 162 cal., 3 g total fat (0 g sat. fat), 1 mg chol., 1,007 mg sodium, 33 g carbo., 7 g fiber, 10 g pro.

Tomato-Basil Panini ♡

Prep: 20 minutes **Cook:** 2 minutes per batch

  Olive oil nonstick cooking spray
8 slices whole wheat bread; four 6-inch whole wheat hoagie rolls, split; or 2 whole wheat pita bread rounds, halved crosswise and split horizontally
4 cups fresh baby spinach leaves
1 medium tomato, cut into 8 slices
1/8 teaspoon salt
1/8 teaspoon black pepper
1/4 cup thinly sliced red onion
2 tablespoons shredded fresh basil
1/2 cup crumbled reduced-fat feta cheese (2 ounces)

1. Lightly coat an unheated electric sandwich press, panini griddle, covered indoor grill, grill pan, or large nonstick skillet with nonstick cooking spray; set aside.

2. Place 4 of the bread slices, roll bottoms, or pita pieces on a work surface; top with half of the spinach leaves. Add a tomato slice to each sandwich; sprinkle lightly with salt and pepper. Add red onion and basil. Top with feta and the remaining spinach. Top with the remaining bread slices, roll tops, or pita pieces. Press down firmly.

3. Preheat sandwich press, panini griddle, or covered indoor grill following manufacturer's directions. (Or heat grill pan or skillet over medium heat.) Add sandwiches, in batches if necessary. If using sandwich press, panini griddle, or covered indoor grill, close lid and grill for 2 to 3 minutes or until bread is toasted. (If using grill pan or skillet, place a heavy skillet on top of sandwiches. Cook over medium heat for 1 to 2 minutes or until bottoms are toasted. Carefully remove top skillet, which may be hot. Turn sandwiches and top again with the skillet. Cook for 1 to 2 minutes more or until bread is toasted.) **MAKES 4 SERVINGS.**

Per serving: 174 cal., 5 g total fat (2 g sat. fat), 5 mg chol., 597 mg sodium, 27 g carbo., 5 g fiber, 10 g pro.

Soups and sandwiches easily lend themselves to a meatless makeup. Legumes, vegetables, and cheeses fill you up but don't weigh you down.

Tomato-Basil
Panini

Edamame
Bread Salad

Edamame Bread Salad

Prep: 30 minutes **Cook:** 6 minutes

¾ cup feta cheese
½ cup Greek yogurt or plain low-fat yogurt
   Salt and black pepper
2 tablespoons snipped fresh basil
1 small clove garlic, minced
2 12-ounce packages frozen soybeans (edamame)
1½ pounds fresh green beans, trimmed
1 recipe Balsamic Dressing
2 cups yellow or red cherry tomatoes, halved
12 slices crusty country bread, toasted
   Fresh basil leaves

1. In a small bowl combine feta cheese and yogurt. Mash into a paste with a fork. Add basil and garlic; mash to blend. Season with salt and pepper. Cover and chill for up to 8 hours.
2. In a large saucepan bring 8 cups lightly salted water to boiling. Add soybeans and green beans; return to boiling. Reduce heat and cook, covered, for 6 to 8 minutes or until tender. Drain; cool. Meanwhile, prepare Balsamic Dressing.
3. Add tomatoes to bean mixture. Drizzle with half of the dressing; toss to coat. Cover and chill up to 8 hours. Toss before serving.
4. Spread feta mixture on bread slices; place slices on serving plate; mound bean mixture on top. Drizzle with remaining dressing and sprinkle with basil leaves. **MAKES 6 SERVINGS.**

Balsamic Dressing In a blender combine ¼ cup extra virgin olive oil, 2 tablespoons balsamic vinegar, 2 tablespoons red wine vinegar, and ¼ cup lightly packed fresh basil leaves. Cover and blend until smooth. Add 2 tablespoons whipping cream; cover and blend just until mixed. Season with salt and black pepper.

Per serving: 474 cal., 24 g total fat (7 g sat. fat), 27 mg chol., 679 mg sodium, 46 g carbo., 10 g fiber, 22 g pro.

Layered Southwestern Salad with Tortilla Strips

Layered Southwestern Salad with Tortilla Strips ♡

Prep: 15 minutes **Bake:** 15 minutes
Oven: 350°F

2 6-inch corn tortillas
   Nonstick cooking spray
½ cup light sour cream
¼ cup snipped fresh cilantro
2 tablespoons fat-free milk
1 teaspoon olive oil
1 large clove garlic, minced
½ teaspoon chili powder
½ teaspoon finely shredded lime peel
¼ teaspoon salt
¼ teaspoon black pepper
6 cups torn romaine lettuce
4 roma tomatoes, chopped (2 cups)
1 15-ounce can black beans, rinsed and drained
1 cup fresh corn kernels
½ cup shredded reduced-fat cheddar cheese (2 ounces)
1 avocado, halved, seeded, peeled, and chopped
   Snipped fresh cilantro (optional)

1. Preheat oven to 350°F. Cut tortillas into ½-inch-wide strips; place in a 15×10×1-inch baking pan. Coat tortillas lightly with cooking spray. Bake for 15 to 18 minutes or until crisp, stirring once. Cool on wire rack.
2. For dressing, in a small bowl stir together sour cream, the ¼ cup cilantro, milk, oil, garlic, chili power, lime peel, salt, and pepper.
3. Place lettuce in a large glass serving bowl. Top with tomatoes, beans, corn, cheese, and avocado. Add dressing and sprinkle with tortilla strips. If desired, garnish with additional cilantro. **MAKES 6 SERVINGS.**

Per serving: 227 cal., 11 g total fat (3 g sat. fat), 12 mg chol., 386 mg sodium, 29 g carbo., 9 g fiber, 11 g pro.

Quick Tip It isn't necessary to cook the corn. However, for a roasted flavor and softer texture, try baking it with the tortilla strips. Place the strips at one end of the baking pan and the corn at the other end.

Meat

Beef Tenderloin with Peppercorns

Beef Tenderloin with Peppercorns

Start to Finish: 20 minutes

    4   4- to 5-ounce beef tenderloin steaks,
        1 inch thick
    4   teaspoons cracked black peppercorns
    3   tablespoons butter
    2   teaspoons all-purpose flour
    ⅛   teaspoon salt
    ⅛   teaspoon ground black pepper
    ⅔   cup half-and-half, light cream, or milk
    2   tablespoons horseradish mustard
        Cracked peppercorns (optional)

1. Trim fat from steaks. Rub both sides of steaks with cracked peppercorns. In a large skillet melt 2 tablespoons of the butter over medium-high heat. Add steaks; reduce heat to medium. Cook for 10 to 13 minutes for medium-rare (145°F) to medium (160°F), turning once halfway through cooking. Transfer steaks to a serving platter; keep warm.
2. Meanwhile, for sauce, in a small saucepan melt remaining 1 tablespoon butter. Stir in flour, salt, and ground pepper. Add half-and-half. Cook and stir until thickened and bubbly. Stir in mustard. Spoon sauce over the steaks. If desired, sprinkle with cracked peppercorns. **MAKES 4 SERVINGS.**

Per serving: 317 cal., 22 g total fat (11 g sat. fat), 96 mg chol., 303 mg sodium, 5 g carbo., 1 g fiber, 26 g pro.

Herbed Steaks with Horseradish

Start to Finish: 20 minutes

    2   12- to 14-ounce beef top loin steaks,
        1 inch thick
        Salt and black pepper
    2   tablespoons prepared horseradish
    1   tablespoon Dijon mustard
    2   teaspoons snipped fresh Italian (flat-leaf)
        parsley
    1   teaspoon snipped fresh thyme
        Broiled cherry tomatoes (optional)
        Broiled sweet pepper strips (optional)
        Herbed mayonnaise (optional)
        Fresh thyme sprigs (optional)

1. Preheat broiler. Trim fat from steaks. Lightly sprinkle steaks with salt and black pepper. Place steaks on the unheated rack of a broiler pan. Broil 3 to 4 inches from heat for 7 minutes.
2. Meanwhile, in a small bowl combine horseradish, mustard, parsley, and thyme.
2. Turn steaks. Broil for 8 to 9 minutes more for medium (160°F). The last 1 minute of broiling, spread steaks with horseradish mixture. If desired, serve with tomatoes, peppers, and herbed mayonnaise; garnish with fresh thyme sprigs. **MAKES 4 SERVINGS.**

Per serving: 284 cal., 15 g total fat (6 g sat. fat), 84 mg chol., 351 mg sodium, 1 g carbo., 0 g fiber, 33 g pro.

Wine- and Balsamic-Glazed Steak

Start to Finish: 30 minutes

    1   pound boneless beef top loin or top sirloin
        steak, cut ½ to ¾ inch thick
    2   teaspoons vegetable oil
    3   cloves garlic, minced
    ⅛   teaspoon crushed red pepper
    ¾   cup dry red wine
    2   cups sliced fresh mushrooms
    3   tablespoons balsamic vinegar
    2   tablespoons soy sauce
    4   teaspoons honey
    2   tablespoons butter

1. Trim fat from steak(s). In a large skillet heat oil over medium-high heat until very hot. Add steak(s). Reduce heat to medium and cook for 10 to 13 minutes or to desired doneness, turning meat occasionally. If meat browns too quickly, reduce heat to medium-low. Transfer meat to platter; keep warm.
2. Add garlic and red pepper to skillet; cook for 10 seconds. Remove skillet from heat. Carefully add wine. Return to heat. Boil, uncovered, about 5 minutes or until most of the liquid is evaporated. Add mushrooms, vinegar, soy sauce, and honey; return to simmer. Cook and stir about 4 minutes or until mushrooms are tender. Stir in butter until melted. Spoon over steak(s).
MAKES 4 SERVINGS.

Per serving: 377 cal., 21 g total fat (9 g sat. fat), 82 mg chol., 588 mg sodium, 12 g carbo., 0 g fiber, 27 g pro.

Herbed Steaks
with
Horseradish

Peppered
Steaks with
Asiago
Cheese

Peppered Steaks with Asiago Cheese

Start to Finish: 20 minutes

- 4 beef tenderloin steaks, cut ¾ inch thick (about 1 pound)
- 1 teaspoon coarsely ground black pepper
- 1 tablespoon olive oil
- ¼ cup lower-sodium beef broth
- 2 4-ounce packages sliced cremini, shiitake, or portobello mushrooms or one 8-ounce package sliced button mushrooms (about 3 cups)
- 1 ounce Asiago cheese, shaved
- ¼ cup fresh spinach leaves, shredded (optional)

1. Trim fat from steaks. Rub both sides of steaks with pepper. In a large skillet heat olive oil over medium-high heat. Add steaks; reduce heat to medium. Cook for 7 to 9 minutes for medium-rare (145°F) to medium (160°F), turning once halfway through cooking. Transfer steaks to serving platter; keep warm.
2. Add beef broth to skillet. Cook until bubbly, stirring to loosen any crusty browned bits in bottom of skillet. Add mushrooms; simmer, uncovered, for 4 minutes. To serve, spoon sauce over steaks. Sprinkle with shaved cheese. If desired, garnish with fresh spinach leaves. **MAKES 4 SERVINGS.**

Per serving: 352 cal., 26 g total fat (10 g sat. fat), 82 mg chol., 165 mg sodium, 3 g carbo., 1 g fiber, 26 g pro.

Quick Tip Slightly reduced beef broth makes a light sauce for this hearty steak. For a thicker sauce, increase the broth to ½ cup and stir in ¼ teaspoon cornstarch before adding the broth to the skillet.

Bistro Beef Steak with Wild Mushroom Ragoût

Start to Finish: 30 minutes

- 3 8-ounce boneless beef top loin steaks, cut ¾ inch thick
- 5 cloves garlic, minced
- 2 teaspoons herbes de Provence
- ½ teaspoon black pepper

Bistro Beef Steak with Wild Mushroom Ragoût

- ¼ teaspoon salt
- 1 tablespoon olive oil
- ⅓ cup finely chopped shallots
- 8 ounces assorted wild mushrooms (oyster, cremini, and/or shiitake), sliced
- ¼ cup dry sherry (optional)
- 1 14.5-ounce can lower-sodium beef broth
- 1 tablespoon cornstarch

1. Preheat broiler. Trim fat from steaks. In a small bowl combine 3 of the minced garlic cloves, 1 teaspoon of the herbes de Provence, the pepper, and salt. Rub herb mixture over steaks. Place steaks on the unheated rack of broiler pan. Broil 3 to 4 inches from the heat for 9 to 11 minutes for medium-rare (145°F) to medium (160°F), turning once.
2. Meanwhile, in a large nonstick skillet heat oil over medium-high heat until hot. Add shallots and 2 minced garlic cloves; cook for 1 to 3 minutes or until tender. Add mushrooms; cook for 6 to 7 minutes or until mushrooms are tender and any liquid evaporates, stirring occasionally. Remove from heat. If desired, stir in sherry. Return to heat. Bring to boiling. Cook, uncovered, for 30 to 60 seconds or until liquid evaporates.
3. In a bowl stir together broth, cornstarch, and the remaining 1 teaspoon herbes de Provence. Stir into mixture in skillet. Cook and stir until thickened and bubbly. Cook and stir for 2 minutes more.
4. Cut each steak in half. Serve steaks with the mushroom mixture. **MAKES 6 SERVINGS.**

Per serving: 206 cal., 8 g total fat (2 g sat. fat), 66 mg chol., 291 mg sodium, 4 g carbo., 1 g fiber, 27 g pro.

Steak with
Sautéed
Onions

Steak with Sautéed Onions

Start to Finish: 25 minutes

6   4-ounce beef tenderloin steaks, 1 inch thick
¼   teaspoon salt
¼   teaspoon black pepper
2   tablespoons butter or margarine
1   small red onion, cut into 6 wedges
2   cloves garlic, minced
1   teaspoon dried basil, crushed
½   teaspoon dried oregano, crushed
2   tablespoons whipping cream
2   tablespoons onion marmalade or orange
     marmalade

1. Trim fat from steaks. Sprinkle steaks with
salt and pepper. In a large skillet melt butter
over medium heat. Add onion and garlic;
cook and stir for 6 to 8 minutes or until onion

is tender but not brown. Remove onion and
garlic from skillet.
2. Increase heat to medium-high. Add steaks
to skillet; cook for 10 to 13 minutes for
medium-rare (145°F) to medium (160°F),
turning and sprinkling meat with basil and
oregano halfway through cooking.
3. Transfer meat to serving plates. Return
onions to skillet. Heat through. Remove skillet
from heat. Stir in whipping cream. Spoon
cream over steaks. Top each steak with
1 teaspoon marmalade. Divide cooked
onions evenly among the steaks.
MAKES 6 SERVINGS.

Per serving: 271 cal., 13 g total fat (4 g sat. fat), 63 mg
chol., 110 mg sodium, 14 g carbo., 0 g fiber, 24 g pro.

Steak with Sweet Potato-Mango Chutney ♡

Start to Finish: 20 minutes

1   large sweet potato, peeled and diced
     (12 ounces)
4   6-ounce boneless beef eye round steaks,
     ¾ inch thick
     Salt
     Steak seasoning blend
⅓   cup mango chutney
¼   cup dried cranberries
     Fresh rosemary sprigs (optional)

1. In a covered medium saucepan cook
sweet potato in lightly salted boiling water for
8 to 10 minutes or until tender; drain and
keep warm.
2. Meanwhile, trim fat from steaks. Lightly
season steaks with salt and steak seasoning
blend. Heat a large nonstick skillet over
medium-high heat. Add steaks to skillet;
reduce heat to medium. Cook for 8 to
10 minutes for medium-rare (145°F) or to
desired doneness. If meat browns too
quickly, reduce heat to medium-low. Transfer
to serving plates; cover to keep warm.
3. Add sweet potato to skillet; cook and stir
for 2 minutes. Add chutney and cranberries to
skillet. Stir gently to heat through. Season
with additional salt and steak seasoning.
Serve with steaks. If desired, garnish with
fresh rosemary. **MAKES 4 SERVINGS.**

Per serving: 344 cal., 5 g total fat (2 g sat. fat), 70 mg
chol., 418 mg sodium, 32 g carbo., 4 g fiber, 40 g pro.

Steak with Sweet Potato-Mango Chutney

Southwestern
Tortilla
Wedges

Southwestern Tortilla Wedges

Prep: 20 minutes **Bake:** 5 minutes **Oven:** 400°F

 Nonstick cooking spray
6 ounces lean ground beef
½ cup bottled salsa or picante sauce
¼ cup water
1 teaspoon fajita seasoning
4 8-inch spinach-flavor, tomato-basil-flavor, or plain flour tortillas
¼ cup light sour cream
½ cup canned red kidney beans, rinsed and drained
¼ cup canned whole kernel corn with sweet peppers, drained
½ cup shredded Monterey Jack cheese with peppers or shredded Colby-Jack cheese (2 ounces)
1 tablespoon snipped fresh cilantro
 Chopped tomato (optional)
 Shredded lettuce (optional)
 Bottled salsa or picante sauce (optional)

1. Preheat oven to 400°F. Coat a medium nonstick skillet with cooking spray. Cook ground beef over medium-high heat until browned. Drain off fat. Stir in the ½ cup salsa, the water, and fajita seasoning. Bring to boiling; reduce heat. Simmer, covered, for 5 minutes.
2. Spread 1 side of each tortilla with some of the sour cream. Top with beef mixture, beans, and corn. In a small bowl combine shredded cheese and cilantro. Sprinkle cheese mixture on tortillas. Place on a very large baking sheet (or use 2 regular baking sheets).
3. Bake for 5 to 7 minutes or until heated through and cheese melts. Cut into wedges to serve. If desired, top with chopped tomato and shredded lettuce and serve with additional salsa. **MAKES 4 SERVINGS.**

Per serving: 275 cal., 12 g total fat (6 g sat. fat), 44 mg chol., 448 mg sodium, 26 g carbo., 3 g fiber, 17 g pro.

Hearty Hamburger Stroganoff

Start to Finish: 25 minutes

1 pound ground beef
½ cup chopped onion (1 medium)
1 clove garlic, minced
8 ounces fresh mushrooms, sliced
1 10.5-ounce can condensed beef broth
3 tablespoons lemon juice
1 tablespoon dry red wine (optional)
4 ounces dried angel hair pasta, broken
1 8-ounce carton sour cream
 Salt and black pepper

1. In an extra-large skillet cook beef, onion, and garlic over medium heat until meat is browned and onion is tender. Drain off fat.
2. Stir in mushrooms; cook and stir about 5 minutes or until mushrooms are tender. Stir in beef broth, lemon juice, and, if desired, wine. Bring to boiling; reduce heat. Stir in uncooked pasta.
3. Simmer, covered, about 5 minutes more or until pasta is tender. Stir in sour cream. Cook and stir until heated through. Season with salt and pepper. **MAKES 4 TO 5 SERVINGS.**

Per serving: 543 cal., 34 g total fat (15 g sat. fat), 106 mg chol., 780 mg sodium, 30 g carbo., 1 g fiber, 31 g pro.

Blackened Skirt Steak

Start to Finish: 20 minutes

1 pound beef plate skirt steak or flank steak
1 tablespoon coarsely ground black pepper
1 teaspoon garlic salt
1 teaspoon paprika
1 teaspoon dried onion flakes
2 tablespoons vegetable oil
2 16-ounce cans sweet potatoes in light syrup
3 tablespoons butter
½ teaspoon garlic salt
¼ teaspoon cayenne pepper

1. Trim fat from steak. In a small bowl combine black pepper, 1 teaspoon garlic salt, paprika, and dried onion flakes. Brush steak with 1 tablespoon of the oil. Rub pepper mixture on both sides of steak.
2. In a large nonstick skillet heat the remaining 1 tablespoon oil over medium-high heat. Add steak; cook about 4 minutes for medium-rare (145°F), turning once halfway through cooking. Remove from heat.
3. Meanwhile, for mashed sweet potatoes, drain sweet potatoes, reserving ½ cup liquid. In a medium saucepan combine sweet potatoes and reserved liquid. Heat over medium-high heat, uncovered, about 5 minutes or until heated through. Add butter, ½ teaspoon garlic salt, and cayenne pepper. Beat until smooth.
4. Thinly slice the steak across the grain and divide among 4 plates. Serve with mashed sweet potatoes. **MAKES 4 SERVINGS.**

Per serving: 534 cal., 26 g total fat (15 g sat. fat), 79 mg chol., 782 mg sodium, 49 g carbo., 6 g fiber, 25 g pro.

Keep staples such as bottled salsa, broth, pasta, and a few canned goods on hand and with the addition of a few fresh ingredients, dinner is done.

Tarragon Pot Roast with Fruit

Tarragon Pot Roast with Fruit

Start to Finish: 25 minutes

1 tablespoon butter
2 tablespoons finely chopped shallot
1 16- to 17-ounce package refrigerated cooked beef roast au jus
2 tablespoons tarragon vinegar
2 cups fresh fruit wedges (such as apples, plums, pears, and/or nectarines or peeled peaches)
 Hot cooked spaetzle or wide noodles (optional)
1 teaspoon snipped fresh tarragon

1. In a large skillet melt butter over medium heat. Add shallot; cook for 1 minute. Add beef roast and juices from package; reduce heat. Simmer, covered, about 10 minutes or until roast is heated through.

2. Add vinegar to skillet. Spoon fruit on top. Cover and heat about 4 minutes or until heated through. If desired, serve with hot cooked noodles. Sprinkle with tarragon.

MAKES 4 SERVINGS.

Per serving: 225 cal., 11 g total fat (6 g sat. fat), 68 mg chol., 422 mg sodium, 12 g carbo., 1 g fiber, 22 g pro.

Quick Tip Tarragon has a licoricelike flavor, similar to basil but a bit more intense. It's often paired with chicken. If you don't have fresh tarragon, basil makes a fine substitute. Its clovelike flavor is a nice match with the fruit in this dish.

Italian-Style Sloppy Joes ♡

Prep: 15 minutes **Cook:** 15 minutes

12 ounces lean ground beef
½ cup chopped onion (1 medium)
1 8-ounce can tomato sauce
¼ teaspoon dried oregano, crushed
¼ teaspoon dried basil, crushed
6 whole wheat hamburger buns, split and toasted
½ cup shredded reduced-fat mozzarella cheese (2 ounces)
¼ cup finely shredded Parmesan cheese (1 ounce)

1. In a large skillet cook ground beef and onion over medium-high heat until meat is browned and onion is tender. Drain off fat. Stir in tomato sauce, oregano, and basil. Bring to boiling; reduce heat. Simmer, covered, for 15 minutes.

2. Divide beef mixture among hamburger bun bottoms; sprinkle with mozzarella and Parmesan cheese. Add bun tops.

MAKES 6 SERVINGS.

Per serving: 281 cal., 10 g total fat (5 g sat. fat), 50 mg chol., 583 mg sodium, 25 g carbo., 3 g fiber, 20 g pro.

Mini Meat Loaves with Green Beans

Mini Meat Loaves with Green Beans

Start to Finish: 22 minutes **Oven:** 450°F

1 egg, lightly beaten
1 cup purchased pasta sauce
½ cup fine dry bread crumbs
2 tablespoons fresh basil leaves, coarsely chopped
¼ teaspoon salt
1 pound lean ground beef
1 cup shredded mozzarella cheese (4 ounces)
1 12-ounce package fresh green beans, trimmed
1 tablespoon olive oil
Crushed red pepper (optional)

1. Preheat oven to 450°F. In a large bowl combine egg, ½ cup of the pasta sauce, the bread crumbs, basil, and the salt. Add beef and ½ cup of the cheese; mix well. Divide beef mixture into 4 equal portions. Shape each portion in a 5½×2-inch oval. Place on a 15×10×1-inch baking pan. Spoon the remaining ½ cup pasta sauce on the loaves.
2. Bake about 15 minutes or until internal temperature registers 160°F on an instant-read meat thermometer. Sprinkle with the remaining ½ cup cheese; bake for 1 to 2 minutes more or until cheese is melted.
3. Meanwhile, in a covered medium saucepan cook green beans in boiling lightly salted water about 10 minutes or until crisp-tender. Drain; toss with 1 tablespoon olive oil and, if desired, crushed red pepper. Serve beans with meat loaves.
MAKES 4 SERVINGS.

Per serving: 496 cal., 29 g total fat (12 g sat. fat), 145 mg chol., 742 mg sodium, 25 g carbo., 5 g fiber, 34 g pro.

Curry Pepper Steak with Sweet Potatoes

Curry Pepper Steak with Sweet Potatoes

Start to Finish: 30 minutes

3 tablespoons vegetable oil
1 pound beef top round steak, cut into thin bite-size strips
1¼ teaspoons salt
2 green sweet peppers, seeded and cut into ½-inch strips
2 sweet potatoes (1 pound), peeled, quartered lengthwise, and sliced crosswise ¼ inch thick
1 large onion, thinly sliced
½ teaspoon curry powder
¼ teaspoon ground ginger
⅛ teaspoon cayenne pepper
½ cup water

1. In a large skillet heat 2 tablespoons of the oil over medium-high heat. Sprinkle meat with ¼ teaspoon of the salt. Add meat to skillet; cook and stir about 3 minutes or to desired doneness. Remove meat from skillet; cover to keep warm.
2. Add the remaining 1 tablespoon oil to the skillet. Add sweet peppers, sweet potatoes, and onion; cook for 6 minutes, stirring frequently. Add curry, ginger, cayenne pepper, and remaining 1 teaspoon salt; cook for 2 minutes. Add the water; cook, covered, about 6 minutes or until sweet potatoes are tender, stirring occasionally. Add meat; heat through. **MAKES 4 SERVINGS.**

Per serving: 375 cal., 15 g total fat (2 g sat. fat), 71 mg chol., 793 mg sodium, 31 g carbo., 4 g fiber, 29 g pro.

Beef and Noodle Casserole

1. In a large saucepan cook potatoes and sweet potato in a small amount of boiling water for 3 minutes. Drain; cool slightly.
2. In a large nonstick skillet heat oil over medium-high heat. Add onion and sweet pepper; cook until tender. Stir in potatoes. Cook and stir about 5 minutes or just until tender. Stir in roast beef.
3. Using the back of a large spoon, make four depressions in the roast beef mixture. Break an egg into each depression. Cook, covered, over medium-low heat about 5 minutes or until egg whites are set and yolks begin to thicken but are not hard. Sprinkle with green onions. Season with salt and black pepper.

MAKES 4 SERVINGS.

Per serving: 420 cal., 19 g total fat (5 g sat. fat), 257 mg chol., 154 mg sodium, 38 g carbo., 4 g fiber, 25 g pro.

Coriander-Studded Tenderloin

Start to Finish: 20 minutes

4	3- to 4-ounce beef tenderloin steaks, cut 1 inch thick
	Salt
1	tablespoon snipped fresh chives
1	tablespoon olive oil
1	tablespoon reduced-sodium soy sauce
2	cloves garlic, minced
½	teaspoon coriander seeds or cumin seeds, crushed
½	teaspoon celery seeds
½	teaspoon coarsely ground black pepper

1. Trim fat from steaks. Sprinkle with salt. In a small bowl combine chives, oil, soy sauce, garlic, coriander, celery seeds, and pepper. Brush mixture onto both sides of each steak.
2. Place steaks on unheated rack of a broiler pan. Broil 3 to 4 inches from heat until desired doneness, turning once. Allow 12 to 14 minutes for medium-rare (145°F) or 15 to 18 minutes for medium (160°F).

MAKES 4 SERVINGS.

Per serving: 164 cal., 9 g total fat (3 g sat. fat), 42 mg chol., 256 mg sodium, 1 g carbo., 0 g fiber, 18 g pro.

Beef and Noodle Casserole

Prep: 15 minutes **Bake:** 30 minutes
Stand: 5 minutes **Oven:** 350°F

1	pound lean ground beef
½	cup milk
½	of an 8-ounce tub cream cheese spread with chives and onion (½ cup)
½	cup shredded carrot (1 medium)
1	4.6-ounce package vermicelli with garlic and olive oil or one 4.8-ounce package angel hair pasta with herbs
1½	cups boiling water

1. Preheat oven to 350°F. Grease a 1½-quart casserole; set aside. In a large skillet cook beef until browned. Drain off fat.
2. In the casserole gradually whisk milk into cream cheese. Stir in carrot and seasoning packet from pasta. Stir in beef. Break pasta into 1-inch pieces; stir into mixture.

3. Slowly pour boiling water over beef mixture. Bake, covered, for 30 to 35 minutes or until pasta is tender, stirring twice. Let stand, covered, for 5 minutes. Stir before serving.

MAKES 4 SERVINGS.

Per serving: 463 cal., 25 g total fat (13 g sat. fat), 101 mg chol., 619 mg sodium, 28 g carbo., 2 g fiber, 28 g pro.

Sweet Potato-Roast Beef Hash

Start to Finish: 30 minutes

2¾	cups diced, peeled potatoes (3 medium)
1	cup diced, peeled sweet potato (1 medium)
½	cup chopped onion (1 medium)
⅓	cup chopped red sweet pepper
2	tablespoons vegetable oil
8	ounces cooked roast beef, cubed
4	eggs
¼	cup chopped green onions (2)

Meatball
Lasagna

Meatball Lasagna

Prep: 25 minutes **Bake:** 45 minutes
Stand: 15 minutes **Oven:** 375°F

    9 dried lasagna noodles
  1/2 of a 15-ounce container ricotta cheese
 1 1/2 cups shredded mozzarella cheese
       (6 ounces)
  1/4 cup grated Parmesan cheese
    1 16-ounce package frozen cooked Italian-
       style meatballs (1/2-ounce size), thawed
    1 26-ounce jar tomato pasta sauce

1. Preheat oven to 375°F. Cook the lasagna
noodles following package directions. Drain
noodles; rinse with cold water. Drain well; set
noodles aside.

2. Meanwhile, for the filling, in a small bowl
stir together ricotta cheese, 1 cup of the
mozzarella cheese, and Parmesan cheese;
set aside. In a medium bowl stir together the
meatballs and one-third (about 1 cup) of the
pasta sauce; set aside.

3. To assemble, spread a small amount
(about 1/2 cup) of the reserved pasta sauce
over the bottom of a 2-quart square baking
dish. Layer 3 of the cooked noodles in the
dish, trimming or overlapping as necessary
to fit. Spoon the meatball mixture over the
noodles. Layer 3 more noodles over the
meatball layer. Spread half of the remaining
sauce over noodles. Spoon ricotta mixture
over the noodles; spread evenly. Layer the
remaining noodles over ricotta mixture. Spread
remaining sauce over noodles. Cover dish
with foil.

4. Bake for 35 minutes. Remove foil and
sprinkle with the remaining 1/2 cup mozzarella
cheese over lasagna. Bake, uncovered, about
10 minutes more or until heated through. Let
stand for 15 to 20 minutes before
serving. **MAKES 8 SERVINGS.**

Per serving: 410 cal., 21 g total fat (11 g sat. fat), 66 mg
chol., 897 mg sodium, 31 g carbo., 4 g fiber, 23 g pro.

Quick
Honey-Garlic
Pot Roast

Quick Honey-Garlic Pot Roast ♡

Prep: 10 minutes **Cook:** 20 minutes

    1 17-ounce package refrigerated cooked
       beef roast au jus or beef pot roast with
       juices
    2 tablespoons honey
    1 tablespoon Worcestershire sauce
    1 to 1 1/2 teaspoons bottled roasted minced
       garlic
  1/4 teaspoon black pepper
    2 cups packaged peeled baby carrots
   12 ounces small red potatoes, quartered
    1 medium red onion, cut into thin wedges
       Snipped fresh parsley (optional)

1. Remove beef from package, reserving
juices. In a medium bowl combine reserved
juices, honey, Worcestershire sauce, roasted
garlic, and pepper. Place beef in a large
nonstick skillet. Arrange carrots, potatoes,
and onion wedges around beef. Pour honey
mixture over beef and vegetables.

2. Bring beef mixture to boiling; reduce heat.
Simmer, covered, for 20 to 25 minutes or until
vegetables are tender and beef is heated
through. Transfer beef and vegetables to a
serving platter. Spoon sauce over beef and
vegetables. If desired, sprinkle with parsley.
MAKES 4 SERVINGS.

Per serving: 305 cal., 9 g total fat (4 g sat. fat), 64 mg
chol., 502 mg sodium, 35 g carbo., 4 g fiber, 26 g pro.

Quick Tip Look for baby red potatoes, also
called new red potatoes, that are firm and
smooth with no dark spots, wrinkles, or
sprouts. Store in a cool, dark, well-ventilated
place. New potatoes should be used within
3 or 4 days of purchase.

Steak 'n' Bake

Steak 'n' Bake

Prep: 20 minutes **Broil:** 15 minutes
Stand: 5 minutes

4 medium baking potatoes
12 to 16 ounces boneless beef sirloin steak, cut 1 inch thick
2 cups fresh baby spinach
¾ cup bottled blue cheese salad dressing
1 small red onion, cut into thin wedges

1. Wash potatoes; pierce with fork. Arrange potatoes on a microwave-safe plate in spoke formation, leaving 1 inch between potatoes. Microwave on high for 14 to 18 minutes or until tender. Let stand for 5 minutes.
2. Meanwhile, preheat broiler. Trim fat from steak. Place steak on the unheated rack of a broiler pan. Broil 3 to 4 inches from heat for 15 to 17 minutes for medium-rare (145°F) or

20 to 22 minutes for medium (160°F), turning once halfway through broiling. Transfer steak to cutting board; let stand for 5 minutes.
3. To serve, roll each potato gently under your hand. Cut an "X" in top of potato. Press in and up on ends of potato. Cut steak into bite-size strips. Top potatoes with steak strips and spinach; drizzle with dressing. Top with onion wedges. **MAKES 4 SERVINGS.**

Per serving: 580 cal., 35 g total fat (9 g sat. fat), 65 mg chol., 577 mg sodium, 35 g carbo., 4 g fiber, 32 g pro.

Peppery Beef with Mushrooms

Start to Finish: 20 minutes

4 beef tenderloin steaks or 2 beef top loin steaks, cut 1 inch thick (about 1 pound)
2 to 3 teaspoons steak seasoning blend

2 tablespoons butter
1 tablespoon olive oil or butter
2 4-ounce packages sliced cremini, shiitake, or portobello mushrooms (3 cups)
1 large leek, thinly sliced
½ teaspoon dried thyme or oregano, crushed
1 5.5- to 6-ounce can tomato juice
1 recipe Easy Roasted Red Potatoes (optional)

1. Trim fat from steaks. If using top loin steaks, cut each steak in half crosswise. Sprinkle both sides of steaks with seasoning blend; rub in with your fingers. In a large skillet melt butter over medium-high heat. Cook steaks in hot butter over medium heat to desired doneness, turning once. For tenderloin steaks, allow 10 to 13 minutes for medium-rare (145°F) to medium (160°F). For top loin steaks, allow 12 to 15 minutes for medium-rare to medium. Transfer steaks to a warm serving platter; reserving the drippings in the skillet. Keep warm.
2. Add oil to drippings in skillet. Add mushrooms, leek, and thyme. Cook and stir for 2 minutes. Stir in tomato juice. Bring to boiling; reduce heat. Simmer, uncovered, for 2 to 3 minutes more or until leek is tender. Spoon mushroom mixture over the steak. If desired, serve with Easy Roasted Red Potatoes. **MAKES 4 SERVINGS.**

Per serving: 296 cal., 20 g total fat (8 g sat. fat), 86 mg chol., 419 mg sodium, 5 g carbo., 1 g fiber, 26 g pro.

Easy Roasted Red Potatoes Preheat oven to 400°F. Place one 20-ounce package refrigerated new potato wedges in a 2-quart square baking dish. Sprinkle with ½ teaspoon dried rosemary, crushed; ½ teaspoon seasoned salt; ¼ teaspoon garlic powder; and ¼ teaspoon black pepper. Drizzle with 2 tablespoons olive oil; toss gently to coat. Roast for 30 minutes, stirring once. Sprinkle with ⅓ cup finely shredded Parmesan cheese. Roast for 5 to 8 minutes more or until cheese is melted and starts to brown.

Peppery Beef
with
Mushrooms

Spicy Beef and Noodle Salad

Spicy Beef and Noodle Salad ♡

Start to Finish: 20 minutes

1 pound beef flank steak
1 tablespoon soy sauce
8 ounces rice noodles
1 medium English cucumber
½ cup Asian sweet chili sauce
½ cup water
1 cup packaged fresh julienned carrots
 Fresh cilantro leaves (optional)

1. Preheat broiler. Trim fat from steak. Brush steak with soy sauce. Place steak on the rack of an unheated broiler pan. Broil 3 to 4 inches from the heat for 15 to 18 minutes or until medium (160°F), turning once halfway through broiling. Thinly slice beef across the grain.

2. Meanwhile, cook noodles following package directions; drain in colander. Rinse with cold water; drain again.

3. Slice cucumber crosswise into 3 pieces. Using a vegetable peeler, cut lengthwise ribbons from cucumber pieces.

4. In a small bowl combine chili sauce and the water. Divide steak, noodles, cucumber ribbons, and carrots among 4 bowls. Drizzle with chili sauce mixture. If desired, sprinkle with cilantro. **MAKES 4 SERVINGS.**

Per serving: 477 cal., 9 g total fat (4 g sat. fat), 40 mg chol., 839 mg sodium, 70 g carbo., 3 g fiber, 27 g pro.

Mexican Beef and Veggies

Mexican Beef and Veggies ♡

Start to Finish: 30 minutes

12 ounces lean ground beef
1 medium (1¼ pounds) butternut squash, peeled, seeded, and cubed (about 3 cups)
2 cloves garlic, minced
1 teaspoon ground cumin
½ teaspoon salt
⅛ teaspoon ground cinnamon
1 14.5-ounce can diced tomatoes
1 medium zucchini, halved lengthwise and sliced ¼ inch thick
¼ cup water
¼ cup chopped fresh cilantro
2 to 3 cups hot cooked white or brown rice
 Bottled hot pepper sauce (optional)

1. In a large skillet cook ground beef, squash, garlic, cumin, salt, and cinnamon over medium heat until beef is browned. Drain off fat.

2. Stir in undrained tomatoes; bring to boiling; reduce heat. Simmer, covered, about 8 minutes or just until squash is tender. Stir in zucchini and the water. Simmer, covered, about 4 minutes more or until zucchini is tender. Stir in cilantro. Serve over hot cooked rice. If desired, pass bottled hot pepper sauce. **MAKES 4 TO 6 SERVINGS.**

Per serving: 313 cal., 9 g total fat (3 g sat. fat), 54 mg chol., 504 mg sodium, 39 g carbo., 3 g fiber, 20 g pro.

Cranberry
Meatball
Skillet

on high about 4 minutes more or until cabbage is crisp-tender. Drain.

2. Preheat broiler. In a 15×10×1-inch baking pan arrange potatoes, carrots, and cabbage. Drizzle with oil; sprinkle with salt and pepper. Broil 3 to 4 inches from heat for 5 minutes.

3. Meanwhile, preheat an extra-large nonstick skillet over medium-high heat. Add corned beef slices; cook for 2 minutes, turning once. Add the remaining 2 tablespoons water; reduce heat to low. Cook, covered, until heated through.

4. In a small bowl combine mustard and honey. Divide cabbage, corned beef, carrots, and potatoes among 4 plates; drizzle with pan juices. Serve with mustard mixture. **MAKES 4 SERVINGS.**

Per serving: 537 cal., 29 g total fat (8 g sat. fat), 111 mg chol., 1,657 mg sodium, 44 g carbo., 8 g fiber, 25 g pro.

Greek Beef and Pasta Skillet
Start to Finish: 30 minutes

  8 ounces dried rotini
 12 ounces boneless beef sirloin steak or top round steak
  1 tablespoon vegetable oil
  1 26-ounce jar ripe olive and mushroom pasta sauce or marinara pasta sauce
 ¼ teaspoon salt
 ¼ teaspoon ground cinnamon
 ½ of a 10-ounce package frozen chopped spinach, thawed and well drained
 ⅓ cup crumbled feta cheese

1. Cook pasta following the package directions; drain. Meanwhile, trim fat from beef. Thinly slice meat across the grain into bite-size strips.

2. In a large skillet heat oil over medium-high heat. Add meat strips; cook and stir for 2 to 3 minutes or until browned. Add pasta sauce, salt, and cinnamon. Cook and stir until bubbly. Add cooked pasta and spinach. Cook and stir until heated through. Sprinkle with feta cheese. **MAKES 4 SERVINGS.**

Per serving: 483 cal., 12 g total fat (3 g sat. fat), 63 mg chol., 1,063 mg sodium, 60 g carbo., 6 g fiber, 32 g pro.

Cranberry Meatball Skillet
Start to Finish: 20 minutes

  1 16-ounce can whole cranberry sauce
 ⅓ cup water
  2 tablespoons cider vinegar
  1 12-ounce package frozen cooked Swedish-style meatballs
  1 cup peeled fresh baby carrots
  8 ounces tiny new potatoes, halved
    Salt and black pepper

1. In a large skillet stir together cranberry sauce, the water, and vinegar. Add frozen meatballs, carrots, and potatoes. Bring to boiling; reduce heat. Simmer, covered, for 12 to 15 minutes or until potatoes are tender. Season with salt and pepper. **MAKES 4 SERVINGS.**

Per serving: 492 cal., 22 g total fat (9 g sat. fat), 30 mg chol., 857 mg sodium, 62 g carbo., 5 g fiber, 12 g pro.

Corned Beef, Cabbage, Carrots, and New Potatoes
Start to Finish: 25 minutes

  1 pound small new potatoes, halved
  1 pound small carrots, halved lengthwise
 ¼ cup water
  1 small head savoy cabbage, cut into wedges
  2 tablespoons olive oil
    Salt and black pepper
  1 pound cooked deli corned beef, sliced
  2 tablespoons spicy brown mustard
  2 tablespoons honey

1. In a 2½- to 3-quart microwave-safe casserole combine potatoes, carrots, and 2 tablespoons of the water. Cover and microwave on high for 8 minutes, stirring once. Add cabbage. Cover and microwave

Corned
Beef,
Cabbage,
Carrots, and
New Potatoes

Balsamic Pork and Dumplings

Balsamic Pork and Dumplings

Start to Finish: 20 minutes

1	16.9-ounce package frozen potato-and-onion-filled pierogi (potato dumplings)
12	ounces green and/or wax beans, trimmed (3 cups)
1	pound pork tenderloin
	Salt and black pepper
2	tablespoons olive oil
1/2	cup balsamic vinegar
2	teaspoons snipped fresh rosemary (optional)

1. Cook pierogi and beans in boiling water following package directions. Drain pierogi and beans; divide among 4 plates.

2. Meanwhile, trim fat from pork. Cut pork crosswise in 1/2-inch medallions. Gently flatten pork slices by hand to 1/4-inch thickness; lightly sprinkle with salt and pepper. In a large skillet heat oil over medium heat. Add pork; cook for 2 to 3 minutes on each side or until pork is slightly pink in the center and juices run clear. Transfer pork to serving plates with pierogi and beans.

3. Drain fat from skillet. Add balsamic vinegar to hot skillet. Cook, uncovered, about 1 minute or until reduced by half. Drizzle over pork, pierogi, and beans. If desired, sprinkle with rosemary. **MAKES 4 SERVINGS.**

Per serving: 419 cal., 11 g total fat (2 g sat. fat), 79 mg chol., 636 mg sodium, 47 g carbo., 4 g fiber, 30 g pro.

Quick Tip Pierogi are Polish and Russian dumplings filled with meat, cheese, mashed potatoes, mushrooms, cabbage, other vegetables, or sweet fillings. As with other types of stuffed pasta or dough pockets (such as ravioli), pierogi are done when they float to the top of the pot.

Pork Medallions with Cherry Sauce

Start to Finish: 20 minutes

1	pound pork tenderloin
	Salt and freshly ground black pepper
	Nonstick cooking spray
3/4	cup cranberry juice or apple juice

Pork Medallions with Cherry Sauce

2	teaspoons spicy brown mustard
1	teaspoon cornstarch
1	cup sweet cherries (such as Rainier or Bing), halved and pitted, or 1 cup frozen pitted dark sweet cherries, thawed

1. Trim fat from pork. Cut pork crosswise into 1-inch slices. Place each slice between two pieces of plastic wrap. With the heel of your hand, press each slice into a 1/2-inch-thick medallion. Discard plastic wrap. Sprinkle pork lightly with salt and pepper.

2. Coat a large unheated nonstick skillet with cooking spray. Heat skillet over medium-high heat. Add pork; cook for 6 minutes or until pork is slightly pink in center and juices run clear, turning once. Transfer pork to a serving platter; keep warm.

3. For cherry sauce, in a small bowl combine cranberry juice, mustard, and cornstarch; add to skillet. Cook and stir until thickened and bubbly. Cook and stir for 2 minutes more. Stir cherries into juice mixture in skillet. Serve sauce over pork. **MAKES 4 SERVINGS.**

Per serving: 197 cal., 5 g total fat (2 g sat. fat), 81 mg chol., 127 mg sodium, 12 g carbo., 0 g fiber, 26 g pro.

Balsamic Pork Chops

Start to Finish: 25 minutes

4	pork loin chops, 1 inch thick (1 1/2 pounds)
	Salt and black pepper
2	teaspoons olive oil
1/4	cup minced shallots
1/2	cup chicken broth
1/4	cup balsamic vinegar
1/4	teaspoon dried thyme, crushed
1	tablespoon butter or margarine

1. Trim fat from pork chops. Sprinkle chops with salt and pepper. In a large skillet heat oil over medium-high heat. Cook chops in hot oil about 10 minutes or until done (160°F), turning chops once halfway through cooking. Transfer chops to a serving platter; cover to keep warm.

2. For sauce, add shallots to drippings in skillet; cook and stir for 1 minute. Add chicken broth, vinegar, and thyme. Cook and stir over high heat for 5 minutes. Remove from heat; stir in butter. Pour sauce over chops.

MAKES 4 SERVINGS.

Per serving: 274 cal., 13 g total fat (5 g sat. fat), 91 mg chol., 306 mg sodium, 5 g carbo., 0 g fiber, 31 g pro.

Breaded Pork
with Cabbage
and Kale

Breaded Pork with Cabbage and Kale

Start to Finish: 20 minutes **Oven:** 250°F

1¼ pounds center-cut pork loin, cut into
      4 slices
2   cups corn bread stuffing mix, crushed
2   tablespoons olive oil
2   cups sliced red cabbage
6   cups coarsely chopped kale
⅓   cup balsamic vinegar
      Salt and black pepper

1. Preheat oven to 250°F. Place each pork slice between two pieces of plastic wrap. Using the flat side of a meat mallet, lightly pound pork to ¼-inch thickness. Place stuffing mix in a shallow dish; coat both sides of pork slices with stuffing mix.

2. In an extra-large skillet heat 1 tablespoon of the olive oil over medium-high heat. Cook 2 of the pork slices for 2 to 3 minutes on each side or until crisp, golden, and cooked through. Transfer to baking sheet; keep warm in oven. Repeat with the remaining oil and pork slices.

3. Wipe skillet with paper towels. Add cabbage. Cook and stir until cabbage is crisp-tender. Add kale and vinegar; cook just until wilted. Lightly sprinkle with salt and pepper. Serve cabbage mixture with pork. **MAKES 4 SERVINGS.**

Per serving: 394 cal., 14 g total fat (2 g sat. fat), 78 mg chol., 769 mg sodium, 35 g carbo., 4 g fiber, 32 g pro.

Pork and Potatoes with Tomato Relish

Start to Finish: 20 minutes

1   24-ounce package refrigerated mashed
      potatoes
4   boneless pork loin chops, ¾ inch thick
      Salt and black pepper
2   tablespoons olive oil or vegetable oil
1   large red onion, quartered and sliced
2   medium tomatoes, cut into thin wedges
¼   cup bottled red wine vinaigrette salad
      dressing

1. Prepare mashed potatoes following microwave package directions.

2. Meanwhile, trim fat from chops. Sprinkle chops lightly with salt and pepper. In an extra-large skillet heat oil over medium-high heat. Add chops; cook for 3 minutes. Turn chops; add onion to skillet. Cook about 10 minutes more or until temperature registers 160°F, turning chops to brown evenly and stirring onion occasionally. Remove chops to serving plates; keep warm.

3. For tomato relish, add tomatoes and vinaigrette to skillet; cook and stir for 1 minute more. Serve chops with mashed potatoes and tomato relish. Sprinkle with *cracked black pepper.* **MAKES 4 SERVINGS.**

Per serving: 433 cal., 20 g total fat (3 g sat. fat), 62 mg chol., 624 mg sodium, 32 g carbo., 3 g fiber, 31 g pro.

Pork and
Potatoes with
Tomato Relish

Pork Cutlets
with Brussels
Sprouts

Pork Cutlets with Brussels Sprouts

Start to Finish: 30 minutes

    4   ½-inch-thick boneless pork chops
    ¼   cup all-purpose flour
    2   teaspoons paprika or smoked paprika
    ½   teaspoon salt
    ½   teaspoon black pepper
    2   tablespoons butter
    1   pound Brussels sprouts, trimmed and
        halved
    1   8-ounce carton light sour cream
    2   tablespoons milk or half-and-half
    1   teaspoon packed brown sugar

1. Place each chop between 2 pieces of plastic wrap. Using the flat side of a meat mallet or heavy rolling pin, pound each chop to ¼-inch thickness. Discard plastic wrap. In a shallow dish combine flour, 1 teaspoon of the paprika, the salt, and pepper. Coat pork in flour mixture; set aside.

2. In a large skillet melt butter over medium-high heat. Add Brussels sprouts and cook in hot butter for 5 to 8 minutes until crisp-tender and edges are brown. Remove from skillet. Cover and keep warm.

3. Add pork to the hot skillet. Cook for 4 to 5 minutes or until golden on the outside and slightly pink in center, turning once and adding additional butter if needed. Remove pork from skillet. Cover and keep warm.

4. For sauce, in a small bowl stir together sour cream, milk, and brown sugar. Whisk into skillet. Heat through (do not boil). Sprinkle paprika on sauce. Serve sauce over pork and sprouts. **MAKES 4 SERVINGS.**

Per serving: 395 cal., 22 g total fat (11 g sat. fat), 108 mg chol., 480 mg sodium, 22 g carbo., 5 g fiber, 29 g pro.

Quick
Mu Shu Pork

Quick Mu Shu Pork

Start to Finish: 20 minutes

    1   tablespoon vegetable oil
    12   ounces boneless pork top loin chops, cut
         into thin strips
    1   8-ounce package sliced button
         mushrooms
    ½   cup bias-sliced green onions (4)
    4   cups packaged shredded cabbage with
         carrot (coleslaw mix)
    2   tablespoons soy sauce
    1   teaspoon toasted sesame oil
    ⅛   teaspoon crushed red pepper
    8   7- to 8-inch flour tortillas, warmed
         Bottled hoisin or plum sauce

1. In a large skillet heat oil over medium-high heat. Add pork strips; cook and stir for 4 to 5 minutes or until no longer pink. Remove meat from skillet. Add mushrooms and green onions to skillet; cook about 3 minutes or until softened. Add coleslaw mix and cook about 1 minute until wilted. Return meat to skillet. Add soy sauce, sesame oil, and crushed red pepper. Heat through.

2. Serve pork mixture with warm tortillas and hoisin sauce. **MAKES 4 SERVINGS.**

Per serving: 412 cal., 14 g total fat (3 g sat. fat), 47 mg chol., 1,066 mg sodium, 43 g carbo., 4 g fiber, 26 g pro.

Quick Tip Warming tortillas in the microwave may be the quickest way, but it's not the best way: You run the risk of toughening them. The best way to warm tortillas is to wrap a stack tightly in foil, then warm them in a 300°F oven for 10 to 12 minutes.

Pork Tenderloin with Quinoa and Greens

tender, stirring occasionally. Using a slotted spoon, transfer kale to a large serving bowl; stir in quinoa.

5. Thinly slice pork. Serve with quinoa mixture and, if desired, yogurt. If desired, garnish with parsley. **MAKES 6 SERVINGS.**

Per serving: 296 cal., 8 g total fat (2 g sat. fat), 74 mg chol., 468 mg sodium, 27 g carbo., 3 g fiber, 30 g pro.

Quick Tip Indian curry paste is available in the ethnic section of many supermarkets. Look for quinoa at a health food store or in the grains section of a large supermarket.

Pork Loin with Vegetables ♡

Prep: 15 minutes **Roast:** 35 minutes
Stand: 10 minutes **Oven:** 425°F

12 ounces packaged, peeled baby carrots (2½ cups)
12 ounces small new potatoes, quartered
1 12- to 16-ounce pork tenderloin
⅔ cup apricot preserves
¼ cup white wine vinegar or white vinegar

1. Preheat oven to 425°F. In a medium saucepan cook the carrots and potatoes in a small amount of boiling water for 4 minutes; drain. Place the pork in a 13×9×2-inch baking pan. Arrange carrots and potatoes in the pan around the meat. Roast, uncovered, for 20 minutes.

2. In a small bowl stir together preserves and vinegar; brush some of the mixture over pork. Drizzle remaining preserves mixture over vegetables; toss to coat. Roast, uncovered, about 15 minutes more or until an instant-read thermometer inserted in center of pork registers 155°F. Stir vegetables. Cover pork and vegetables and let stand for 15 minutes. The temperature of the pork after standing should be 160°F.

3. Transfer pork to a serving platter; slice pork. Using a slotted spoon, transfer vegetables to the platter. Drizzle pan juices over pork and vegetables.

MAKES 4 SERVINGS.

Per serving: 365 cal., 2 g total fat (1 g sat. fat), 50 mg chol., 84 mg sodium, 62 g carbo., 5 g fiber, 23 g pro.

Pork Tenderloin with Quinoa and Greens ♡

Prep: 20 minutes **Roast:** 25 minutes
Stand: 15 minutes **Oven:** 425°F

2 tablespoons curry paste
2 12- to 16-ounce pork tenderloins
2 14.5-ounce cans chicken broth
1 cup quinoa
1 tablespoon olive oil
2 cloves garlic, minced
12 ounces fresh kale, stemmed and torn
½ cup plain low-fat yogurt (optional)
Chopped fresh parsley (optional)

1. Preheat oven to 425°F. Rub curry paste over all sides of pork tenderloins. Place pork on a rack in a shallow roasting pan.

2. Roast pork for 25 to 35 minutes or until an instant-read thermometer inserted in thickest part of tenderloin registers 155°F. Remove pork from oven. Cover with foil and let stand for 10 minutes. The temperature of the pork after standing should be 160°F.

3. Meanwhile, in a medium saucepan bring 1 can of the broth to boiling over medium-high heat. Add quinoa, olive oil, and garlic; reduce heat. Simmer, covered, about 15 minutes or until liquid is absorbed and quinoa is tender. Remove from heat; let stand, covered, for 5 minutes.

4. Meanwhile, in a large saucepan bring the remaining 1 can broth and the kale to boiling over medium-high heat; reduce heat. Simmer, covered, about 20 minutes or until kale is

Pork Loin with Vegetables

Pork
Medallions
with Fennel and
Pancetta

Ham and Asparagus Pasta

Start to Finish: 20 minutes

- 4 cups dried bow tie pasta, rotini, or other medium-size pasta
- 1 10-ounce package frozen cut asparagus or broccoli
- 8 ounces sliced cooked ham, cut into thin strips
- 1 8-ounce tub cream cheese spread with chives and onion
- 1/3 cup milk

1. Cook pasta following package directions, adding the frozen asparagus for the last 5 minutes and the ham for the last 1 minute of cooking time. Drain and return to the pan.
2. In a medium bowl whisk together cream cheese and milk; add to the pasta mixture in the pan. Cook and stir gently over medium heat until heated through. If necessary, add additional milk to reach desired consistency. Serve immediately. **MAKES 4 SERVINGS.**

Per serving: 459 cal., 24 g total fat (15 g sat. fat), 89 mg chol., 1,001 mg sodium, 38 g carbo., 3 g fiber, 19 g pro.

Pork Medallions with Fennel and Pancetta

Start to Finish: 30 minutes

- 1 12-ounce pork tenderloin
- 1/4 cup all-purpose flour
  Dash salt
  Dash black pepper
- 2 tablespoons olive oil
- 2 ounces pancetta (Italian bacon) or bacon, finely chopped
- 2 fennel bulbs, trimmed and cut crosswise into 1/4-inch slices
- 1 small onion, thinly sliced
- 2 cloves garlic, minced
- 2 tablespoons lemon juice
- 1/2 cup whipping cream

1. Trim fat from pork. Cut pork crosswise into 1-inch slices. Place each slice between 2 pieces of plastic wrap. Pound pork lightly with the flat side of a meat mallet to a 1/4-inch thickness. Discard plastic wrap. In a shallow dish combine flour, salt, and pepper. Dip pork slices into flour mixture to coat.
2. In a large heavy skillet heat oil over high heat. Add pork, half at a time, and cook for 2 to 3 minutes or until pork is slightly pink in center, turning once. (If necessary, add more oil.) Remove meat from skillet; set aside.
3. In the same skillet cook pancetta over medium-high heat until crisp. Add fennel, onion, and garlic and cook for 3 to 5 minutes or until crisp-tender. Add lemon juice; stir in whipping cream. Bring to boiling; return pork to pan. Cook until pork is heated through and sauce is slightly thickened.
4. Transfer the meat to a serving platter. Spoon the sauce over the meat.
MAKES 4 SERVINGS.

Per serving: 341 cal., 23 g total fat (10 g sat. fat), 105 mg chol., 175 mg sodium, 12 g carbo., 12 g fiber, 22 g pro.

Sausage,
Beans, and
Greens

Thai Pork Stir-Fry

Start to Finish: 30 minutes

- 2 tablespoons olive oil
- 1 tablespoon reduced-sodium soy sauce
- ½ teaspoon garlic powder
- ½ teaspoon finely chopped fresh ginger or
  ¼ teaspoon ground ginger
- ½ teaspoon black pepper
- ½ teaspoon ground cardamom
- ½ teaspoon chili powder
- 1½ pounds pork loin, cut into bite-size strips
- 2 cups broccoli florets
- 1 cup cauliflower florets
- 1 cup thinly sliced carrots (2 medium)
- 2 tablespoons white vinegar
- 1 tablespoon curry powder
- 2 cups hot cooked brown rice

1. In an extra-large skillet combine olive oil, soy sauce, garlic powder, ginger, pepper, cardamom, and chili powder. Add half the pork; cook and stir over medium-high heat for 3 minutes. Using a slotted spoon, remove pork from skillet. Repeat with the remaining pork. Return all of the pork to the skillet.

2. Add broccoli, cauliflower, carrots, vinegar, and curry powder to pork mixture. Bring to boiling; reduce heat. Simmer, covered, for 3 to 5 minutes or until vegetables are crisp-tender, stirring occasionally.

3. Serve pork and vegetables over brown rice.

MAKES 6 SERVINGS.

Per serving: 301 cal., 11 g total fat (3 g sat. fat), 71 mg chol., 206 mg sodium, 21 g carbo., 3 g fiber, 28 g pro.

Sausage, Beans, and Greens

Start to Finish: 25 minutes

- 8 ounces hot or mild fresh Italian sausage links, bias-sliced into ½-inch pieces
- ½ cup chopped onion (1 medium)
- 2 19-ounce cans cannellini (white kidney) beans, rinsed and drained
- 2 cups coarsely chopped escarole or spinach
- ¾ cup reduced-sodium chicken broth
- ¼ cup dry white wine or reduced-sodium chicken broth
- 2 tablespoons snipped fresh thyme or 1 teaspoon dried thyme, crushed
- ¼ cup finely shredded Parmesan cheese (optional)

1. In a large saucepan cook sausage and onion over medium heat about 5 minutes or until onion is tender. Drain off fat.

2. Add beans, escarole, chicken broth, wine, and thyme to sausage mixture in skillet. Bring to boiling; reduce heat. Simmer, covered, for 5 minutes. Ladle into serving bowls. If desired, sprinkle with Parmesan cheese.

MAKES 4 SERVINGS.

Per serving: 397 cal., 14 g total fat (5 g sat. fat), 38 mg chol., 993 mg sodium, 41 g carbo., 12 g fiber, 20 g pro.

Thai Pork
Stir-Fry

Kielbasa
and Orzo

Kielbasa and Orzo

Start to Finish: 16 minutes

- 1 tablespoon vegetable oil
- 1 pound cooked kielbasa, halved lengthwise and cut into 2-inch pieces
- 1 cup dried orzo (rosamarina)
- 1 14.5-ounce can beef broth
- ½ cup water
- 1 teaspoon dried Italian seasoning, crushed
- 2½ cups zucchini, halved lengthwise and coarsely chopped (2 medium)
- ⅓ cup 1-inch pieces green onions and/or finely chopped red sweet pepper (optional)
- Salt and black pepper

1. In a large skillet heat oil over medium-high heat. Cook kielbasa in hot oil about 2 minutes or until browned. Stir in orzo. Cook and stir for 1 minute.

2. Stir in beef broth, the water, and Italian seasoning. Bring to boiling; reduce heat. Simmer, covered, about 8 minutes or until orzo is tender, adding the zucchini for the last 4 minutes of cooking time and stirring occasionally.

3. If desired, stir in green onions and/or sweet pepper. Season with salt and pepper. **MAKES 4 SERVINGS.**

Per serving: 467 cal., 24 g total fat (8 g sat. fat), 79 mg chol., 1,630 mg sodium, 40 g carbo., 3 g fiber, 23 g pro.

Cuban Fried Rice

Start to Finish: 20 minutes

- 1 peeled fresh pineapple, packed in juice
- 1 tablespoon olive oil
- 1 14.8-ounce pouch cooked long grain rice
- 12 ounces cooked ham, coarsely chopped
- 1 cup chopped or sliced sweet pepper (1 large)
- 1 jalapeño, sliced (see note, page 31)
- ½ of a 15-ounce can black beans, rinsed and drained (¾ cup)
- Lime wedges (optional)

Cuban Fried Rice

1. Remove pineapple from container, reserving juice. Cut pineapple into ¾-inch slices; discard core if present. In an extra-large skillet heat oil over medium-high heat. Add pineapple slices; cook for 3 to 4 minutes or until pineapple begins to brown. Divide pineapple among 4 plates.

2. Meanwhile, prepare rice following package directions.

3. Add ham, sweet pepper, and jalapeño to skillet; cook for 3 minutes, stirring occasionally. Add beans and rice. Cook about 3 minutes or until heated through, stirring occasionally. Stir in reserved pineapple juice. If desired, serve with lime wedges. **MAKES 4 SERVINGS.**

Per serving: 375 cal., 9 g total fat (1 g sat. fat), 38 mg chol., 1,549 mg sodium, 58 g carbo., 6 g fiber, 24 g pro.

Apricot Pork and Garlicky Green Beans

Start to Finish: 20 minutes

- 4 pork rib chops, ½ inch thick
- 1 tablespoon olive oil
- 4 apricots, pitted and cut in wedges
- 2 tablespoons honey
- 3 cloves garlic, sliced
- 1 pound green beans, trimmed

1. Trim fat from chops. Sprinkle chops with salt and black pepper. In an extra-large nonstick skillet cook chops in hot oil for 5 minutes, turning once. Add apricots, honey, and garlic. Cook, covered, for 5 to 7 minutes or until pork is slightly pink in center.

2. In a covered 2-quart microwave-safe casserole microwave beans and ¼ cup water on high about 6 minutes or until beans are crisp-tender, stirring once; drain.

3. Transfer pork, apricots, and beans to a serving platter. Spoon juices from skillet over beans. **MAKES 4 SERVINGS.**

Per serving: 295 cal., 14 g total fat (4 g sat. fat), 57 mg chol., 207 mg sodium, 20 g carbo., 4 g fiber, 22 g pro.

Wilted Cabbage and Brats
Start to Finish: 20 minutes

- 2 tablespoons olive oil
- ½ of a 2-pound head napa cabbage, cut into 4 wedges, leaving the core intact to hold wedges together
- 14 to 16 ounces cooked smoked bratwurst links, halved diagonally
- 2 small apples, cored and cut into thin wedges
- ¼ cup water
- 2 tablespoons Dijon mustard
- ½ cup sour cream or light sour cream
- 1 tablespoon snipped fresh sage
  Fresh sage leaves (optional)

1. In an extra-large skillet heat 1 tablespoon of the olive oil over medium heat. Add cabbage wedges; cook for 8 to 10 minutes or until lightly browned and tender, turning occasionally to brown evenly.
2. Meanwhile, in a 4- to 5-quart Dutch oven heat the remaining 1 tablespoon olive oil over medium-high heat. Add bratwurst and apples; cook for 2 minutes. In a small bowl whisk together the water and mustard. Add mustard mixture to bratwurst mixture. Bring to boiling; reduce heat. Simmer, covered, for 4 to 6 minutes or until apples are tender, stirring occasionally.
3. Transfer cabbage to a serving platter or bowl. Use a slotted spoon to remove bratwurst and apples to the platter, reserving juices in Dutch oven. In a small bowl combine sour cream and snipped sage. Gradually whisk in bratwurst cooking juices until well combined. Serve over bratwurst mixture. If desired, sprinkle fresh sage leaves.
MAKES 4 SERVINGS.

Per serving: 456 cal., 38 g total fat (10 g sat. fat), 88 mg chol., 1,046 mg sodium, 13 g carbo., 2 g fiber, 15 g pro.

Pork and Pear Stir-Fry ♡
Start to Finish: 30 minutes

- 1½ cups fresh pea pods or one 6-ounce package frozen pea pods
- 1 pound pork tenderloin
- ½ cup plum preserves or plum jam
- 3 tablespoons soy sauce
- 2 tablespoons lemon juice
- 1 tablespoon prepared horseradish
- 2 teaspoons cornstarch
- ½ teaspoon crushed red pepper
- 1 tablespoon vegetable oil
- 2 teaspoons grated fresh ginger
- 1 medium yellow or red sweet pepper, cut into thin strips
- 1 medium pear, cored and sliced
- ½ of an 8-ounce can sliced water chestnuts, drained (about ½ cup)
- 1 to 2 tablespoons sliced almonds, toasted (see note, page 54) (optional)
- 2 cups hot cooked rice

1. Thaw pea pods, if frozen. Trim fat from pork. Cut pork into thin bite-size strips. Set aside.
2. For sauce, in a small bowl stir together preserves, soy sauce, lemon juice, horseradish, cornstarch, and crushed red pepper. Set aside.
3. In a wok or large skillet heat oil over medium-high heat. (Add more oil as necessary during cooking.) Add ginger; cook for 15 seconds. Add sweet pepper and pear; cook and stir for 1½ minutes. Remove pepper strips and pear from wok. Add pork to wok; cook and stir for 2 to 3 minutes or until meat is no longer pink. Push pork from center of wok. Stir sauce; add to wok. Cook and stir until thickened and bubbly. Add water chestnuts. Return pepper strips and pear to wok; stir to coat. Cook and stir about 2 minutes more. Top with pea pods; cover and heat through. If desired, sprinkle with almonds. Serve with hot cooked rice.
MAKES 4 SERVINGS.

Per serving: 482 cal., 7 g total fat (2 g sat. fat), 73 mg chol., 504 mg sodium, 72 g carbo., 4 g fiber, 29 g pro.

Pecan Pork Tenderloin
Start to Finish: 30 minutes

- 12 ounces pork tenderloin
- 1 egg, lightly beaten
- 2 tablespoons Dijon mustard
- 1 tablespoon water
- ¼ to ½ teaspoon cayenne pepper
- ½ cup fine dry bread crumbs
- ½ cup ground pecans, toasted (see note, page 54)
- ⅓ cup all-purpose flour
- 2 tablespoons olive oil or vegetable oil

1. Trim fat from pork. Cut pork crosswise into ¼-inch slices. In a shallow bowl combine egg, mustard, the water, and cayenne pepper. In another shallow bowl combine bread crumbs and pecans. Coat pork slices with flour. Dip slices into egg mixture; coat with the crumb mixture.
2. In an extra-large skillet heat oil over medium heat. (If necessary, add additional oil during cooking.) Cook pork in the hot oil for 5 to 6 minutes or until slightly pink in center, turning once. **MAKES 4 SERVINGS.**

Per serving: 351 cal., 21 g total fat (3 g sat. fat), 108 mg chol., 488 mg sodium, 17 g carbo., 2 g fiber, 23 g pro.

Apple
Butter-Glazed
Ham

Apple Butter-Glazed Ham

Start to Finish: 20 minutes

  2 medium sweet potatoes, peeled and cut
     into 1-inch cubes
 12 ounces Brussels sprouts, trimmed and
     halved
  2 tablespoons butter
  1 to 1¼ pounds sliced cooked ham, about
     ¼ inch thick
     Salt and black pepper
 ½ cup apple butter
  2 tablespoons cider vinegar
     Baguette slices (optional)

1. In a large saucepan cook sweet potatoes
and Brussels sprouts in lightly salted boiling
water for 8 or 10 minutes or just until tender.
Drain.

2. Meanwhile, in an extra-large skillet melt
butter over medium-high heat. Add ham;
cook for 4 to 5 minutes, turning occasionally.
Arrange ham and vegetables on serving
plates; season with salt and pepper. Stir
apple butter and vinegar into skillet; heat
through. Serve with ham, vegetables, and, if
desired, baguette slices. **MAKES 4 SERVINGS.**

Per serving: 513 cal., 16 g total fat (7 g sat. fat), 80 mg
chol., 1,664 mg sodium, 71 g carbo., 8 g fiber, 23 g pro.

Quick Tip When trimming Brussels sprouts,
be sure to nip the very tip off the stem end
with a small sharp knife. If you cut off too
much, when you cut the sprouts in half, there
will be nothing to hold the individual leaves
together, and they will fall apart.

Tex-Mex
Skillet

Tex-Mex Skillet

Start to Finish: 30 minutes

  8 ounces ground pork
  4 ounces bulk chorizo sausage
  1 10-ounce can diced tomatoes and green
     chile peppers, undrained
  1 cup frozen whole kernel corn
 ¾ cup water
 ½ cup chopped red sweet pepper
  1 cup instant rice
 ½ cup shredded cheddar cheese or
     Monterey Jack cheese (2 ounces)
     Flour tortillas, warmed (optional)
     Sour cream (optional)

1. In a large skillet cook pork and sausage
until browned. Drain off fat. Stir in undrained
tomatoes, corn, the water, and sweet pepper.
Bring to boiling.

2. Stir uncooked rice into tomato mixture in
skillet. Remove from heat. Top with cheese.
Cover and let stand about 5 minutes or until
rice is tender. If desired, serve in flour tortillas
and top with sour cream. **MAKES 4 SERVINGS.**

Per serving: 395 cal., 20 g total fat (9 g sat. fat), 66 mg
chol., 748 mg sodium, 33 g carbo., 1 g fiber, 21 g pro.

Greek Lamb
Salad with
Yogurt
Dressing

Greek Lamb Salad with Yogurt Dressing ♡

Start to Finish: 30 minutes

 8 ounces boneless lamb leg sirloin chops, ½ inch thick
 2 teaspoons snipped fresh rosemary or ½ teaspoon dried rosemary, crushed
 2 cloves garlic, minced
 8 cups torn fresh spinach or torn mixed salad greens
 1 15-ounce can garbanzo beans (chickpeas), rinsed and drained
 ¼ cup chopped, seeded cucumber
 ½ cup plain low-fat yogurt
 ¼ cup chopped green onions (2)
 ⅛ to ¼ teaspoon salt
 ⅛ teaspoon black pepper
 ¼ cup golden raisins or dried tart cherries

1. Preheat broiler. Trim fat from lamb chops. Combine rosemary and half of the minced garlic; rub evenly onto chops. Place chops on the unheated rack of a broiler pan. Broil 4 to 5 inches from heat for 12 to 15 minutes for medium (160°F), turning once halfway through cooking. Cut lamb chops into thin bite-size slices.

2. Meanwhile, in a large bowl toss together spinach, garbanzo beans, and cucumber. Divide spinach mixture among 4 plates. Arrange lamb slices on the spinach mixture.

3. For dressing, in a small bowl combine yogurt, green onions, salt, pepper, and the remaining minced garlic clove. Drizzle dressing on salads. Sprinkle with raisins.

MAKES 4 SERVINGS.

Per serving: 243 cal., 6 g total fat (2 g sat. fat), 36 mg chol., 569 mg sodium, 29 g carbo., 8 g fiber, 20 g pro.

Pan-Seared Lamb Chops with Mint Salad

Start to Finish: 30 minutes

 ¼ cup snipped fresh mint
 ¼ cup snipped fresh parsley
 ¼ cup crumbled feta cheese (1 ounce)
 ¼ cup chopped pecans, toasted (see note, page 54)
 8 lamb rib chops or loin chops, 1 inch thick (about 2 pounds)
 2 teaspoons olive oil
 ¼ teaspoon salt
 ⅛ teaspoon black pepper
 Olive oil (optional)
 Lemon juice (optional)
 Mixed salad greens (optional)

1. In a small bowl combine mint, parsley, feta cheese, and pecans; set aside.

2. Trim fat from chops. Rub chops with the 2 teaspoons olive oil, salt, and pepper. Preheat a large heavy skillet over medium-high heat until hot. Add chops. Cook for 8 to 10 minutes or until medium-rare (145°F), turning once halfway through cooking.

3. To serve, sprinkle chops with mint mixture. If desired, drizzle additional olive oil and/or lemon juice over mint mixture and serve with salad greens.

Per serving: 252 cal., 17 g total fat (5 g sat. fat), 72 mg chol., 311 mg sodium, 2 g carbo., 1 g fiber, 22 g pro.

Pan-Seared
Lamb Chops
with Mint
Salad

Poultry

Buffalo-Style
Chicken Strips
with Blue
Cheese

Buffalo-Style Chicken Strips with Blue Cheese

Start to Finish: 25 minutes

⅓ cup all-purpose flour
¾ teaspoon salt
½ teaspoon black pepper
¼ cup milk
1 pound chicken breast tenderloins
½ cup olive oil or vegetable oil
4 teaspoons butter, melted
2 teaspoons bottled hot pepper sauce
⅓ cup bottled blue cheese salad dressing

1. In a shallow dish combine flour, salt, and pepper. Pour milk into another shallow dish. Dip chicken in milk; coat with flour mixture.
2. In a large skillet heat oil over medium heat. Add half of the chicken; cook about 4 minutes or until no longer pink (170°F), turning once. Remove chicken from skillet. Repeat with remaining chicken.
3. Meanwhile, in a small bowl stir together melted butter and hot pepper sauce. Drizzle butter mixture over chicken strips. Serve chicken strips with blue cheese salad dressing for dipping. **MAKES 4 SERVINGS.**

Per serving: 369 cal., 24 g total fat (6 g sat. fat), 81 mg chol., 784 mg sodium, 10 g carbo., 0 g fiber, 29 g pro.

Herbed Cheese-Stuffed Chicken Breasts

Start to Finish: 30 minutes

1 tablespoon snipped dried tomatoes (not oil-packed)
  Boiling water
4 skinless, boneless chicken breast halves (about 1¼ pounds)
¼ cup crumbled feta cheese (1 ounce)
2 tablespoons softened cream cheese (1 ounce)
½ teaspoon dried basil, crushed
½ teaspoon black pepper
1 teaspoon olive oil or vegetable oil

1. Place tomatoes in a small bowl. Cover with boiling water. Let stand for 10 minutes. Drain and pat dry; set aside. Meanwhile, using a sharp knife, cut a pocket in each chicken breast by cutting horizontally through the thickest portion to, but not through, the opposite side; set aside.
2. In a small bowl combine feta cheese, cream cheese, basil, and tomatoes. Spoon about 1 rounded tablespoon into each chicken pocket. If necessary, secure openings with wooden toothpicks. Sprinkle chicken with pepper.
3. In a large nonstick skillet heat oil over medium-high heat. Add chicken; cook for 12 to 14 minutes or until chicken is no longer pink (170°F), turning once (reduce heat to medium if chicken browns too quickly).
MAKES 4 SERVINGS.

Per serving: 186 cal., 7 g total fat (4 g sat. fat), 82 mg chol., 203 mg sodium, 1 g carbo., 0 g fiber, 28 g pro.

Herb-Rubbed Roaster

Prep: 20 minutes **Roast:** 1¼ hours
Stand: 10 minutes **Marinate:** 2 to 24 hours
Oven: 375°F

1 3½- to 4-pound whole broiler-fryer chicken
¼ cup olive oil
2 tablespoons herbes de Provence
1 teaspoon salt or smoked salt
1 teaspoon crushed red pepper
¾ teaspoon coarsely ground black pepper
1½ pounds tiny yellow and purple potatoes and/or fingerling potatoes, halved

1. Remove the neck and giblets from chicken. Rinse chicken; pat dry with paper towels. Skewer neck skin to back; tie legs to tail with 100%-cotton kitchen string. Twist wings under back. Brush chicken with 2 tablespoons of the olive oil.
2. In a small bowl stir together herbes de Provence, salt, crushed red pepper, and black pepper. Rub 2 tablespoons of the herb mixture onto the chicken. Cover the remaining herb mixture; set aside. Place chicken in a large resealable plastic bag. Seal bag and place in the refrigerator for 2 to 24 hours.
3. Preheat oven to 375°F. Remove chicken from bag. Place chicken, breast side up, on a rack in a shallow roasting pan. Insert an ovenproof meat thermometer into center of an inside thigh muscle. Do not allow thermometer bulb to touch bone.
4. In a large bowl combine the remaining 2 tablespoons oil and remaining herb mixture. Add the potatoes and toss to combine. Arrange potatoes around the chicken. Roast, uncovered, for 1¼ to 1¾ hours or until drumsticks move easily in their sockets and meat thermometer registers 180°F. Remove chicken from oven. Cover and let stand for 10 minutes before carving.
5. To serve, place the chicken on a large serving platter. Arrange the potatoes around the chicken. **MAKES 6 SERVINGS.**

Per serving: 543 cal., 35 g total fat (9 g sat. fat), 134 mg chol., 492 mg sodium, 18 g carbo., 3 g fiber, 37 g pro.

Couscous
Chicken Salad

Couscous Chicken Salad ♡

Start to Finish: 15 minutes

- 1   14.5-ounce can chicken broth
- 1¼ cups quick-cooking couscous
- ½   cup mango chutney, large pieces cut up
- ¼   cup bottled olive oil and vinegar salad dressing, white wine vinaigrette salad dressing, or roasted garlic vinaigrette salad dressing
- 1   6-ounce package refrigerated cooked lemon-pepper chicken breast strips, cut into bite-size pieces (about 1½ cups)
- ½   cup golden raisins or raisins (optional)
- 1   cup coarsely chopped radishes or seeded cucumber
     Salt
     Freshly ground black pepper
- 1   small cucumber, cut into spears

1. In a medium saucepan bring chicken broth to boiling. Stir in couscous. Cover and remove from heat. Let stand for 5 minutes. Fluff couscous lightly with a fork.

2. In a medium bowl combine chutney and salad dressing. Add chicken, raisins (if desired), radishes, and cooked couscous. Toss to coat. Season with salt and pepper. Serve with cucumber spears.

MAKES 4 SERVINGS.

Per serving: 411 cal., 10 g total fat (2 g sat. fat), 22 mg chol., 848 mg sodium, 63 g carbo., 4 g fiber, 16 g pro.

Quick Tip Choose radishes that feel firm when gently squeezed. If a radish gives to pressure when pressed, the inside will likely be pithy instead of crisp. Any attached leaves should be green and unwilted. Store radishes in a plastic bag in the refrigerator for up to 1 week.

Plum Wonderful Chicken

Prep: 40 minutes **Bake:** 35 minutes
Oven: 350°F

- 2   tablespoons olive oil or vegetables oil
- 2½ to 3 pounds meaty chicken pieces (breast halves, thighs, and/or drumsticks), skinned
- ¼   cup chopped onion
- 1   teaspoon grated fresh ginger
- 1   clove garlic, minced
- ⅓   cup bottled plum sauce

Plum Wonderful Chicken

- ¼   cup frozen lemonade concentrate
- ¼   cup bottled chili sauce
- 2   tablespoons reduced-sodium soy sauce
- 1   tablespoon lemon juice
- 1   teaspoon dry mustard
- 3   cups hot cooked rice
     Thinly sliced green onions (optional)
     Sesame seeds, toasted (see note, page 54) (optional)

1. Preheat oven to 350°F. In a large skillet heat oil over medium heat. Add half of the chicken; cook about 10 minutes or until browned, turning often to brown evenly on all sides. Transfer browned chicken pieces to a 3-quart rectangular baking dish. Repeat with remaining chicken. Drain fat from skillet, reserving 1 tablespoon in the skillet. Add onion, ginger, and garlic to skillet. Cook and stir about 5 minutes or until onion is tender.

2. Meanwhile, for the sauce, in a small bowl stir together plum sauce, lemonade concentrate, chili sauce, soy sauce, lemon juice, and dry mustard. Carefully stir into onion mixture in skillet. Bring to boiling; reduce heat. Simmer, covered, for 5 minutes; spoon sauce over chicken in dish.

3. Bake, uncovered, for 35 to 40 minutes or until chicken is tender and no longer pink (170°F for breast pieces; 180°F for thighs and drumsticks), spooning sauce over chicken twice during baking. Serve chicken and sauce over hot cooked rice. If desired, sprinkle with green onions and sesame seeds.

MAKES 6 SERVINGS.

Per serving: 366 cal., 12 g total fat (2 g sat. fat), 77 mg chol., 405 mg sodium, 37 g carbo., 1 g fiber, 28 g pro.

Thai Chicken Pasta

3. In a medium nonstick skillet heat oil over medium-high heat. Add chicken to skillet; cook about 5 minutes, turning to brown evenly. Add broth. Bring to boiling; reduce heat. Simmer, covered, for 7 to 8 minutes or until chicken is no longer pink (170°F). To serve, spoon juices over chicken.
MAKES 4 SERVINGS.

Per serving: 265 cal., 11 g total fat (5 g sat. fat), 107 mg chol., 449 mg sodium, 2 g carbo., 0 g fiber, 37 g pro.

Spicy Chicken Breasts with Fruit ♡
Start to Finish: 25 minutes

- 1 tablespoon Jamaican jerk seasoning
- 4 skinless, boneless chicken breast halves (about 1¼ pounds)
- 1 tablespoon vegetable oil
- 3 green onions, cut into 1-inch pieces
- ½ cup peach nectar
- 1 teaspoon cornstarch
- 2 cups frozen peach slices
- ½ cup frozen unsweetened pitted dark sweet cherries
- 1 tablespoon packed brown sugar
- ⅛ teaspoon salt
- 1 cup sliced plums
  Hot cooked rice (optional)

1. Sprinkle jerk seasoning evenly over both sides of chicken; rub in with your fingers. Add oil to a large skillet; heat over medium heat. Add chicken. Cook for 10 to 12 minutes or until chicken is tender and no longer pink (170°F), turning once and adding the green onions the last 2 to 3 minutes of cooking. Transfer chicken to a serving platter; cover and keep warm.
2. Meanwhile, in a medium bowl combine nectar and cornstarch. Add peaches, cherries, brown sugar, and salt. Add to skillet. Cook and stir about 3 minutes or until slightly thickened and bubbly. Stir in plums; cook and stir for 1 minute more.
3. To serve, spoon fruit mixture over chicken. If desired, serve with hot cooked rice.
MAKES 4 SERVINGS.

Per serving: 294 cal., 6 g total fat (1 g sat. fat), 82 mg chol., 380 mg sodium, 26 g carbo., 3 g fiber, 34 g pro.

Thai Chicken Pasta
Start to Finish: 20 minutes

- 8 ounces dried angel hair or vermicelli pasta
- 3 cups cooked chicken (about 1 pound), cut into strips
- 1 14-ounce can unsweetened coconut milk
- 1 teaspoon Thai seasoning
- ¼ cup roasted peanuts
- 2 tablespoons snipped fresh cilantro

1. Cook pasta following package directions. Drain and return pasta to warm pan.
2. Meanwhile, in a large skillet combine chicken, coconut milk, and Thai seasoning. Cook and stir over medium heat until heated through. Pour hot chicken mixture over pasta in pan. Add peanuts and cilantro. Toss gently to coat. **MAKES 4 SERVINGS.**

Per serving: 644 cal., 31 g total fat (19 g sat. fat), 93 mg chol., 236 mg sodium, 47 g carbo., 2 g fiber, 42 g pro.

Feta-Stuffed Chicken Breasts
Prep: 25 minutes **Cook:** 12 minutes

- 4 skinless, boneless chicken breast halves (about 1¼ pounds)
- 4 ounces crumbled feta cheese with peppercorn, feta cheese with garlic and herb, or plain feta cheese
- ½ of a 7-ounce jar roasted red sweet peppers, drained and cut into strips (½ cup)
- 1 tablespoon olive oil
- ¼ cup chicken broth

1. Place each chicken breast half between 2 pieces of plastic wrap. Pound lightly with the flat side of a meat mallet to ¼-inch thickness. Remove plastic wrap; discard.
2. Sprinkle each chicken breast half with cheese. Place sweet pepper strips in center of each breast half. Fold narrow ends over filling; fold in sides. Roll up each breast half from a short side. Secure with wooden toothpicks.

Spicy
Chicken
Breasts
with Fruit

Lemon
Chicken

Lemon Chicken

Prep: 20 minutes **Cook:** 15 minutes

    4 skinless, boneless chicken breast halves
       (about 1¼ pounds)
    ¼ cup fat-free milk
    ⅔ cup fine dry bread crumbs
    2 teaspoons adobo seasoning*
    2 tablespoons vegetable oil
  1¾ cups water
    1 clove garlic, minced
    1 lemon, halved crosswise
    1 tablespoon snipped fresh parsley
       Shredded lemon peel (optional)
       Lemon slices (optional)

1. Split chicken breast halves in half horizontally. Place milk in a shallow bowl. In a shallow dish combine bread crumbs and adobo seasoning. Dip chicken pieces into milk, allowing excess to drip off. Dip chicken pieces into crumb mixture, turning to coat evenly.
2. In a very large nonstick skillet heat oil over medium heat. Add chicken; cook about 5 minutes or until browned, turning occasionally.
3. Add the water and garlic to skillet. Squeeze juice from 1 of the lemon halves over chicken. Bring to boiling; reduce heat. Simmer, uncovered, about 15 minutes or until sauce is thickened, stirring occasionally. Cut the remaining lemon half in half and then into slices.
4. Sprinkle chicken with parsley and, if desired, lemon peel. If desired, serve with the lemon slices. **MAKES 4 SERVINGS.**

Per serving: 254 cal., 8 g total fat (2 g sat. fat), 66 mg chol., 999 mg sodium, 15 g carbo., 1 g fiber, 29 g pro.

*Note Look for this seasoning blend at a market that specializes in Hispanic foods.

Quick Tip Before you halve the lemon for this recipe, finely shred the peel to sprinkle onto the finished dish for additional flavor. When shredding peel, be sure to remove only the yellow part of the rind; the white pith could impart a bitter flavor.

Tuscan Chicken

Tuscan Chicken

Prep: 5 minutes **Cook:** 45 minutes

    2 tablespoons olive oil
    2 to 2½ pounds meaty chicken pieces
       (breast halves, thighs, and drumsticks)
  1¼ teaspoons pesto seasoning or dried Italian
       seasoning, crushed
    ½ cup whole pitted kalamata olives
    ½ cup white wine or chicken broth
       Fresh arugula leaves sautéed in olive oil
       (optional)

1. In a very large skillet heat oil over medium heat. Add chicken to skillet; cook for 15 minutes, turning to brown evenly. Reduce heat. Drain off excess oil in skillet. Sprinkle pesto seasoning evenly over chicken. Add olives to skillet. Pour wine over all. Bring to boiling; reduce heat.
2. Cook, covered, for 25 minutes. Uncover; cook for 5 to 10 minutes more or until chicken is no longer pink (170°F for breasts; 180°F for thighs and drumsticks). If desired, serve chicken on sautéed arugula.
MAKES 4 SERVINGS.

Per serving: 334 cal., 18 g total fat (4 g sat. fat), 104 mg chol., 280 mg sodium, 2 g carbo., 1 g fiber, 34 g pro.

Chicken with Onions, Tomatoes, and Pasta

Chicken with Onions, Tomatoes, and Pasta

Start to Finish: 30 minutes

1½ teaspoons coarsely ground pepper blend
¾ teaspoon salt
1 clove garlic, minced
4 skinless, boneless chicken breasts (about 1¼ pounds total)
2 tablespoons olive oil
2 large onions, sliced
1½ cups chopped tomatoes (3 medium)
1 tablespoon tomato paste
2 to 3 teaspoons grated fresh ginger
8 ounces dried spaghetti
¼ cup purchased pesto
   Parmesan cheese shavings (optional)

1. In a bowl combine 1 teaspoon of the pepper blend, ½ teaspoon of the salt, and the garlic. Sprinkle over chicken. In a large skillet heat oil over medium heat. Add chicken and onions; cook about 15 minutes or until chicken is no longer pink (170°F), turning chicken once and stirring onions occasionally. Remove chicken from skillet; slice into strips.
2. Return chicken to the skillet; add tomatoes, tomato paste, ginger, the remaining ½ teaspoon pepper blend, and the remaining ¼ teaspoon salt. Cook and stir just until heated through.

3. Meanwhile, cook spaghetti following package directions. Drain. Return spaghetti to the hot pan. Stir pesto into pasta. Serve the chicken and tomato on spaghetti. If desired, top with shavings of Parmesan cheese. **MAKES 4 SERVINGS.**

Per serving: 597 cal., 20 g total fat (2 g sat. fat), 84 mg chol., 641 mg sodium, 59 g carbo., 4 g fiber, 44 g pro.

Peruvian-Style Chicken Tacos ♡

Start to Finish: 30 minutes **Oven:** 350°F

1 pound uncooked ground chicken
½ cup chopped onion (1 medium)
2 teaspoons ground coriander
2 teaspoons ground cumin
1 teaspoon salt
1 14.5-ounce can diced tomatoes
¾ cup finely chopped, peeled potato (1 medium)
¼ cup snipped pitted dried plums
¼ cup chopped pimiento-stuffed green olives
12 6- to 7-inch corn or flour tortillas
4 to 6 ounces Cotija or Monterey Jack cheese, shredded

1. Preheat oven to 350°F. In a large skillet cook chicken and onion until chicken is no longer pink. If necessary, drain off fat. Add coriander, cumin, and salt; cook and stir for 1 to 2 minutes.
2. Add undrained tomatoes, potato, dried plums, and olives. Bring to boiling; reduce heat. Simmer, covered, for 12 to 15 minutes or until potatoes are tender. Uncover; cook about 5 minutes more or until most of the liquid has evaporated. Wrap tortillas in foil; bake about 15 minutes or until heated.
3. To assemble, place ⅓ cup chicken mixture in center of each tortilla; top with cheese. Fold tortillas in half.
MAKES 4 SERVINGS.

Per serving (3 tacos): 194 cal., 10 g total fat (0 g sat. fat), 9 mg chol., 328 mg sodium, 18 g carbo., 3 g fiber, 11 g pro.

Chicken with Cherry Tomatoes

Prep: 15 minutes **Cook:** 10 minutes

4 skinless, boneless chicken breast halves (about 1¼ pounds)
½ teaspoon salt
¼ teaspoon black pepper
2 teaspoons olive oil
2 cups red and/or yellow cherry tomatoes, halved
2 tablespoons water
½ teaspoon dried parsley, basil, or tarragon, crushed
1 tablespoon white wine vinegar

1. Sprinkle chicken with ¼ teaspoon of the salt and ⅛ teaspoon of the pepper. In a large nonstick skillet heat oil over medium-high heat. Add chicken; cook for 10 to 12 minutes or until no longer pink (170°F), turning once. Transfer chicken to a serving platter; cover and keep warm.
2. Drain fat from skillet. Add tomatoes, the water, parsley, vinegar, the remaining ¼ teaspoon salt, and the remaining ⅛ teaspoon pepper to skillet.
3. Bring to boiling; reduce heat. Simmer, uncovered, for 3 to 4 minutes or until tomatoes begin to soften, stirring occasionally. Serve tomato mixture over chicken.
MAKES 4 SERVINGS.

Per serving: 163 cal., 4 g total fat (1 g sat. fat), 66 mg chol., 320 mg sodium, 4 g carbo., 1 g fiber, 27 g pro.

Chicken with Cherry Tomatoes

Chicken and Pasta Stack

Start to Finish: 20 minutes

- 6 ounces dried angel hair pasta
- 3 ears fresh sweet corn
- 4 small skinless, boneless chicken breast halves (1 to 1¼ pounds)
- 1½ teaspoons chili powder
- ¼ teaspoon salt
- ¼ teaspoon freshly ground black pepper
- 4 tablespoons olive oil
- 3 tablespoons fresh lime or lemon juice
- 2 medium tomatoes, sliced
  Snipped fresh parsley (optional)
  Lime halves (optional)

1. Cook pasta and corn in lightly salted boiling water following pasta package directions. Drain in colander; rinse with cold water until cool.
2. Meanwhile, sprinkle chicken with 1 teaspoon of the chili powder, the salt, and pepper. In a large skillet heat 1 tablespoon of the oil over medium heat. Add chicken; cook for 8 to 10 minutes or until tender and no longer pink (170°F), turning once halfway through cooking.
3. For dressing, in a screw top jar combine the remaining 3 tablespoons oil, the remaining ½ teaspoon chili powder, and the lime juice; shake to combine.
4. Cut corn from cob. Arrange pasta, chicken, corn, and tomatoes on 4 dinner plates. Drizzle dressing over all. Lightly sprinkle with additional salt and pepper. If desired, sprinkle with parsley and serve with lime halves. **MAKES 4 SERVINGS.**

Per serving: 515 cal., 17 g total fat (3 g sat. fat), 66 mg chol., 226 mg sodium, 58 g carbo., 5 g fiber, 36 g pro.

Chicken Wellington

Prep: 10 minutes **Bake:** 25 minutes
Oven: 425°F

- 1 10-ounce package frozen chopped broccoli, thawed and drained
- 1 5.2-ounce package semisoft cheese with garlic and fine herbs
- 1 17.25-ounce package frozen puff pastry sheets, thawed

Chicken Wellington

- 6 skinless, boneless chicken breast halves (2 pounds)
- ½ teaspoon salt
- ¼ cup fine dry bread crumbs
- 1 egg, lightly beaten
- 1 tablespoon water

1. Preheat oven to 425°F. In a medium bowl stir together broccoli and cheese; set aside.
2. On lightly floured surface roll out each pastry sheet to a 14×12-inch rectangle. Cut each sheet into four 7×6-inch rectangles.
3. Sprinkle both sides of chicken with salt. Spread ¼ cup of the broccoli mixture on 1 pastry rectangle. Place a chicken breast half on top. Sprinkle with 2 teaspoons bread crumbs. In a small bowl combine egg and the water. Brush some egg mixture onto edges of rectangle; fold pastry over chicken. Press

edges to seal. Place, seam side down, in ungreased shallow baking pan. Repeat with remaining chicken, 5 of the remaining pastry rectangles, broccoli mixture, bread crumbs, and egg mixture.
4. Using a small cookie cutter, cut shapes from remaining pastry rectangles. Brush egg mixture on pastry packets. Place cutouts on packets; brush with additional egg mixture.
5. Bake about 25 minutes or until pastry is golden and an instant-read thermometer inserted in chicken breasts registers 170°F.
MAKES 6 SERVINGS.

Per serving: 701 cal., 35 g total fat (11 g sat. fat), 163 mg chol., 751 mg sodium, 52 g carbo., 8 g fiber, 44 g pro.

Cucumber-Yogurt Chicken

¼ teaspoon black pepper
12 ounces skinless, boneless chicken breast halves
2 tablespoons vegetable oil
2 cups frozen mixed vegetables
1 14.5-ounce can reduced-sodium chicken broth
½ cup milk
1 11-ounce package (8) refrigerated breadsticks
⅓ cup cornmeal
½ cup shredded Mexican-style four-cheese blend (2 ounces)

1. Preheat oven to 450°F. In a large resealable plastic bag combine flour, sage, salt, and pepper. Cut chicken into bite-size pieces. Add chicken to bag; seal bag. Shake to coat.
2. In a large skillet heat oil over medium-high heat. Add chicken to hot oil; sprinkle any remaining flour mixture on chicken. Cook for 2 minutes (chicken will not be completely cooked), stirring to brown evenly. Place vegetables in a sieve or colander. Run cold water over vegetables to thaw. Add vegetables, broth, and milk to skillet. Bring to boiling, stirring once. Open package of breadsticks and separate into 16 pieces.
3. Divide chicken mixture among four 16-ounce au gratin dishes or individual casserole dishes. Cut breadsticks in half lengthwise; roll in cornmeal. Arrange breadsticks on top. Sprinkle with cheese. Bake for 9 to 10 minutes or until breadsticks are golden brown. **MAKES 4 SERVINGS.**

Per serving: 612 cal., 25 g total fat (7 g sat. fat), 64 mg chol., 1,259 mg sodium, 60 g carbo., 3 g fiber, 34 g pro.

Quick Tip Dividing a large casserole that serves 4 or 6 into individual servings and baking it in au gratin dishes or individual casseroles reduces baking time. Try it with some of your favorite casserole recipes. A large casserole that bakes at about 375°F for 25 to 30 minutes until golden brown and bubbly can be baked in individual dishes at 375°F for about half the time.

Cucumber-Yogurt Chicken

Prep: 20 minutes **Bake:** 8 minutes
Oven: 350°F

1 cup plain low-fat yogurt
1 cup chopped, peeled seedless cucumber
½ cup finely chopped radishes
2 tablespoons mayonnaise or salad dressing
¼ teaspoon finely shredded lemon peel
1 tablespoon lemon juice
1 teaspoon salt
¼ teaspoon minced garlic
¼ teaspoon bottled cayenne pepper sauce
1 tablespoon vegetable oil
4 skinless, boneless chicken breast halves (1½ to 1¾ pounds)
½ teaspoon cayenne pepper

1. Preheat oven to 350°F. For yogurt sauce, in a medium bowl stir together yogurt, cucumber, radishes, mayonnaise, lemon peel, lemon juice, ½ teaspoon of the salt, the garlic, and cayenne pepper sauce.

2. In a very large nonstick, ovenproof skillet heat oil over medium heat. Sprinkle chicken with the remaining ½ teaspoon salt and the cayenne pepper. Add chicken to the hot skillet; cook about 6 minutes or until browned, turning once.
3. Bake chicken in skillet for 8 to 9 minutes or until no longer pink (170°F). Serve with yogurt sauce. **MAKES 4 SERVINGS.**

Per serving: 321 cal., 13 g total fat (3 g sat. fat), 105 mg chol., 760 mg sodium, 6 g carbo., 1 g fiber, 43 g pro.

Chicken with Quick Cornmeal Crust

Start to Finish: 22 minutes

½ cup all-purpose flour
½ teaspoon ground sage
¼ teaspoon salt

Quick Chicken
Panzanella

Quick Chicken Panzanella

Start to Finish: 20 minutes

- 1 14.5-ounce can diced tomatoes with green pepper, celery, and onions, undrained
- 3 tablespoons olive oil
  Dash salt and black pepper
- 1 2- to 2¼-pound purchased whole roasted chicken
- 4 cups cubed Italian bread
- 2 medium cucumbers, halved lengthwise and sliced
- 1 cup torn fresh basil or spinach

1. Spoon off 2 tablespoons of the liquid from the diced tomatoes. Combine liquid with 1 tablespoon of the olive oil, the salt, and pepper; set aside. Remove meat from roasted chicken. Cut meat into pieces.

2. In a large skillet heat the remaining 2 tablespoons olive oil over medium heat. Add bread cubes; cook and stir about 5 minutes or until golden. Remove skillet from heat. Add diced tomatoes; toss to mix. Divide bread mixture among 4 plates. Add chicken, cucumber, and basil. Pass tomato-oil mixture.
MAKES 4 SERVINGS.

Per serving: 596 cal., 27 g total fat (6 g sat. fat), 92 mg chol., 824 mg sodium, 50 g carbo., 4 g fiber, 37 g pro.

Quick Tip Next time you're grocery shopping, pick up a rotisserie chicken—even if you don't plan to use it that night. When you get home, let it cool, then refrigerate it. The meat from a rotisserie chicken can be used in many healthful dishes. Keep a whole bird in the refrigerator for 3 to 4 days.

Chicken with Cherry-Ginger Chutney

Chicken with Cherry-Ginger Chutney ♡

Start to Finish: 20 minutes

- 4 medium skinless, boneless chicken breast halves, each cut into 4 pieces
  Salt and black pepper
- ½ teaspoon ground ginger
- 1 tablespoon olive oil
- 1 large apple, thinly sliced horizontally
- ½ cup dried tart red cherries
- ⅓ cup coarsely chopped walnuts
- ¼ cup water
- 3 tablespoons cider vinegar
- 4 teaspoons packed brown sugar

1. Sprinkle chicken with salt, pepper, and ¼ teaspoon of the ginger.

2. In a large skillet heat oil over medium heat. Add chicken; cook for 8 to 12 minutes or until tender and no longer pink (170°F). Transfer chicken to a serving platter; keep warm.

3. For cherry-ginger chutney, add apple, cherries, and walnuts to skillet; cook for 2 minutes, stirring frequently. In a small bowl stir together the water, vinegar, brown sugar, and the remaining ¼ teaspoon ginger. Add to skillet. Cook and stir for 1 minute. Serve chutney with chicken. **MAKES 4 SERVINGS.**

Per serving: 364 cal., 12 g total fat (2 g sat. fat), 82 mg chol., 249 mg sodium, 30 g carbo., 3 g fiber, 35 g pro.

Chicken and
Asparagus
Skillet Supper

Chicken with Parmesan Noodles

Start to Finish: 20 minutes

- 1 9-ounce package refrigerated angel hair pasta
- 2 tablespoons butter
- 2 cups thinly sliced carrots (4 large)
- 1½ pounds skinless, boneless chicken breast halves, cut into 1-inch cubes
- ¼ cup purchased basil pesto
- ¼ cup finely shredded Parmesan cheese (1 ounce)
  Freshly ground black pepper
  Olive oil (optional)
  Fresh basil (optional)

1. Cook pasta following package directions.

2. Meanwhile, in a very large skillet melt 1 tablespoon of the butter over medium heat. Add carrots; cook for 3 minutes. Add chicken; cook and stir for 4 to 5 minutes or until chicken is no longer pink. Add pesto; toss to coat.

3. Drain pasta; return to pan. Toss pasta with the remaining 1 tablespoon butter. Serve with chicken mixture. Sprinkle with Parmesan cheese and pepper. If desired, drizzle with olive oil and top with basil. **MAKES 4 SERVINGS.**

Per serving: 567 cal., 19 g total fat (8 g sat. fat), 164 mg chol., 452 mg sodium, 47 g carbo., 5 g fiber, 52 g pro.

Chicken and Asparagus Skillet Supper

Start to Finish: 20 minutes

- 8 skinless, boneless chicken thighs
  Salt and black pepper
- 3 slices bacon, coarsely chopped
- ½ cup chicken broth
- 1 pound fresh asparagus spears, trimmed
- 1 small yellow summer squash, halved crosswise and cut into ½-inch strips
- 2 tablespoons water
- 4 green onions, cut into 2-inch pieces

1. Lightly sprinkle chicken with salt and pepper. In an extra-large skillet cook chicken and bacon over medium-high heat for

12 minutes, turning to brown evenly. Carefully add chicken broth; cook, covered, for 3 to 5 minutes more or until chicken is no longer pink (180°F).

2. Meanwhile, in a microwave-safe 2-quart dish combine asparagus, squash, and the water. Sprinkle with salt and pepper. Cover with vented plastic wrap. Microwave on high for 3 to 5 minutes or until vegetables are crisp-tender, stirring once. Transfer vegetables to 4 plates. Drizzle with cooking liquid from skillet; top with chicken, bacon, and green onions. **MAKES 4 SERVINGS.**

Per serving: 320 cal., 18 g total fat (6 g sat. fat), 134 mg chol., 626 mg sodium, 5 g carbo., 2 g fiber, 32 g pro.

Chicken with
Parmesan
Noodles

Ginger-Chicken and Garden-Vegetable Fried Rice

Ginger-Chicken and Garden-Vegetable Fried Rice

Start to Finish: 29 minutes

- 1 tablespoon vegetable oil
- 4 chicken drumsticks
- 2 tablespoons soy sauce
- 1 1-inch piece fresh ginger, peeled and finely chopped (2 tablespoons)
- ½ cup water
- 1 cup sliced or coarsely chopped carrots (2 large)
- 2 tablespoons water
- 1 14.8-ounce pouch cooked long grain rice
- 8 ounces fresh sugar snap peas
- ½ cup chopped red sweet pepper (optional)
- 4 eggs, lightly beaten
  Sliced green onions (optional)
  Soy sauce and/or dark sesame oil (optional)

1. In a large nonstick skillet heat oil over medium-high heat. Add chicken, 2 tablespoons soy sauce, and 1 tablespoon of the ginger; stir to coat chicken. Cook until browned, turning chicken to brown evenly. Add the ½ cup water. Cook, covered, about 15 minutes or until chicken is no longer pink (180°F).

2. Meanwhile, in a 2-quart microwave-safe casserole combine carrots, the remaining 1 tablespoon ginger, and 2 tablespoons water. Microwave, covered, on high for 4 minutes. Add rice from pouch, sugar snap peas, and, if desired, sweet pepper. Cook, covered, about 5 minutes or until heated through, stirring twice.

3. Remove chicken and pan juices from skillet; cover to keep warm. Using paper towels, wipe out skillet. Return skillet to heat; add eggs. Cook, stirring occasionally, for 30 seconds or just until scrambled. Stir in rice mixture. Divide among 4 shallow bowls or plates; top each with a chicken drumstick. If desired, top with green onions and pass reserved pan juices and soy sauce.

MAKES 4 SERVINGS.

Per serving: 421 cal., 17 g total fat (4 g sat. fat), 271 mg chol., 666 mg sodium, 42 g carbo., 4 g fiber, 25 g pro.

Chicken and Lemon-Broccoli Alfredo

Chicken and Lemon-Broccoli Alfredo

Start to Finish: 20 minutes

- 4 small skinless, boneless chicken breast halves (1 to 1¼ pounds)
  Salt and black pepper
- 1 tablespoon olive oil
- 8 ounces fresh mushrooms, halved
- 1 lemon
- 3 cups broccoli florets
- 1 10-ounce container refrigerated light Alfredo pasta sauce

1. Lightly sprinkle chicken with salt and pepper. In a large skillet heat oil over medium heat. Add chicken and mushrooms; cook about 4 minutes or until chicken is browned, turning chicken once.

2. Meanwhile, finely shred 2 teaspoons lemon peel; set aside. Slice lemon. Add broccoli and lemon slices to skillet. Cook, covered, about 8 minutes or until chicken is tender and no longer pink (170°F).

3. Place chicken and vegetables on 4 plates. Add Alfredo sauce to skillet; heat through. Serve with chicken. Sprinkle with lemon peel and pepper. **MAKES 4 SERVINGS.**

Per serving: 295 cal., 12 g total fat (5 g sat. fat), 91 mg chol., 705 mg sodium, 16 g carbo., 4 g fiber, 35 g pro.

Lemon
Chicken with
Olives and
Ricotta

Lemon Chicken with Olives and Ricotta

Start to Finish: 27 minutes

 8 no-boil lasagna noodles
 1 teaspoon olive oil
 1 Meyer lemon or lemon
 4 small skinless, boneless chicken breast
   halves, halved crosswise (1 to 1¼ pounds)
   Salt and black pepper
 1 tablespoon olive oil
 1 cup garlic-stuffed or pitted green olives
 1 cup ricotta cheese
 ½ teaspoon salt
 ½ teaspoon black pepper
   Snipped fresh rosemary (optional)

1. In a Dutch oven bring 3 inches water to boiling. Add noodles and 1 teaspoon olive oil. Cover and cook about 6 minutes or until tender; drain. Lay noodles in single layer on waxed paper. Cover; set aside.

2. Meanwhile, shred peel from lemon; halve lemon. Juice 1 half; cut remaining half into wedges. Sprinkle chicken with salt, pepper, and half of lemon peel. In a large skillet heat oil over medium-high heat. Add chicken. Cook about 10 minutes or until no longer pink, turning once. Add olives; heat through. Remove from heat.

3. In a microwave-safe bowl combine ricotta, lemon juice, ½ teaspoon salt, and ½ teaspoon pepper. Microwave on high for 30 seconds, stirring once.

4. Spoon ricotta mixture into bowls. Top with noodles, chicken, olives, the remaining lemon peel, and, if desired, the fresh rosemary. Serve with the lemon wedges.

MAKES 4 SERVINGS.

Per serving: 443 cal., 19 g total fat (7 g sat. fat), 130 mg chol., 1,053 mg sodium, 30 g carbo., 4 g fiber, 39 g pro.

Lickety-Split Lemon Chicken ♡

Start to Finish: 30 minutes

 2 tablespoons butter
 12 ounces chicken breast tenderloins
 1 8-ounce package sliced fresh mushrooms
 1 medium red sweet pepper, cut into strips
 2 tablespoons all-purpose flour
 1 14.5-ounce can chicken broth
 1 teaspoon finely shredded lemon peel
 2 tablespoons lemon juice
 1 teaspoon dried thyme, crushed
   Salt and black pepper
 1 14.8-ounce pouch cooked long grain
   white rice
   Lemon wedges (optional)

1. In a very large skillet melt butter over medium heat. Add chicken; cook for 6 to 8 minutes or until no longer pink (170°F), adding mushrooms and sweet pepper for the last 5 minutes of cooking time. Stir in flour. Cook and stir for 1 minute more. Add chicken broth, lemon peel, lemon juice, and thyme. Cook and stir until thickened and bubbly. Cook and stir for 2 minutes more. Season with salt and black pepper.

2. Meanwhile, prepare rice following package directions. Serve chicken mixture over rice. If desired, serve with lemon wedges.

MAKES 4 SERVINGS.

Per serving: 361 cal., 10 g total fat (4 g sat. fat), 66 mg chol., 643 mg sodium, 41 g carbo., 2 g fiber, 25 g pro.

Lickety-Split
Lemon
Chicken

Pecan-Crusted Chicken Thighs with Braised Greens

Pecan-Crusted Chicken Thighs with Braised Greens

Start to Finish: 30 minutes

1 pound skinless, boneless chicken thighs
Salt and black pepper
1 egg
⅓ cup finely chopped pecans
⅓ cup crushed saltine or wheat crackers
¼ teaspoon ground nutmeg
4 teaspoons olive oil
1 10-ounce package mixed salad greens
4 small grape clusters
⅓ cup frozen harvest blend or white grape juice concentrate, thawed

1. Place each of the chicken thighs between 2 pieces of waxed paper. Using the flat side of a meat mallet, pound chicken thighs to flatten pieces slightly. Sprinkle lightly with salt and pepper. Beat egg in a shallow dish. In another shallow dish combine pecans, crackers, and nutmeg. Dip chicken into egg and then into pecan mixture, pressing to coat both sides.

2. In a very large skillet heat 3 teaspoons of the olive oil over medium heat. Add chicken; cook for 10 to 12 minutes or until golden and crisp (180°F), turning once halfway through cooking. Remove chicken; cover and keep warm. Add greens to skillet; cook and stir just until greens begin to wilt. Remove from heat; season with salt and pepper.

3. Meanwhile, in a medium skillet heat the remaining 1 teaspoon oil. Add grapes and cook for 3 to 4 minutes or just until grapes are warmed and some of the skins begin to burst. Add juice concentrate; cook for 1 minute more. Remove from heat.

4. To serve, divide greens among 4 plates; serve with chicken and grape clusters. Drizzle with the remaining juice from skillet. **MAKES 4 SERVINGS.**

Per serving: 367 cal., 18 g total fat (3 g sat. fat), 147 mg chol., 485 mg sodium, 27 g carbo., 3 g fiber, 27 g pro.

Mediterranean
Pizza Skillet

Mediterranean Pizza Skillet

Start to Finish: 30 minutes

2 tablespoons olive oil
3 skinless, boneless chicken breast halves, cut into ¾-inch pieces
2 cloves garlic, minced
4 roma tomatoes, chopped
1 14-ounce can artichoke hearts, drained and quartered
1 2.25-ounce can sliced pitted ripe olives, drained
½ teaspoon dried Italian seasoning, crushed
¼ teaspoon freshly ground black pepper
2 cups coarsely chopped romaine lettuce or hearty mesclun
1 cup crumbled feta cheese (4 ounces)
⅓ cup fresh basil leaves, shredded or torn
Crusty Italian or French bread, sliced

1. In a large skillet heat oil over medium-high heat. Add chicken and garlic; cook and stir until chicken is browned. Stir in tomatoes, artichokes, olives, seasoning, and pepper. Bring to boiling; reduce heat. Simmer, covered, about 10 minutes or until chicken is no longer pink (170°F).

2. Top chicken with lettuce and cheese. Cook, covered, for 1 to 2 minutes more or until lettuce starts to wilt. Sprinkle with basil. Serve with bread. **MAKES 4 SERVINGS.**

Per serving: 395 cal., 17 g total fat (6 g sat. fat), 82 mg chol., 1,003 mg sodium, 27 g carbo., 6 g fiber, 33 g pro.

Soft Shell
Chicken
Tacos

Soft Shell Chicken Tacos

Start to Finish: 20 minutes

1 2¼- to 2½-pound purchased whole
   roasted chicken
4 7- to 8-inch flour tortillas
½ cup sour cream salsa- or Mexican-flavor
   dip
1 large red, green, or yellow sweet pepper,
   cut into bite-size strips
1½ cups shredded lettuce

1. Remove skin and bones from chicken and
discard. Coarsely shred 2 cups of the
chicken. Reserve remaining chicken for
another use.
2. Spread 1 side of each tortilla with dip. Top
with chicken, sweet pepper, and lettuce. Fold
each tortilla in half. **MAKES 4 TACOS.**

Per taco: 284 cal., 13 g total fat (5 g sat. fat), 82 mg
chol., 479 mg sodium, 19 g carbo., 1 g fiber, 23 g pro.

Green Chile and Chicken Enchiladas

Start to Finish: 28 minutes

1¼ pounds chicken breast tenderloins
1½ cups bottled green salsa
 1 4-ounce can diced green chiles
1½ cups shredded Mexican-style four-cheese
    blend (6 ounces)
 8 6- to 7-inch flour tortillas
    Refrigerated fresh salsa (optional)
    Lime wedges (optional)

1. Preheat broiler. Cut chicken into 1-inch
pieces and place in a microwave-safe bowl.
Microwave, covered, on high for 7 minutes or
until no pink remains, stirring twice. Drain
liquid. Break up the chicken slightly in a bowl
with back of wooden spoon. Add salsa and
chiles. Cook 3 minutes more or until heated
through, stirring once. Stir in 1 cup of the
cheese.
2. Spoon chicken mixture evenly down center
of tortillas. Roll tortillas around filling and
place in 13×9×2-inch baking pan. Sprinkle
remaining ½ cup cheese over enchiladas.
Broil 3 to 4 inches from heat for 1 to
2 minutes or until cheese melts.
3. To serve, if desired, top enchiladas with
salsa and lime wedges. **MAKES 4 SERVINGS.**

Per serving: 569 cal., 24 g total fat (8 g sat. fat), 120 mg
chol., 1,081 mg sodium, 33 g carbo., 1 g fiber, 49 g pro.

Quick Tip Refrigerated salsa has a fresher
taste and chunkier texture than most of the
bottled varieties—close to that of pico de
gallo. You can usually find it in the produce
section in both mild and hot versions.

Green Chile
and Chicken
Enchiladas

Turkey-Pesto
Pot Pie

Turkey-Pesto Pot Pie

Prep: 15 minutes **Bake:** 15 minutes
Oven: 375°F

    1 12-ounce jar turkey gravy
  ⅓ cup purchased basil or dried tomato pesto
    3 cups cubed cooked turkey (about 1 pound)
    1 16-ounce package frozen peas and carrots
    1 11-ounce package refrigerated
       breadsticks (12)

1. Preheat oven to 375°F. In a large saucepan combine turkey gravy and pesto; stir in turkey and vegetables. Bring to boiling, stirring frequently. Divide turkey mixture evenly among six 8-ounce casseroles.
2. Cut 6 of the breadsticks into 6 pieces. Place remaining breadsticks onto a baking sheet. Divide breadstick pieces among the dishes.
3. Bake casseroles about 15 minutes or until breadsticks are golden. Bake remaining breadsticks following package directions.
MAKES 6 SERVINGS.

Per serving: 365 cal., 16 g total fat (5 g sat. fat), 52 mg chol., 964 mg sodium, 36 g carbo., 4 g fiber, 20 g pro.

Turkey and Soba Noodle Stir-Fry ♡

Start to Finish: 25 minutes

    6 ounces dried soba (buckwheat) noodles
       or whole wheat spaghetti pasta
    2 teaspoons olive oil
    2 cups fresh sugar snap peas
    1 medium red sweet pepper, cut into thin
       strips
    2 teaspoons minced fresh ginger
    4 cloves garlic, minced (2 teaspoons
       minced)
    4 green onions, bias-sliced into 1-inch pieces
  12 ounces turkey breast tenderloin, cut into
       bite-size strips

Turkey and Soba Noodle Stir-Fry

    1 teaspoon toasted sesame oil
  ½ cup bottled plum sauce
  ¼ teaspoon crushed red pepper

1. Cook soba noodles following package directions; drain. Return to hot pan; cover and keep warm.
2. Meanwhile, pour oil into a wok or large skillet. (Add more olive oil as necessary during cooking.) Heat over medium-high heat. Stir-fry peas, sweet pepper, ginger, and garlic in hot oil for 2 minutes. Add green onion. Stir-fry for 1 to 2 minutes more or until vegetables are crisp-tender. Remove vegetables from wok.
3. Add turkey and sesame oil to the hot wok. Stir-fry for 3 to 4 minutes or until turkey is no longer pink. Add plum sauce and crushed red pepper. Return cooked vegetables to wok; stir to coat all ingredients with sauce. Heat through. Serve immediately over noodles. **MAKES 4 SERVINGS.**

Per serving: 368 cal., 5 g total fat (1 g sat. fat), 53 mg chol., 409 mg sodium, 55 g carbo., 4 g fiber, 29 g pro.

Quick Tip If your supermarket doesn't carry soba noodles, look for them at Asian food stores. Or opt for whole wheat spaghetti for a similar nutty flavor.

Turkey Roulade

Creamy Turkey Fettuccine

Start to Finish: 35 minutes

- 1 pound dried spinach fettuccine and/or plain fettuccine
- 2 8-ounce cartons fat-free sour cream
- ¼ cup all-purpose flour
- 1 cup reduced-sodium chicken broth
- 1 teaspoon dried sage, crushed
- ¼ teaspoon black pepper
- 1½ pounds turkey breast tenderloin
- ¼ teaspoon salt
  Nonstick cooking spray
- 3 cups sliced fresh mushrooms
- 1 cup sliced green onions (8)
- 4 cloves garlic, minced

1. Cook pasta following package directions; drain. Meanwhile, in a large bowl stir together sour cream and flour. Gradually stir in chicken broth, sage, and pepper. Cut turkey in bite-size strips; sprinkle with salt. Set aside.
2. Coat a large skillet with cooking spray. Heat over medium-high heat. Add half of the turkey; cook and stir for 3 to 5 minutes or until no longer pink (170°F). Remove turkey from skillet. Add remaining turkey, mushrooms, green onions, and garlic to skillet. Cook and stir for 3 to 5 minutes or until turkey is no longer pink (170°F). Return all of the turkey to the skillet.
3. Stir the sour cream mixture into turkey mixture in skillet. Cook and stir until thickened and bubbly. Cook and stir for 1 minute more. Serve over hot cooked pasta. **MAKES 8 SERVINGS.**

Per serving: 400 cal., 3 g total fat (1 g sat. fat), 51 mg chol., 327 mg sodium, 58 g carbo., 1 g fiber, 34 g pro.

Turkey Roulade ♡

Start to Finish: 25 minutes

- 1 4.1- to 6-ounce package long grain and wild rice mix
- 2 turkey breast tenderloins (about 1 pound)
- ½ of a 6-ounce package frozen pea pods
- 2 tablespoons vegetable oil
- ⅓ cup bottled barbecue sauce
- ⅓ cup orange juice
  Orange slices, quartered (optional)

1. Prepare rice mix following package directions.
2. Meanwhile, cut each turkey tenderloin in half horizontally to make 2 steaks each. Place each turkey steak between 2 pieces of plastic wrap. Using the flat side of a meat mallet, pound turkey lightly to ¼-inch thickness. Discard plastic wrap. Arrange the pea pods across the turkey steaks. Roll up and secure with wooden toothpicks.
3. In a large skillet heat oil over medium-high heat. Add turkey rolls; cook until browned, turning to brown evenly.
4. Meanwhile, in a small bowl stir together the barbecue sauce and orange juice. Add orange juice mixture to skillet with turkey rolls. Bring to boiling; reduce heat. Simmer, covered, for 10 to 15 minutes or until turkey is no longer pink (170°F). Serve with rice. If desired garnish with orange slices.
MAKES 4 SERVINGS.

Per serving: 332 cal., 8 g total fat (1 g sat. fat), 70 mg chol., 701 mg sodium, 34 g carbo., 2 g fiber, 31 g pro.

Creamy
Turkey
Fettuccine

Ham and Apricot Turkey Spirals

Ham and Apricot Turkey Spirals ♡

Prep: 30 minutes **Roast:** 35 minutes
Oven: 425°F

2 12-ounce turkey breast tenderloins
4 ounces thinly sliced reduced-sodium cooked ham
½ cup finely chopped dried apricot halves
2 tablespoons Dijon mustard
1 teaspoon dried rosemary, crushed
1 teaspoon honey
1 egg white, lightly beaten
½ teaspoon black pepper
½ cup whole wheat panko (Japanese-style bread crumbs)
   Fresh spinach (optional)
   Bottled raspberry vinaigrette salad dressing (optional)

1. Preheat oven to 425°F. Using a sharp knife, split each tenderloin almost in half horizontally, cutting to within ½ inch of the opposite side. Open each tenderloin like a book and place each between 2 pieces of plastic wrap so it lies almost flat. Using the flat side of a meat mallet, pound each tenderloin to ½ inch thick. Remove top pieces of plastic wrap.
2. Layer ham slices evenly on top of turkey pieces. In a small bowl combine apricots, mustard, rosemary, and honey. Spread evenly over ham. Starting from a short side, roll up each turkey piece into a spiral. Tie each spiral at 2-inch intervals with clean 100%-cotton kitchen string.
3. Brush egg white over turkey spirals. Sprinkle with pepper. Spread panko in an even layer on a piece of waxed paper. Roll each turkey spiral in the panko to coat. Place turkey spirals on a rack in a shallow roasting pan. Roast for 35 minutes or until turkey is no

Teriyaki-Glazed Turkey Tenderloin Steaks

longer pink (170°F). To serve, cut each spiral into 6 slices. If desired, toss spinach with vinaigrette dressing and serve with turkey.
MAKES 6 SERVINGS.

Per serving: 214 cal., 2 g total fat (1 g sat. fat), 81 mg chol., 372 mg sodium, 13 g carbo., 2 g fiber, 34 g pro.

Teriyaki-Glazed Turkey Tenderloin Steaks

Start to Finish: 30 minutes

2 turkey breast tenderloins
1 tablespoon vegetable oil
1 12-ounce package frozen broccoli, carrots, sugar snap peas, and water chestnuts in microwavable steaming bag
½ cup bottled stir-fry sauce
1 14.8-ounce pouch cooked long grain white rice
¼ cup chopped dry-roasted peanuts

1. Split each turkey tenderloin in half horizontally to make four ½-inch-thick steaks. In a very large skillet heat oil over medium-high heat. Add turkey to the skillet. Cook for 14 to 16 minutes or until no longer pink (170°F), turning once halfway through cooking. (Reduce heat to medium if turkey becomes too brown during cooking.) Remove turkey from skillet; keep warm.
2. Meanwhile, prepare vegetables following package directions. Transfer vegetables to the skillet. Add stir-fry sauce; heat through.
3. Heat rice following package directions. Serve turkey and vegetable mixture over rice. Sprinkle with peanuts. **MAKES 4 SERVINGS.**

Per serving: 447 cal., 11 g total fat (1 g sat. fat), 70 mg chol., 1,127 mg sodium, 48 g carbo., 4 g fiber, 35 g pro.

Turkey
Cranberry
Fried Rice

Turkey Cranberry Fried Rice

Start to Finish: 25 minutes

1 pound uncooked ground turkey
½ cup chopped celery (1 stalk)
½ cup chopped onion (1 medium)
1 8.8-ounce package cooked long grain and wild rice
½ cup apple cider
⅓ cup dried cranberries
½ teaspoon dried thyme, crushed
⅓ cup chopped pecans, toasted (see note, page 54)
 Salt and black pepper

1. In a very large skillet cook and stir turkey, celery, and onion over medium heat until turkey is browned and vegetables are tender.
2. Meanwhile, prepare long grain and wild rice following package directions.
3. Stir rice, cider, cranberries, and thyme into mixture in skillet. Cook and stir until liquid is absorbed. Stir in pecans. Season with salt and pepper. **MAKES 4 SERVINGS.**

Per serving: 385 cal., 18 g total fat (3 g sat. fat), 90 mg chol., 395 mg sodium, 34 g carbo., 2 g fiber, 23 g pro.

Turkey Dinner Burgers

Prep: 15 minutes **Broil:** 14 minutes

1 egg, lightly beaten
½ teaspoon salt
¼ teaspoon black pepper
1 pound uncooked lean ground turkey or ground chicken
¼ cup fine dry bread crumbs
¼ cup jalapeño pepper jelly, melted
 Shredded green cabbage, thinly sliced red onion, and/or other desired toppings
4 ciabatta rolls, potato rolls, kaiser rolls, or hamburger buns, split and toasted

1. Preheat broiler. In a large bowl combine egg, salt, and pepper. Add turkey and bread crumbs; mix well. Shape the poultry mixture into four ¾-inch-thick patties.
2. Place patties on the unheated rack of a broiler pan. Broil 4 to 5 inches from the heat for 12 to 14 minutes or until done (165°F), turning once halfway through cooking time. Brush patties with half of the jalapeño jelly. Broil 1 minute; turn and brush with remaining jelly. Broil 1 minute more.
3. To assemble, place cabbage, red onion, and/or other toppings on bottoms of rolls and top with patties and roll tops.

MAKES 4 SERVINGS.

Per serving: 504 cal., 20 g total fat (2 g sat. fat), 55 mg chol., 900 mg sodium, 52 g carbo., 2 g fiber, 28 g pro.

Quick Tip To ensure that you get the leanest ground turkey, look for fresh ground turkey made from the breast only. It will be light in color—almost white—rather than dark pink. Regular ground turkey is made with dark and light meat. Frozen ground turkey, which is made from dark meat only, can also contain skin and can be as high in fat and calories as ground beef.

Turkey Dinner
Burgers

Turkey and Pasta with Peanut Sauce

Turkey and Pasta with Peanut Sauce ♡

Start to Finish: 30 minutes

- 6 ounces dried fettuccine or linguine pasta
- 2 cups fresh pea pods, tips trimmed, or one 6-ounce package frozen pea pods
- 1 cup cooked turkey or chicken strips
- 1 cup coarsely chopped fresh pineapple or one 8-ounce can pineapple chunks, drained
- ¼ cup reduced-sodium chicken broth
- 2 tablespoons creamy peanut butter
- 1 tablespoon reduced-sodium soy sauce
- 1 tablespoon lime juice or lemon juice
- ¼ teaspoon crushed red pepper
- 1 clove garlic, minced

1. Cook pasta following package directions. Meanwhile, halve the fresh pea pods diagonally. Place the pea pods and turkey in a large colander. Pour hot cooking liquid from pasta over pea pods and turkey in colander; drain well. Return pasta, pea pods, and turkey to the hot pan. Add the pineapple.
2. Meanwhile, for the sauce, in a small saucepan stir chicken broth into peanut butter. Heat and stir with a whisk until peanut butter melts. Stir in soy sauce, lime juice, red pepper, and garlic; heat through.
3. Add sauce to the pasta mixture. Gently stir to coat pasta with sauce. **MAKES 4 SERVINGS.**

Per serving: 317 cal., 7 g total fat (2 g sat. fat), 30 mg chol., 254 mg sodium, 44 g carbo., 3 g fiber, 21 g pro.

Turkey Burgers with Cranberry Sauce

Turkey Burgers with Cranberry Sauce

Prep: 12 minutes **Broil:** 11 minutes

- ⅓ cup herb-seasoned stuffing mix, crushed (¼ cup)
- 2 tablespoons milk
- 1 tablespoon snipped fresh sage or ½ teaspoon dried sage, crushed
- ¼ teaspoon salt
- 1 pound uncooked ground turkey or ground chicken
- 1 cup torn mixed salad greens, watercress leaves, or shredded fresh spinach
- 4 whole wheat hamburger buns, split and toasted
- ½ cup whole cranberry sauce

1. Preheat broiler. In a large bowl combine stuffing mix, milk, sage, and salt. Add ground turkey; mix well. Shape into four ½-inch patties. Place patties on the unheated rack of a broiler pan. Broil 4 to 5 inches from the heat for 11 to 13 minutes or until done (165°F),* turning once halfway through broiling.
2. Divide greens among bottoms of buns; top with patties and cranberry sauce. Top with bun tops. **MAKES 4 SERVINGS.**

Per serving: 350 cal., 11 g total fat (3 g sat. fat), 71 mg chol., 503 mg sodium, 37 g carbo., 3 g fiber, 28 g pro.

*Note The internal color of a burger is not a reliable doneness indicator. A turkey or chicken patty cooked to 165°F is safe, regardless of color. To measure the doneness of a patty, insert an instant-read thermometer through the side of the patty to a depth of 2 to 3 inches.

Spiced Jerk Turkey with Mango Salsa

Spiced Jerk Turkey with Mango Salsa ♡

Start to Finish: 30 minutes

- 4 teaspoons Jamaican jerk seasoning
- 1 teaspoon ground cumin
- ½ teaspoon salt
- ½ teaspoon ground ginger
- ⅛ teaspoon cayenne pepper
- 2 tablespoons olive oil
- 2 cloves garlic, minced
- 8 turkey breast slices, cut ¼ to ⅜ inch thick (about 1 pound)
- 1 cup chopped, peeled mango, peach, or nectarine
- ¼ cup finely chopped red sweet pepper
- ¼ cup finely chopped red onion
- 2 tablespoons snipped fresh cilantro
- 1 tablespoon fresh lime juice
- 1 teaspoon finely chopped, seeded fresh serrano chile (see note, page 31)
  Torn mixed salad greens

1. In a small bowl combine Jamaican jerk seasoning, cumin, salt, ginger, and cayenne pepper; remove and set aside 1 teaspoon of the cumin mixture. Add 1 tablespoon of the olive oil and the garlic to the remaining cumin mixture. Using your fingers, rub the cumin mixture evenly onto both sides of turkey slices. Set turkey aside.

2. For salsa, in a small bowl combine mango, sweet pepper, onion, cilantro, lime juice, serrano chile, and the reserved 1 teaspoon cumin mixture. Set salsa aside.

3. In a large skillet heat the remaining 1 tablespoon olive oil over medium heat. Add half the turkey slices; cook for 4 to 6 minutes or until turkey is no longer pink, turning once halfway through cooking. Repeat with remaining turkey slices. (Add more olive oil if necessary during cooking.) If desired, cut turkey into bite-size strips. Serve on salad greens; top with salsa. **MAKES 4 SERVINGS.**

Per serving: 243 cal., 8 g total fat (1 g sat. fat), 70 mg chol., 648 mg sodium, 13 g carbo., 3 g fiber, 30 g pro.

Sautéed Apple and Smoked Turkey Salad

Start to Finish: 30 minutes

- 1 red or green tart apple
- 1 tablespoon butter
- 1 tablespoon pure maple or maple-flavor syrup
- ¼ cup fresh or dried cranberries
- 1 6- to 8-ounce package torn mixed salad greens
- 2 cups cubed smoked turkey (10 ounces)
- 2 ounces goat cheese, crumbled
- 1 recipe Apple Cider Vinaigrette
- 1 to 2 tablespoon coarsely chopped pecans or almonds, toasted (see note, page 54), and/or snipped fresh chives

1. Core and thinly slice apple. In a large skillet melt butter over medium heat. Stir in maple syrup. Add apple slices; cook for 6 to 8 minutes or until apple slices are golden on both sides and still slightly crisp, turning as needed. Stir in cranberries; set aside.

2. Arrange greens on a large platter. Top with turkey and apple mixture. Sprinkle with goat cheese. Drizzle with Apple Cider Vinaigrette. Sprinkle with toasted nuts.

MAKES 4 SERVINGS.

Apple Cider Vinaigrette In a small bowl whisk together ½ cup cider vinegar, 2 tablespoons pure maple or maple-flavor syrup, 1 teaspoon grainy mustard, ¼ teaspoon salt, and ¼ teaspoon black pepper. Gradually whisk in ⅓ cup nut oil (such as pecan or almond). Use at once. Makes about 1 cup.

Per serving: 424 cal., 28 g total fat (7 g sat. fat), 53 mg chol., 1,107 mg sodium, 25 g carbo., 2 g fiber, 19 g pro.

Fish & Seafood

Roasted
Salmon and
Tomatoes

Sesame-Crusted Salmon

Start to Finish: 30 minutes

- 1 1-pound fresh or frozen skinless salmon or halibut fillet
- ½ cup mayonnaise
- ⅓ cup chopped roasted red sweet pepper
- 2 teaspoons lemon juice
- 1 teaspoon snipped fresh chives
  Salt and black pepper
- ⅓ cup all-purpose flour
- 1 tablespoon white sesame seeds
- 1 tablespoon black sesame seeds
- ¼ teaspoon salt
- ¼ cup milk
- 2 tablespoons vegetable oil
  Lemon or lime wedges (optional)
  Fresh watercress (optional)

1. Thaw fish, if frozen. Rinse fish; pat dry with paper towels. Cut into 4 serving-size pieces. Set aside.

2. In a small bowl combine mayonnaise, sweet pepper, lemon juice, and chives. Season with salt and black pepper. Cover and chill until serving time.

3. In another small bowl combine flour, white sesame seeds, black sesame seeds, and the ¼ teaspoon salt. Place milk in a shallow dish. Dip salmon in milk. Firmly press both sides of fish in sesame seed mixture.

4. In a large skillet heat oil over medium-high heat; cook coated fish fillets in hot oil for 8 to 10 minutes or until fish flakes when tested with a fork, turning once. To serve, spoon sweet pepper sauce on dinner plates; top with fish. If desired, garnish with lemon or lime wedges and fresh watercress.

MAKES 4 SERVINGS.

Per serving: 539 cal., 44 g total fat (8 g sat. fat), 78 mg chol., 404 mg sodium, 10 g carbo., 1 g fiber, 25 g pro.

Make-Ahead Directions Prepare sweet pepper sauce; cover and chill up to 24 hours. Stir before serving; if necessary, stir in a little extra water.

Quick Tip If you can't find black sesame seeds, just use all white sesame seeds. Mix all of the sesame seeds with all of the flour and salt in one bowl and dredge both sides of fish in mixture.

Roasted Salmon and Tomatoes

Prep: 15 minutes **Bake:** 12 minutes
Oven: 450°F

- 1 1¼-pound fresh salmon fillet, about 1 inch thick
  Nonstick cooking spray
- ¼ teaspoon salt
- 6 roma tomatoes, seeded and chopped (about 1 pound)
- 1 tablespoon Worcestershire-style marinade for chicken
- ¼ teaspoon black pepper
- 1 tablespoon Dijon mustard
- 1 tablespoon snipped fresh marjoram or oregano

1. Thaw fish, if frozen. Preheat oven to 450°F. Coat a 13×9×2-inch baking pan with cooking spray. Rinse fish; pat dry with paper towels.

Cut fish into 4 serving-size pieces. Sprinkle with ⅛ teaspoon of the salt. Place fillets in pan, skin sides up, tucking under any thin edges to make fish uniform thickness. Arrange tomatoes around salmon. Sprinkle tomatoes with Worcestershire-style marinade, pepper, and the remaining ⅛ teaspoon salt.

2. Bake, uncovered, for 12 to 16 minutes or until fish flakes when tested with a fork. Remove skin from fish; discard skin. Transfer fish to 4 dinner plates. Stir mustard and marjoram into tomatoes. Serve tomato mixture with fish. **MAKES 4 SERVINGS.**

Per serving: 231 cal., 10 g total fat (2 g sat. fat), 75 mg chol., 370 mg sodium, 6 g carbo., 1 g fiber, 30 g pro.

Sesame-
Crusted
Salmon

Maple
Salmon with
Greens,
Edamame, and
Walnuts

Maple Salmon with Greens, Edamame, and Walnuts

Start to Finish: 29 minutes

- 4   5- to 6-ounce fresh or frozen skinless salmon fillets, about 1 inch thick
- 3   tablespoons pure maple syrup
- 2   tablespoons balsamic vinegar
- 1   tablespoon lemon juice
- 1   tablespoon Dijon mustard
- 1   tablespoon finely chopped shallot
- ¼   teaspoon kosher salt or salt
- ¼   teaspoon freshly ground black pepper
- 2   teaspoons snipped fresh rosemary
- 2   tablespoons olive oil
- 1   6-ounce package fresh baby spinach
- ½   cup cooked sweet soybeans (edamame)
- ½   cup red sweet pepper strips
- ¼   cup chopped walnuts, toasted (see note, page 54)

1. Thaw fish, if frozen. Rinse fish; pat dry with paper towels; set fish aside. Preheat broiler.
2. In a small saucepan combine maple syrup, vinegar, lemon juice, mustard, shallot, salt, and black pepper. Transfer 2 tablespoons of the maple syrup mixture to a small bowl; set aside. For glaze, heat remaining maple syrup mixture to boiling; reduce heat. Simmer, uncovered, about 5 minutes or until syrupy. Remove from heat; stir in rosemary.
3. Meanwhile, for dressing, stir olive oil into the 2 tablespoons reserved syrup. Set dressing aside.
4. Place fish on the greased unheated rack of a broiler pan, tucking under thin edges to make fish uniform thickness. Brush fish with half of the glaze. Broil 6 to 7 inches from heat for 5 minutes. Turn fish over; brush with remaining glaze. Broil for 3 to 5 minutes more or until fish flakes when tested with a fork.
4. Meanwhile, in a large bowl combine spinach, edamame, sweet pepper, and nuts. Drizzle with dressing; toss to coat. Arrange spinach mixture on 4 serving plates. Add a fillet to each plate. **MAKES 4 SERVINGS.**

Per serving: 460 cal., 28 g total fat (5 g sat. fat), 84 mg chol., 313 mg sodium, 18 g carbo., 3 g fiber, 33 g pro.

Herb-Crusted Salmon with Roasted Pepper Cream

Herb-Crusted Salmon with Roasted Pepper Cream

Prep: 10 minutes **Bake:** 20 minutes
Cook: 15 minutes **Oven:** 400°F

- 4   5- to 6-ounce fresh or frozen skinless, boneless salmon fillets
- 3   tablespoons honey-Dijon mustard
- 3   tablespoons seasoned fine dry bread crumbs
- ½   cup chopped bottled roasted red sweet peppers, drained
- 1   cup whipping cream

1. Thaw fish, if frozen. Rinse fish; pat dry with paper towels. Preheat oven to 400°F. Brush 1 side of each fillet with 2 tablespoons of the mustard. Sprinkle with bread crumbs. Place fish, coated sides up, in a 3-quart rectangular baking dish.

2. Bake, uncovered, for 20 to 25 minutes or until crumbs are golden and fish flakes when tested with a fork.
3. Meanwhile, for sauce, in a medium saucepan combine the remaining 1 tablespoon mustard, the roasted peppers, and cream. Bring to boiling; reduce heat. Boil gently, uncovered, about 15 minutes or until reduced to 1 cup. Serve sauce over fish.
MAKES 4 SERVINGS.

Per serving: 576 cal., 32 g total fat (15 g sat. fat), 227 mg chol., 359 mg sodium, 11 g carbo., 0 g fiber, 57 g pro.

Seared Sesame Salmon

Start to Finish: 20 minutes

- 4 4- to 5-ounce fresh or frozen skinless salmon fillets, ³/₄ inch thick
- ¼ cup seasoned fine dry bread crumbs
- 2 tablespoons sesame seeds
- 1 tablespoon soy sauce
  Salt and ground black pepper
- 2 to 3 tablespoons vegetable oil
- 12 ounces fresh asparagus spears, trimmed
- ¼ cup bottled hollandaise or tartar sauce

1. Thaw fish, if frozen. Rinse fish; pat dry with paper towels. In a shallow dish combine bread crumbs and sesame seeds; set aside.
2. Brush both sides of fish with soy sauce. Sprinkle lightly with salt and pepper. Coat fish with crumb mixture.
3. In a very large skillet heat 2 tablespoons of the oil over medium heat. Add fish to hot oil in skillet. Cook for 4 minutes; turn fish over. Cook for 3 to 4 minutes more or until fish flakes when tested with a fork. Transfer fish to a serving platter; cover to keep warm.
4. Add remaining oil to skillet if needed. Add asparagus; cook about 3 minutes or until crisp-tender, turning occasionally. Add asparagus to serving platter. Serve with hollandaise sauce. **MAKES 4 SERVINGS.**

Per serving: 347 cal., 23 g total fat (4 g sat. fat), 70 mg chol., 615 mg sodium, 9 g carbo., 2 g fiber, 26 g pro.

Salmon Steaks with Pistachios

Start to Finish: 25 minutes **Oven:** 450°F

- 4 5- to 6-ounce fresh or frozen salmon steaks, cut ³/₄ inch thick, or 1 pound salmon, cut into serving-size pieces
- ¼ cup finely chopped natural pistachios, toasted
- 1 tablespoon vegetable oil
- 1 pound asparagus, bias-sliced into 1-inch pieces
- 4 ounces shiitake mushrooms or button mushrooms, sliced (about 1½ cups)
- 6 green onions, cut into bite-size pieces (1 cup)
- 1 recipe Barbecue Sauce

1. Thaw fish, if frozen. Rinse fish; pat dry with paper towels. Preheat oven to 450°F. Place fish in a greased shallow baking pan. Sprinkle with pistachios.
2. Bake for 8 to 12 minutes or until fish flakes when tested with a fork.
3. Meanwhile, in a skillet or wok heat oil over medium-high heat. Add asparagus; cook and stir for 3 minutes. Add mushrooms and green onions. Cook and stir for 1 to 2 minutes or until the vegetables are crisp-tender. Stir in ½ cup of the Barbecue Sauce; heat through.
4. Spoon vegetable mixture on 4 plates; place salmon on top. **MAKES 4 SERVINGS.**

Per serving: 445 cal., 27 g total fat (5 g sat. fat), 78 mg chol., 304 mg sodium, 19 g carbo., 4 g fiber, 33 g pro.

Barbecue Sauce In a covered container combine ½ cup hoisin sauce; ½ cup honey; 3 tablespoons soy sauce; 2 to 3 tablespoons sesame seeds, toasted (see note, page 54); 1 jalapeño, Asian, or other hot chile, diced (see note, page 31); 4 teaspoons finely shredded orange peel, 2 teaspoons finely shredded lemon peel or 1½ teaspoons finely shredded lime peel; 1 tablespoon dry sherry; 1 tablespoon triple sec or Grand Marnier (optional); 1 teaspoon grated fresh ginger; 1 teaspoon dark sesame oil; and 1 clove garlic, minced. Mix well. Cover and chill for up to 2 weeks. Use with fish, chicken, pork, or beef. Makes 3 cups.

Salmon with Matzo Crust

Start to Finish: 20 minutes **Oven:** 450°F

- 4 4- to 5-ounce fresh or frozen skinless salmon fillets, 1 inch thick
- 1½ 6-inch squares matzo (1½ ounces), broken up
- 2 tablespoons snipped fresh dill or 1½ teaspoon dried dill
- ½ teaspoon salt
- ¼ teaspoon black pepper
- 3 tablespoons olive oil

1. Thaw fish, if frozen. Rinse fish; pat dry with paper towels. Preheat oven to 450°F. In a blender or food processor combine matzo, the 2 tablespoons dill, the salt, and pepper. Cover; blend or process until coarse crumbs form. Transfer crumb mixture to a sheet of waxed paper or shallow dish.
2. Brush shallow baking pan with oil. Brush fish with oil. Roll in crumb mixture; place in prepared pan. Drizzle with remaining oil.
3. Bake, uncovered, for 10 to 12 minutes or until fish flakes when tested with a fork. If desired, serve with *lemon wedges,* fresh *dill sprigs,* and steamed *green beans.*
MAKES 4 SERVINGS.

Per serving: 340 cal., 23 g total fat (4 g sat. fat), 67 mg chol., 358 mg sodium, 9 g carbo., 0 g fiber, 24 g pro.

With its mild and adaptable flavor, meaty texture, and heart healthiness, salmon has become one of the country's most popular fish.

Salmon with
Matzo Crust

Salmon-
Buckwheat
Noodle Bowl

Salmon-Buckwheat Noodle Bowl

Start to Finish: 30 minutes

1¼ pounds fresh or frozen skinless salmon fillets, about 1 inch thick
¼ cup olive oil
¼ cup balsamic vinegar
1½ teaspoons cracked black pepper
8 ounces dried buckwheat (soba) noodles or whole wheat noodles
2 oranges, peeled, sectioned, and chopped
⅓ cup fresh orange juice
½ of a red onion or 2 green onions, thinly sliced
2 teaspoons anise seeds, crushed
1 clove garlic, minced

1. Thaw fish, if frozen. Cut fish into 4 pieces. Preheat broiler. In a small bowl combine 1 tablespoon of the oil, 1 tablespoon of the balsamic vinegar, and the cracked pepper. Place salmon on the unheated rack of a broiler pan. Brush both sides of fish with olive oil mixture. Broil 4 inches from the heat for 8 to 12 minutes or until fish flakes when tested with a fork.
2. Meanwhile, in a large saucepan cook buckwheat noodles in boiling water about 4 minutes or until slightly chewy. (Cook whole wheat noodles for 8 to 10 minutes.) Drain; place noodles in a large bowl. Add the remaining 3 tablespoons oil, the remaining 3 tablespoons vinegar, the chopped oranges, orange juice, onion, anise seeds, and garlic; toss to coat.
3. To serve, divide the noodle mixture among 4 bowls. Top each with a piece of salmon.
MAKES 4 SERVINGS.

Per serving: 548 cal., 19 g total fat (3 g sat. fat), 74 mg chol., 549 mg sodium, 59 g carbo., 5 g fiber, 38 g pro.

Cold Roasted Salmon

Cold Roasted Salmon

Prep: 30 minutes **Bake:** 15 minutes
Chill: 4 to 24 hours **Oven:** 475°F

6 5- to 6-ounce fresh or frozen center-cut salmon fillets, skinned
Olive oil
2 tablespoons peppercorn or tarragon mustard
6 slices bacon, crisp-cooked, drained, and coarsely crumbled
3 ounces goat cheese (chèvre), crumbled
Snipped fresh chives (optional)

1. Thaw fish, if frozen. Rinse fish; pat dry with paper towels. Preheat oven to 475°F. Lightly brush a 15×10×1-inch baking pan with olive oil. Arrange fish in prepared pan, tucking under any thin edges to make uniform thickness. Spread mustard on fillets.

2. Bake for 15 to 18 minutes or until fish flakes when tested with a fork. Transfer to plate; cover and chill for 4 to 24 hours.
3. To serve, arrange fish on a serving plate. Sprinkle with bacon, goat cheese, and, if desired, chives. **MAKES 6 SERVINGS.**

Per serving: 407 cal., 26 g total fat (8 g sat. fat), 118 mg chol., 387 mg sodium, 1 g carbo., 0 g fiber, 40 g pro.

Roasted Salmon Sandwiches Roast and chill fish as above. Spread 6 split French rolls with mayonnaise and mustard. Top with fish, bacon, goat cheese, and, if desired, chives. Makes 6 sandwiches.

Salmon with Wilted Greens

Remove from heat. Pour over greens mixture; toss to coat.

5. To serve, divide the greens mixture among 4 plates. Top with the fish. Serve immediately. **MAKES 4 SERVINGS.**

Per serving: 281 cal., 14 g total fat (2 g sat. fat), 70 mg chol., 383 mg sodium, 14 g carbo., 5 g fiber, 27 g pro.

Quick Tip To section an orange, cut a slice off the top and bottom of the fruit to expose the flesh. Stand the orange on one end and cut down to the bottom of the fruit, removing pieces of peel as you cut. When the fruit is peeled, take a very thin knife and cut toward the center of the fruit on either side of the membranes, slipping the sections out. Work over a bowl to catch both the fruit and juice.

Chipotle Salmon Tacos

Prep: 10 minutes **Bake:** 18 minutes
Oven: 450°F

- 1 1¼-pound fresh or frozen salmon fillet, with skin
- ¼ teaspoon salt
- 1 canned chipotle pepper in adobo sauce, seeded, chopped, and mixed with 1 tablespoon adobo sauce (see note, page 31)
- 8 taco shells
- 1 11-ounce can whole kernel corn with sweet peppers
- 1 cup hot salsa

1. Thaw fish, if frozen. Rinse fish; pat dry with paper towels. Preheat oven to 450°F. Place fish, skin side down, in a 2-quart rectangular baking dish. Sprinkle with salt. Spread chipotle pepper and sauce over fish.

2. Bake about 18 minutes or until fish flakes when tested with a fork. Place taco shells in the oven the last 3 minutes of baking.

3. Meanwhile, in a small saucepan heat corn over medium heat. Remove fish from oven; flake fish. Divide corn and fish among warm taco shells. Serve with salsa.

MAKES 4 SERVINGS (2 TACOS EACH).

Per serving: 349 cal., 10 g total fat (2 g sat. fat), 66 mg chol., 1,079 mg sodium, 31 g carbo., 5 g fiber, 32 g pro.

Salmon with Wilted Greens

Start to Finish: 21 minutes

- 1 pound fresh or frozen salmon steaks, cut ¾ inch thick
- 3 tablespoons orange juice concentrate
- 3 tablespoons water
- 2 tablespoons reduced-sodium soy sauce
- 1 tablespoon honey
- 2 teaspoons vegetable oil
- 1 teaspoon dark sesame oil
- ½ teaspoon grated fresh ginger or ¼ teaspoon ground ginger
- 6 cups torn mixed salad greens (such as spinach, Swiss chard, radicchio, mustard, and collard)
- 1 medium orange, peeled and sectioned
- 1 small red sweet pepper, cut into thin strips

1. Thaw fish, if frozen. Preheat broiler. Rinse fish; pat dry with paper towels. Cut fish into 4 pieces. Set aside.

2. For dressing, in a small bowl combine orange juice concentrate, the water, soy sauce, honey, vegetable oil, sesame oil, and ginger.

3. Place fish on the greased unheated rack of a broiler pan. Broil 4 inches from the heat for 6 to 9 minutes or until fish flakes when tested with a fork, brushing with 1 tablespoon of the dressing halfway through broiling. (Or grill fish on the greased rack of an uncovered grill directly over medium coals for 6 to 9 minutes, gently turning and brushing with 1 tablespoon of the dressing halfway through grilling.) Cover to keep warm while preparing the greens.

4. In a large bowl combine greens and orange sections. In a large skillet bring the remaining dressing to boiling. Boil gently, uncovered, for 1 minute. Add pepper strips.

Chipotle
Salmon
Tacos

Peppered
Salmon with
Quick
Ratatouille

Peppered Salmon with Quick Ratatouille

Start to Finish: 20 minutes **Oven:** 450°F

4 6-ounce fresh or frozen skinless
    salmon fillets
    Salt and freshly ground black pepper
2 tablespoons vegetable oil
1 large red sweet onion, cut into thin
    wedges
2 medium zucchini, halved lengthwise and
    cut into 1-inch pieces
1 small eggplant, peeled and cubed
1 14.5-ounce can Italian-style stewed
    tomatoes, undrained

1. Preheat oven to 450°F. Rinse fish; pat dry with paper towels. Measure thickness of fish. Sprinkle fish lightly with salt; sprinkle generously with pepper. Place fish on a baking sheet. Bake until fish flakes when tested with a fork. (Allow 4 to 6 minutes per ½-inch thickness of fish.)
2. Meanwhile, in a very large skillet heat oil over medium-high heat. Add onion to skillet; cook for 2 minutes. Add zucchini, eggplant, and undrained tomatoes. Bring to boiling; reduce heat. Simmer, covered, for 5 minutes. Serve vegetable mixture with fish.

MAKES 4 SERVINGS.

Per serving: 450 cal., 26 g total fat (5 g sat. fat), 100 mg chol., 601 mg sodium, 19 g carbo., 7 g fiber, 37 g pro.

Quick Tip When the fish counter doesn't have skinless salmon fillets, just ask the butcher to skin them for you. It's easy to destroy a perfect piece of fish trying to do it yourself.

Poached Salmon with Citrus Salad

Start to Finish: 25 minutes

4 4-ounce fresh or frozen skinless salmon,
    cod, or haddock fillets, about 1 inch thick
1 lime
6 oranges (navel, blood, Cara Cara, and/or
    tangerines)
½ cup water

Poached Salmon with Citrus Salad

¼ cup olive oil
1 teaspoon sugar
    Salt and black pepper
2 tablespoons vegetable oil
6 wonton wrappers, cut into ½-inch strips
1 7-ounce bunch watercress, trimmed, or
    4 cups arugula or baby spinach

1. Thaw fish, if frozen. Rinse fish; pat dry with paper towels. Finely shred 1 teaspoon peel from lime; set aside. Squeeze juice from the lime and 2 of the oranges; combine juices. Measure ¼ cup juice for dressing and set aside. Pour the remaining juice into a large nonstick skillet; add the water and the lime peel. Bring to boiling. Add salmon; reduce heat to medium. Simmer, covered, for 8 to 12 minutes or until fish flakes when tested with a fork.

2. Meanwhile, for dressing, in a small bowl whisk together the reserved ¼ cup juice, olive oil, and sugar; season with salt and pepper.
3. For wonton strips, in another large skillet heat vegetable oil over medium-high heat. Add wonton strips; cook about 1 to 2 minutes or until crisp, stirring often.
4. Peel and section or slice remaining oranges; arrange oranges, watercress, and salmon on dinner plates. Drizzle with dressing. Pass wonton strips.

MAKES 4 SERVINGS.

Per serving: 553 cal., 36 g total fat (6 g sat. fat), 63 mg chol., 303 mg sodium, 32 g carbo., 5 g fiber, 27 g pro.

Fresh Feta
Salmon Pasta

Fresh Feta Salmon Pasta

Start to Finish: 35 minutes

- 6 ounces whole wheat penne or rotini pasta
  Nonstick cooking spray
- 2 cloves garlic, minced
- 4 large roma tomatoes, chopped
- ½ cup sliced green onions (4)
- 12 ounces cooked salmon, broken into chunks, or two 6-ounce cans water-pack skinless, boneless salmon, drained
- ⅛ teaspoon salt
- 3 tablespoons snipped fresh basil
- ½ teaspoon black pepper
- 2 teaspoons olive oil
- ¾ cup crumbled feta cheese (3 ounces)
  Fresh basil sprigs

1. In a 4-quart Dutch oven cook pasta following package directions. Drain well. Return pasta to pan; cover to keep warm.

2. Lightly coat an unheated large nonstick skillet with cooking spray. Heat skillet over medium-high heat. Add garlic; cook and stir for 15 seconds. Add tomatoes and green onions to skillet; cook and stir just until tender. Sprinkle salmon with salt. Add salmon, snipped basil, and pepper to skillet. Heat through.

3. Add oil to drained pasta; toss to mix. Add salmon mixture and feta cheese to pasta; toss gently. Garnish with basil sprigs.

MAKES 4 SERVINGS.

Per serving: 442 cal., 20 g total fat (6 g sat. fat), 86 mg chol., 384 mg sodium, 37 g carbo., 6 g fiber, 31 g pro.

Hawaiian Tuna Toss

Start to Finish: 15 minutes

- 5 cups packaged shredded broccoli (broccoli slaw mix)
- 2 5-ounce pouches sweet and spicy marinated chunk light tuna
- ½ cup bottled honey-Dijon salad dressing
- ½ of a small fresh pineapple, cut into 4 slices
- ½ cup macadamia nuts, chopped

1. In a large bowl toss together broccoli slaw, tuna, and salad dressing.

2. Arrange a quartered pineapple slice on each of 4 plates. Spoon broccoli mixture over pineapple. Sprinkle with nuts.

MAKES 4 SERVINGS.

Per serving: 399 cal., 25 g total fat (3 g sat. fat), 31 mg chol., 480 mg sodium, 27 g carbo., 5 g fiber, 18 g pro.

Quick Tip If you don't have honey-Dijon salad dressing, any salad dressing that's on the sweet side, including balsamic vinaigrette, Asian-ginger vinaigrette, or poppy seed dressing, works on this salad.

Hawaiian
Tuna Toss

Bacon, Egg,
and Tuna
Salad

Bacon, Egg, and Tuna Salad

Start to Finish: 25 minutes

- 12 ounces fresh or frozen tuna steaks
- 4 eggs
- 6 slices bacon
- ½ cup white wine vinegar
- 2 to 3 tablespoons honey
- 1 tablespoon Dijon mustard
- 1 6-ounce package fresh baby spinach
  Black pepper (optional)

1. Thaw fish, if frozen. Place eggs in a saucepan; cover with water. Bring to boiling. Remove from heat. Cover; let stand for 10 to 15 minutes. Drain. Rinse with cold water and let cool. Peel and halve eggs.

2. In a large skillet cook bacon until crisp. Remove bacon from skillet; remove 2 tablespoons drippings for dressing. Crumble bacon; set aside. Rinse fish; pat dry. Add fish to skillet; cook over medium-high heat 3 minutes per side or until slightly pink in center. Remove fish from skillet; keep warm.

3. Wipe skillet clean. Whisk in reserved drippings, vinegar, honey, and mustard to skillet. Bring to boiling.

4. Slice tuna. Line plates with spinach. Top with tuna, bacon, and eggs. Drizzle with dressing. If desired, sprinkle with pepper. **MAKES 4 SERVINGS.**

Per serving: 481 cal., 32 g total fat (10 g sat. fat), 289 mg chol., 702 mg sodium, 11 g carbo., 1 g fiber, 34 g pro.

Curried Tuna on Biscuits

Start to Finish: 20 minutes

- 3 tablespoons butter
- 3 tablespoons all-purpose flour
- 2 to 3 teaspoons curry powder
- 2 cups milk
- 1 12-ounce can chunk white tuna, drained and broken into chunks
- 1 cup frozen peas
- ½ cup coarsely shredded carrot
- 4 warm biscuits, split

Tuna Salad with Capers

1. In a large saucepan melt butter over medium heat. Stir in flour, curry powder, and ¼ teaspoon salt. Cook and stir 30 seconds. Add milk all at once. Cook and stir until thickened and bubbly; cook and stir 1 minute more. Stir in tuna, peas, and carrot; cook and stir until heated through. Serve tuna mixture over split biscuits. **MAKES 4 SERVINGS.**

Per serving: 494 cal., 23 g total fat (10 g sat. fat), 68 mg chol., 1,208 mg sodium, 39 g carbo., 3 g fiber, 31 g pro.

Tuna Salad with Capers

Start to Finish: 25 minutes

- ½ cup mayonnaise or salad dressing
- 2 tablespoons capers, drained
- 2 tablespoons lemon juice
- 1 tablespoon snipped fresh tarragon
- 1 teaspoon Cajun seasoning
- 1 12-ounce can solid white tuna, drained and broken into chunks
- 2 tablespoons milk
- 8 cups torn romaine
- 2 cups shredded cabbage with carrot (coleslaw mix)
- 2 small tomatoes, cut into wedges

1. In a bowl combine mayonnaise, capers, lemon juice, tarragon, and Cajun seasoning. In a large bowl toss tuna with 3 tablespoons of the mayonnaise mixture. Stir milk into the remaining mayonnaise mixture.

2. Divide greens among 6 plates; top with shredded cabbage, tuna, and tomato wedges. Serve with remaining mayonnaise mixture. **MAKES 6 SERVINGS.**

Per serving: 228 cal., 17 g total fat (3 g sat. fat), 38 mg chol., 455 mg sodium, 5 g carbo., 2 g fiber, 15 g pro.

Oven-Fried
Fish

Baked Fish in White Wine

Prep: 10 minutes **Bake:** 17 minutes
Oven: 450°F

- 4 4- to 5-ounce fresh or frozen flounder or sole fillets
   Nonstick cooking spray
- 2 cups chopped, seeded tomatoes (2 large)
- 1/3 cup dry white wine
- 3 tablespoons capers packed in oil, drained and chopped
- 3 tablespoons snipped fresh mint
- 1/2 teaspoon salt
- 1/4 teaspoon black pepper
- 4 slices lemon
- 1 1/2 cups couscous
- 1 1/2 cups water
- 4 tablespoons butter

1. Thaw fish, if frozen. Rinse fish; pat dry with paper towels. Preheat oven to 450°F. Coat a shallow baking pan that is just large enough to hold the fish with cooking spray.
2. In a medium bowl gently stir together tomatoes, wine, capers, and mint. Set tomato mixture aside.
3. Sprinkle fish with 1/4 teaspoon of the salt and 1/8 teaspoon of the pepper. Place fish in the prepared pan. Spoon tomato mixture on fish. Place a lemon slice on each fillet.
4. Bake, uncovered, for 17 to 18 minutes or until fish flakes when tested with a fork.
5. Meanwhile, prepare couscous following package directions, using the water, 2 tablespoons of the butter, the remaining 1/4 teaspoon salt, and the remaining 1/8 teaspoon pepper.
6. Transfer fish to 4 plates. Divide couscous among the plates. Whisk the remaining 2 tablespoons butter into pan juices; spoon pan juices over couscous. **MAKES 4 SERVINGS.**

Per serving: 492 cal., 14 g total fat (8 g sat. fat), 98 mg chol., 599 mg sodium, 55 g carbo., 4 g fiber, 33 g pro.

Oven-Fried Fish

Prep: 15 minutes
Bake: 4 minutes per 1/2-inch thickness
Oven: 450°F

- 1 pound fresh or frozen skinless cod, orange roughy, or catfish fillets
- 1/4 cup milk
- 1/3 cup all-purpose flour
- 1/2 cup fine dry bread crumbs
- 2 tablespoons grated Parmesan cheese
- 1/4 teaspoon lemon-pepper seasoning
- 2 tablespoons butter or margarine, melted
   Lemon wedges (optional)

1. Thaw fish, if frozen. Preheat oven to 450°F. Rinse fish; pat dry with paper towels. If necessary, cut into 4 serving-size pieces. Measure the thickness of each piece. Place milk in a shallow dish. Place flour in another shallow dish. In a third shallow dish combine bread crumbs, Parmesan cheese, and lemon-pepper seasoning. Add melted butter to bread crumb mixture; stir until well mixed.
2. Grease a shallow baking pan; set aside. Dip fish in the milk; coat with flour. Dip again in the milk; dip in the crumb mixture, turning to coat all sides. Place fish in a single layer in prepared baking pan. Bake, uncovered, for 4 to 6 minutes per 1/2-inch thickness or until fish flakes when tested with a fork. If desired, serve with lemon wedges.
MAKES 4 SERVINGS.

Per serving: 254 cal., 9 g total fat (5 g sat. fat), 75 mg chol., 565 mg sodium, 15 g carbo., 1 g fiber, 26 g pro.

Baked Fish in
White Wine

Tilapia Vera Cruz

Tilapia Vera Cruz

Start to Finish: 25 minutes

4   6- to 8-ounce fresh or frozen skinless
    tilapia, red snapper, mahi mahi, or other
    fish fillets
1   tablespoon olive oil
1   small onion, cut into thin wedges
1   jalapeño, seeded and finely chopped
    (see note, page 31) (optional)
1   clove garlic, minced
1   14.5-ounce can diced tomatoes,
    undrained
1   cup sliced fresh cremini or button
    mushrooms
³⁄₄   cup pimiento-stuffed olives, coarsely
    chopped
1   tablespoon snipped fresh oregano or
    ¹⁄₂ teaspoon dried oregano, crushed
¹⁄₄   teaspoon salt
¹⁄₈   teaspoon black pepper
2   cups hot cooked rice and/or 8 crusty
    bread slices

1. Thaw fish, if frozen. Rinse fish; pat dry with
paper towels. Set fish aside.
2. For sauce, in a very large skillet heat olive
oil over medium heat. Add onion, jalapeño (if
desired), and garlic; cook and stir for 2 to
3 minutes or until onion is tender. Add
undrained tomatoes, mushrooms, olives,
oregano, salt, and black pepper. Bring to
boiling.
3. Add fish to skillet, spooning the sauce over
fish. Return to boiling; reduce heat. Simmer,
covered, for 8 to 10 minutes or until fish
flakes when tested with a fork. If desired,
serve fish and sauce with hot cooked rice.
MAKES 4 SERVINGS.

Per serving: 363 cal., 10 g total fat (2 g sat. fat), 84 mg
chol., 1,111 mg sodium, 31 g carbo., 3 g fiber, 38 g pro.

Cajun Snapper with Red Beans and Rice

Cajun Snapper with Red Beans and Rice

Start to Finish: 20 minutes

2   10-ounce fresh or frozen red snapper
    fillets with skin or other firm white fish
    fillets with skin
2   teaspoons Creole or Cajun seasoning
1   14.8-ounce pouch cooked long grain rice
1   15-ounce can red beans, rinsed and
    drained
2   lemons
2   tablespoons butter, melted
    Snipped fresh parsley (optional)

1. Thaw fish, if frozen. Rinse fish; pat dry with
paper towels. Cut fillets in half crosswise.
Sprinkle fish with 1 teaspoon of the Creole
seasoning. Heat a very large heavy nonstick
skillet over medium-high heat. Add fish, skin
sides up; cook for 4 minutes; turn. Cook for
2 to 4 minutes more or until fish flakes when
tested with fork.
2. Meanwhile, in a large microwave-safe bowl
combine rice, red beans, and the remaining
1 teaspoon Creole seasoning. Cover with
vented plastic wrap. Microwave on high for
3 to 3¹⁄₂ minutes or until hot, stirring twice.
3. Finely shred 2 teaspoons peel from
1 lemon; cut the remaining lemon into wedges.
4. Drizzle melted butter over fish; sprinkle
with lemon peel and, if desired, parsley.
Serve fish with rice and beans. Pass lemon
wedges. **MAKES 4 SERVINGS.**

Per serving: 447 cal., 11 g total fat (4 g sat. fat), 68 mg
chol., 1,055 mg sodium, 51 g carbo., 6 g fiber, 38 g pro.

Prosciutto-
Wrapped
Trout

the remaining 2 tablespoons lemon juice, the beans, the 1 tablespoon olive oil, garlic, the 2 teaspoons snipped rosemary, and salt. Serve fish with bean mixture. **MAKES 4 SERVINGS.**

Per serving: 332 cal., 15 g total fat (3 g sat. fat), 77 mg chol., 731 mg sodium, 21 g carbo., 7 g fiber, 36 g pro.

Cornmeal-Crusted Catfish Rolls

Start to Finish: 30 minutes

1 ½ pounds fresh or frozen catfish fillets
¼ cup cornmeal
2 teaspoons Cajun or blackening seasoning
¼ cup vegetable oil
2 baby sweet peppers or ¼ of a large sweet pepper, thinly sliced
½ cup thinly sliced celery (1 stalk)
¼ of a small red or sweet onion, thinly sliced (optional)
⅓ cup mayonnaise
1 tablespoon ketchup
¼ to ½ teaspoon bottled hot pepper sauce (optional)
8 cocktail-size rolls, split and toasted

1. Thaw fish, if frozen. Rinse fish; pat dry. Cut into 8 pieces. In a shallow dish combine cornmeal and 1½ teaspoons of the Cajun seasoning; coat fish with cornmeal mixture.
2. In a large skillet heat oil over medium-high heat. Cook fish in hot oil for 8 to 10 minutes or until coating is golden and fish flakes when tested with fork.
3. Meanwhile, in a medium bowl combine peppers, celery, and, if desired, onion. In a small bowl combine mayonnaise, ketchup, the remaining ½ teaspoon Cajun seasoning, and, if desired, hot pepper sauce. Add 1 tablespoon of the mayonnaise mixture to pepper-celery mixture. Spread some of remaining mayonnaise mixture on cut sides of rolls. Place catfish pieces on roll bottoms. Top with celery mixture and roll tops. Pass any remaining mayonnaise mixture.
MAKES 4 SERVINGS.

Per serving: 636 cal., 38 g total fat (7 g sat. fat), 88 mg chol., 638 mg sodium, 38 g carbo., 2 g fiber, 34 g pro.

Prosciutto-Wrapped Trout

Prep: 20 minutes **Cook:** 10 minutes

4 fresh or frozen skinless trout, flounder, or catfish fillets, about ¼ inch thick, or 2 fresh or frozen orange roughy or cod fillets, ½ inch thick
4 2-inch sprigs fresh rosemary or 2 teaspoons dried rosemary, crushed
4 slices thinly sliced prosciutto or thinly sliced cooked ham
3 tablespoons lemon juice
Freshly ground black pepper
2 medium roma tomatoes
Olive oil
1 19-ounce can cannellini (white kidney) beans, rinsed and drained
1 tablespoon olive oil
1 clove garlic, minced
2 teaspoons snipped fresh rosemary or ½ teaspoon dried rosemary, crushed
¼ teaspoon smoked sea salt, crushed, or ⅛ teaspoon salt

1. Thaw fish, if frozen. Rinse fish; pat dry with paper towels. Cut each fillet in half crosswise. If using trout, flounder, or catfish,

place rosemary sprigs on half the pieces (or sprinkle with dried rosemary) and top with remaining pieces to make 4 stacks. (If using roughy or cod, place a rosemary sprig on each fillet half or sprinkle with the 2 teaspoons dried rosemary.) Wrap 1 slice of prosciutto around fish and rosemary. Sprinkle with 1 tablespoon of the lemon juice and the pepper; set aside.
2. Heat a nonstick or well-seasoned grill pan on stovetop over medium heat until hot. Meanwhile, cut tomatoes in half lengthwise. Brush tomatoes lightly with olive oil. Add tomato halves to grill pan, cut sides down. Cook for 6 to 8 minutes or until very tender, turning once. Remove tomatoes from grill; set aside to cool slightly.
3. Place the fish fillets on grill pan, rosemary sprig sides up. Cook for 4 to 6 minutes or until fish flakes when tested with a fork, turning once halfway through cooking.
4. Coarsely chop grilled tomatoes. In a medium bowl gently toss together tomatoes,

Cornmeal-Crusted Catfish Rolls

Shrimp with
Vermicelli

Shrimp with Vermicelli ♡

Start to Finish: 30 minutes

12 ounces fresh or frozen medium shrimp, peeled and deveined
 4 ounces dried multigrain angel hair pasta
 2 tablespoons butter
 1 large onion, halved and thinly sliced
¼ to ½ teaspoon crushed red pepper
 1 8-ounce can tomato sauce with basil, garlic, and oregano
 1 medium yellow summer squash or zucchini, halved lengthwise and thinly sliced
⅛ teaspoon salt
 4 cups baby spinach
 1 cup cherry tomatoes, halved
 2 tablespoons finely shredded Parmesan cheese

1. Thaw shrimp, if frozen. Cook pasta following package directions; drain.

2. Meanwhile, in a very large skillet melt butter over medium heat. Add onion; cook until tender. Add shrimp and crushed red pepper; cook and stir for 1 minute. Add tomato sauce, squash, and salt. Bring to boiling; reduce heat. Simmer, covered, for 5 minutes.

3. Stir drained pasta, spinach, and cherry tomatoes into skillet. Toss gently on medium heat until heated through. Sprinkle with Parmesan cheese. **MAKES 4 SERVINGS.**

Per serving: 279 cal., 8 g total fat (4 g sat. fat), 114 mg chol., 588 mg sodium, 31 g carbo., 5 g fiber, 21 g pro.

Lemon Shrimp Salad

Lemon Shrimp Salad

Start to Finish: 20 minutes

 1 pound cooked shrimp in shells
¼ cup low-fat mayonnaise or salad dressing
 2 tablespoons lemon juice
 1 tablespoon water
¼ to ½ teaspoon Cajun seasoning
½ of a small red onion, thinly sliced
 1 5-ounce package mixed baby salad greens (6 cups)

1. Peel and devein shrimp, leaving tails intact if desired. For dressing, in a small bowl stir together mayonnaise, lemon juice, the water, and Cajun seasoning.

2. In a large bowl combine shrimp and red onion. Add dressing; toss gently to coat. To serve, divide salad greens among 4 serving plates; top with shrimp mixture.

MAKES 4 SERVINGS.

Per serving: 148 cal., 6 g total fat (1 g sat. fat), 171 mg chol., 310 mg sodium, 5 g carbo., 0 g fiber, 19 g pro.

Quick Tip Shrimp are classified as small, medium, extra-large, or jumbo depending on how many of them it takes to equal a pound. For instance, if you see a number on the package that reads "12/15," that means there are between 12 and 15 shrimp per pound. (Those are considered jumbo shrimp.) Generally there are 36 to 45 small shrimp per pound; 30 to 35 medium shrimp per pound; 24 to 30 large shrimp per pound; and 14 to 20 extra-large shrimp per pound.

Linguine with Garlic Shrimp ♡
Start to Finish: 25 minutes

- 8 ounces fresh or frozen shrimp, thawed, peeled, and deveined
- 8 ounces refrigerated linguine or fettuccine pasta
- ½ cup chicken broth
- 1 tablespoon snipped fresh basil or ½ teaspoon dried basil, crushed
- 2 teaspoons cornstarch
- 1 tablespoon olive oil
- 2 cups sliced fresh mushrooms
- 1 medium yellow or green sweet pepper, chopped (1 cup)
- 2 tablespoons bottled minced garlic
- 1 14.5-ounce can Italian-style stewed tomatoes, undrained
- ¼ cup finely shredded Parmesan cheese (1 ounce)
  Fresh basil leaves (optional)

1. Thaw shrimp, if frozen. Cook pasta following package directions; drain and return to pan to keep warm.
2. In a small bowl combine broth, snipped basil, and cornstarch; set aside.
3. Meanwhile, rinse shrimp; pat dry with paper towels. In a large skillet heat oil over medium heat. Add mushrooms, sweet pepper, and garlic; cook about 3 minutes or just until pepper is tender. Add broth mixture and undrained tomatoes; cook and stir until boiling. Add the shrimp; cook, covered, about 2 minutes or until shrimp turn opaque.
4. To serve, spoon shrimp mixture over pasta. Top with Parmesan cheese. If desired, garnish with fresh basil leaves.
MAKES 4 SERVINGS.

Per serving: 420 cal., 9 g total fat (2 g sat. fat), 92 mg chol., 482 mg sodium, 59 g carbo., 3 g fiber, 25 g pro.

Quick Tip When purchasing shrimp, look for firm meat, translucent and moist shells without black spots, and a fresh scent (ammonia indicates spoilage). To store, refrigerate shrimp for up to 2 days. Keep frozen shrimp in the freezer for up to 6 months.

Quick Coconut Shrimp
Prep: 10 minutes **Bake:** 8 minutes
Oven: 450°F

- 1 pound fresh or frozen peeled and deveined large shrimp
  Nonstick cooking spray
  Salt and black pepper
- ⅓ cup bottled sweet-and-sour sauce
- 1½ cups shredded coconut
- 2 medium yellow summer squash

1. Thaw shrimp, if frozen. Rinse shrimp and pat dry with paper towels. Preheat oven to 450°F. Lightly coat a baking sheet and a 15×10×1-inch baking pan with cooking spray; set aside. Sprinkle shrimp lightly with salt and pepper. Place sweet-and-sour sauce in a medium bowl; place coconut in a small bowl. Add shrimp to bowl with sauce and stir to coat. Add shrimp, a few at a time, to dish with coconut; turn shrimp to coat. Arrange shrimp in a single layer on the prepared baking sheet.
2. Trim ends from squash; cut squash into ½-inch slices. Arrange squash in a single layer in the prepared pan. Sprinkle squash with salt and pepper; lightly coat with cooking spray.
3. Bake for 8 to 10 minutes or until shrimp are opaque and squash is tender. Serve shrimp with squash slices. **MAKES 4 SERVINGS.**

Per serving: 380 cal., 17 g total fat (14 g sat. fat), 172 mg chol., 659 mg sodium, 31 g carbo., 4 g fiber, 27 g pro.

Shrimp Celeste
Start to Finish: 25 minutes

- 1 pound fresh or frozen prawns or jumbo shrimp in shells (6 to 8)
- 3 tablespoons butter
- ½ cup sliced fresh mushrooms
- ½ cup chopped tomato (1 medium)
- ¼ cup sliced green onions (2)
- 1 tablespoon minced garlic (9 cloves)
- 1 teaspoon curry powder
- ¼ teaspoon salt
- ¼ teaspoon black pepper
- ½ cup half-and-half or light cream
- 1 tablespoon all-purpose flour
- ¼ cup brandy
- 1½ cups hot cooked rice or couscous
  Snipped fresh parsley (optional)

1. Thaw prawns, if frozen. Peel and devein prawns. Rinse prawns; pat dry with paper towels. In a large skillet melt butter over medium heat. Add prawns; cook for 5 minutes, turning once. Add mushrooms, tomato, green onions, garlic, curry powder, salt, and pepper. Cook and stir for 2 to 3 minutes more or until prawns turn opaque.
2. Meanwhile, in a small bowl whisk together half-and-half and flour until smooth. Add flour mixture and brandy to shrimp mixture in skillet. Cook and stir until thickened and bubbly; cook and stir for 1 minute more. Serve in shallow bowls with rice. If desired, sprinkle with parsley. **MAKES 2 SERVINGS.**

Per serving: 767 cal., 29 g total fat (16 g sat. fat), 413 mg chol., 781 mg sodium, 53 g carbo., 2 g fiber, 54 g pro.

Quick Tip To peel and devein shrimp, first remove the legs from the underside of the shrimp, then slip the tip of your fingers under the shell and gently peel it off. Use the tip of a paring knife to make a shallow cut down the back of the shrimp, from the top to the bottom. Use the tip of the knife to scrape and pull out the vein—discard it—then thoroughly rinse the shrimp under cold running water.

Linguine with Garlic Shrimp

Spinach-Pasta
Salad with
Shrimp

Spinach-Pasta Salad with Shrimp ♡
Start to Finish: 20 minutes

- 4 ounces shell pasta or elbow macaroni
- 1 pound frozen cooked shrimp, thawed, or 1 pound cooked deli shrimp
- 1 cup chopped red sweet pepper (1 large)
- 1/3 cup bottled creamy onion or Caesar salad dressing
- 2 tablespoons snipped fresh dill (optional) Salt and black pepper
- 1 6-ounce package baby spinach
- 4 ounces goat cheese, sliced, or feta cheese, crumbled Bottled creamy onion or Caesar dressing (optional)

1. Cook pasta following package directions. Drain and rinse with cold water.
2. In a very large bowl combine cooked pasta, shrimp, and sweet pepper. Drizzle with 1/3 cup salad dressing. If desired, sprinkle with dill. Toss to mix. Season with salt and pepper. Divide spinach between salad plates or bowls. Top with shrimp mixture and cheese. If desired, drizzle with additional dressing. **MAKES 6 SERVINGS.**

Per serving: 247 cal., 10 g total fat (4 g sat. fat), 156 mg chol., 435 mg sodium, 17 g carbo., 2 g fiber, 23 g pro.

Pesto Pasta with Shrimp
Start to Finish: 20 minutes

- 12 ounces fresh or frozen, peeled and deveined medium shrimp (leave tails intact, if desired)
- 1 9-ounce package refrigerated linguine pasta
- 1 7-ounce container refrigerated basil pesto
- 2 teaspoons finely shredded lemon peel
- 2 tablespoons snipped fresh chives
- 1 teaspoon finely shredded lemon peel (optional)

1. Thaw shrimp, if frozen. Rinse shrimp; pat dry with paper towels. In a large saucepan cook linguine in a large amount of boiling water for 1 minute. Add shrimp; cook about 2 minutes more or until shrimp turn opaque. Drain well.
2. Meanwhile, in a small bowl stir together pesto and the 2 teaspoons lemon peel.
3. To serve, divide pasta mixture among 4 shallow bowls or dinner plates. Spoon pesto mixture over pasta mixture. Sprinkle with chives and, if desired, the 1 teaspoon lemon peel. **MAKES 4 SERVINGS.**

Per serving: 497 cal., 23 g total fat (6 g sat. fat), 186 mg chol., 562 mg sodium, 42 g carbo., 3 g fiber, 30 g pro.

Spanish-Style Rice with Seafood ♡
Start to Finish: 25 minutes

- 1 5.6- to 6.2-ounce package Spanish-style rice mix
- 1¾ cups water
- 1 tablespoon butter Several dashes bottled hot pepper sauce
- 1 12-ounce package frozen peeled, deveined shrimp
- 1 cup frozen peas
- ½ cup chopped tomato (1 medium)

1. In a large skillet stir together rice mix, the water, butter, and hot pepper sauce. Bring to boiling; reduce heat. Simmer, covered, for 5 minutes.
2. Stir shrimp into rice mixture. Return to boiling; reduce heat. Simmer, covered, for 2 to 3 minutes more or until shrimp turn opaque. Remove from heat. Stir in peas. Cover and let stand for 10 minutes. Sprinkle with chopped tomato before serving. **MAKES 4 SERVINGS.**

Per serving: 197 cal., 6 g total fat (2 g sat. fat), 137 mg chol., 414 mg sodium, 15 g carbo., 2 g fiber, 21 g pro.

With their delicate flavor and tender texture, shrimp infuse a dish with a sense of specialness—even for a quick weeknight supper.

Seafood Curry

Start to Finish: 20 minutes

1 tablespoon vegetable oil
1 medium sweet onion (such as Vidalia), cut into thin wedges
2 teaspoons curry powder
2 8.8-ounce pouches cooked garden vegetable-flavor rice
½ cup orange juice
1 8-ounce package flake-style imitation crabmeat
½ of a purchased peeled and cored pineapple, cut into bite-size pieces

1. In a large skillet heat oil over medium heat. Add onion; cook until tender. Add curry powder; cook and stir for 1 minute. Stir in rice and orange juice; heat through. Add imitation crabmeat and pineapple. Cook, covered, about 4 minutes or until heated through. **MAKES 4 SERVINGS.**

Per serving: 331 cal., 7 g total fat (1 g sat. fat), 11 mg chol., 1,141 mg sodium, 60 g carbo., 2 g fiber, 9 g pro.

Crab Louis

Start to Finish: 20 minutes

½ cup mayonnaise
¼ cup chili sauce
1 tablespoon finely chopped green sweet pepper
1 tablespoon finely snipped fresh parsley
1 tablespoon prepared horseradish
1 tablespoon finely chopped green onion
⅛ teaspoon cayenne pepper
⅛ teaspoon Worcestershire sauce
¼ teaspoon salt
6 cups torn lettuce
3 ripe avocados, halved, seeded, peeled, and sliced
1 tablespoon lemon juice
1 pound fresh cooked crabmeat, picked over, rinsed, and patted dry, or canned lump crabmeat
Lemon slices (optional)
Cherry tomatoes (optional)

1. For dressing, in a medium bowl whisk together mayonnaise, chili sauce, sweet pepper, parsley, horseradish, green onion, cayenne pepper, Worcestershire sauce, and salt.
2. Arrange lettuce on 6 serving plates. Brush avocado slices with lemon juice; divide among plates. Arrange crabmeat on plates; spoon about 2 tablespoons of dressing over each serving. If desired, garnish with lemon slices and cherry tomatoes. **MAKES 6 SERVINGS.**

Per serving: 290 cal., 18 g total fat (3 g sat. fat), 81 mg chol., 604 mg sodium, 16 g carbo., 6 g fiber, 18 g pro.

Peanut-Sauced Shrimp and Pasta ♡

Start to Finish: 20 minutes

12 ounces fresh or frozen peeled, deveined medium shrimp with tails
½ of a 14-ounce package dried medium rice noodles
4 cups boiling water
1 tablespoon vegetable oil
12 ounces fresh asparagus spears, trimmed and cut into 2-inch pieces (3 cups)
1 cup ¾-inch pieces red and/or yellow sweet pepper
½ cup bottled peanut sauce

1. Thaw shrimp, if frozen. Rinse shrimp; pat dry with paper towels. Place noodles in a large bowl. Pour boiling water over noodles; let stand for 10 minutes.
2. Meanwhile, in a large skillet heat oil over medium-high heat. Add shrimp, asparagus, and sweet pepper. Cook and stir for 3 to 5 minutes or until shrimp are opaque. Add peanut sauce; stir to coat shrimp and vegetables. Cook until heated through.
3. Drain noodles; divide among 4 shallow bowls. Using a fork, twist noodles into nests. Top with shrimp mixture. **MAKES 4 SERVINGS.**

Per serving: 396 cal., 9 g total fat (2 g sat. fat), 129 mg chol., 642 mg sodium, 55 g carbo., 5 g fiber, 21 g pro.

Perfect for a warm summer evening, cool and crisp Crab Louis features lump crab on lettuce with a creamy chili-and-scallion-infused dressing.

Peanut-Sauced Shrimp and Pasta

Honey- and
Rum-Glazed
Shrimp

Honey- and Rum-Glazed Shrimp

Start to Finish: 30 minutes

¼ cup honey
3 tablespoons lime juice
3 tablespoons dark rum
1 tablespoon orange juice
1½ teaspoons cornstarch
1 teaspoon grated fresh ginger
1 tablespoon snipped fresh cilantro
½ teaspoon finely shredded lime peel
½ teaspoon finely shredded orange peel
20 fresh extra-jumbo shrimp in shells (about 1¼ pounds), peeled and deveined
¼ teaspoon salt
¼ teaspoon black pepper

1. For glaze, in a small saucepan combine honey, lime juice, rum, orange juice, cornstarch, and ginger. Cook and stir medium heat until thickened and bubbly. Cook and stir for 2 minutes more. Cool to room temperature. Stir in cilantro, lime peel, and orange peel.
2. Rinse shrimp; pat dry with paper towels. On four 10- to 12-inch skewers thread shrimp, leaving ¼ inch between pieces. Season shrimp with salt and pepper. Remove and reserve half of the glaze. Brush shrimp with half of the glaze.
3. For a charcoal grill, grill kabobs on the rack of an uncovered grill directly over medium coals for 2 to 3 minutes or until shrimp are opaque, turning once halfway through grilling. (For a gas grill, preheat grill. Reduce heat to medium. Place kabobs on grill rack over heat. Cover and grill as above.)
4. Brush shrimp with the reserved glaze.
MAKES 4 SERVINGS.

Per serving: 248 cal., 2 g total fat (0 g sat. fat), 215 mg chol., 357 mg sodium, 21 g carbo., 0 g fiber, 29 g pro.

Spicy Jalapeño Shrimp Pasta

Spicy Jalapeño Shrimp Pasta ♡

Start to Finish: 30 minutes

12 ounces fresh or frozen large shrimp in shells
8 ounces dried linguine pasta
2 tablespoons extra virgin olive oil
1 or 2 fresh jalapeños, finely chopped (see note, page 31)
1 teaspoon bottled minced garlic (2 cloves)
½ teaspoon salt
⅛ teaspoon black pepper
2 cups chopped tomato and/or cherry tomatoes, halved or quartered
Finely shredded Parmesan cheese (optional)

1. Thaw shrimp, if frozen. Peel and devein shrimp. Rinse shrimp; pat dry with paper towels. Cook linguine according to package directions; drain well. Return to pan. Cover and keep warm.
2. In a large skillet heat oil over medium-high heat. Add jalapeño, garlic, salt, and black pepper; cook and stir for 1 minute. Add shrimp; cook about 3 minutes more or until shrimp are opaque. Stir in tomato; heat through.
3. Toss cooked linguine with shrimp mixture. If desired, sprinkle with Parmesan cheese.
MAKES 4 SERVINGS.

Per serving: 363 cal., 9 g total fat (1 g sat. fat), 97 mg chol., 396 mg sodium, 48 g carbo., 3 g fiber, 21 g pro.

Chipotle-
Topped Crab
Cakes

Chipotle-Topped Crab Cakes

Start to Finish: 30 minutes

    1 egg, lightly beaten
  ¾ cup soft bread crumbs (1 slice)
    2 tablespoons sliced green onion (1)
    2 tablespoons mayonnaise or salad dressing
    1 tablespoon milk
  ½ teaspoon lemon-pepper seasoning
    2 6.5-ounce cans crabmeat, drained, flaked,
        and cartilage removed
        Nonstick cooking spray
    4 cups torn mixed salad greens
    1 recipe Chipotle Sauce
        Lime wedges (optional)

1. In a large bowl stir together egg, bread crumbs, green onion, mayonnaise, milk, and lemon-pepper seasoning. Add crabmeat; mix well. Shape into eight 2½-inch patties.
2. Lightly coat an unheated large nonstick skillet with cooking spray. Preheat over medium heat. Add patties. Cook for 6 to 8 minutes or until browned, turning once. Serve crab cakes on greens with Chipotle Sauce. If desired, garnish with lime wedges.
MAKES 4 SERVINGS.

Chipotle Sauce In a small bowl combine ⅓ cup mayonnaise or salad dressing; ¼ cup sour cream; 2 tablespoons milk; 2 teaspoons snipped fresh cilantro; 1 canned chipotle chile pepper in adobo sauce, drained and finely chopped (see note, page 31); and a dash of salt.

Per serving: 359 cal., 26 g total fat (6 g sat. fat), 150 mg chol., 712 mg sodium, 8 g carbo., 1 g fiber, 23 g pro.

Citrus Scallops

Start to Finish: 15 minutes

    1 pound fresh or frozen sea scallops
    1 medium orange
    1 tablespoon olive oil
    2 cloves garlic, minced, or 1 teaspoon
        bottled minced garlic
  ½ teaspoon snipped fresh thyme
        Salt and black pepper

1. Thaw scallops, if frozen. Rinse scallops; pat dry with paper towels. Set scallops aside. Finely shred 1 teaspoon peel from the orange. Cut orange in half; squeeze to get ⅓ cup juice.
2. In a large skillet heat oil over medium-high heat. Add scallops. Cook, stirring frequently, for 2 to 3 minutes or until scallops turn opaque. Remove scallops; keep warm.
3. For the sauce, add garlic to the skillet; cook and stir for 30 seconds (add more oil to skillet if necessary). Add orange peel, orange juice, and thyme to skillet. Bring to boiling; reduce heat. Simmer, uncovered, for 1 to 2 minutes or until desired consistency. Season with salt and pepper. Pour sauce over scallops. **MAKES 4 SERVINGS.**

Per serving: 142 cal., 4 g total fat (1 g sat. fat), 37 mg chol., 218 mg sodium, 5 g carbo., 0 g fiber, 19 g pro.

Grilled Scallop Kabobs

Prep: 15 minutes **Grill:** 5 minutes

  12 ounces fresh or frozen sea scallops
  16 cherry tomatoes
    1 medium yellow summer squash, halved
        lengthwise and sliced ½ inch thick
    3 tablespoons bottled sesame-ginger
        stir-fry sauce

1. Thaw scallops, if frozen. Rinse scallops; pat dry with paper towels. On eight 8-inch skewers alternately thread scallops, cherry tomatoes, and squash, leaving ¼ inch between pieces.
2. For a charcoal grill, grill kabobs on the greased rack of an uncovered grill directly over medium coals for 5 to 8 minutes or until scallops are opaque, turning once and brushing frequently with stir-fry sauce during the last half of grilling. (For a gas grill, preheat grill. Reduce heat to medium. Place kabobs on greased grill rack over heat. Cover and grill as above.) **MAKES 4 SERVINGS.**

Per serving: 108 cal., 1 g total fat (0 g sat. fat), 28 mg chol., 421 mg sodium, 9 g carbo., 1 g fiber, 16 g pro.

Quick Tip If using wooden skewers, soak them in water for at least 30 minutes before grilling.

Grilled Scallop Kabobs

CHAPTER 6

Sides

Grapefruit-
Avocado
Salad

Grapefruit-Avocado Salad ♡

Start to Finish: 15 minutes

    4   cups packaged fresh baby spinach
    1   grapefruit, peeled and sectioned
    1   small avocado, halved, seeded, peeled,
          and sliced
    1   cup canned sliced beets
    1   tablespoon sliced almonds, toasted
    1   recipe Orange Vinaigrette

1. Divide spinach among 4 salad plates.
Arrange grapefruit, avocado, and beets on
spinach. Top with almonds. Drizzle with
Orange Vinaigrette. **MAKES 6 SERVINGS.**

Orange Vinaigrette In a screw-top jar
combine 1 teaspoon finely shredded orange
peel, ⅓ cup orange juice, 2 teaspoons red
wine vinegar, 2 teaspoons salad oil,
⅛ teaspoon salt, and a dash of black pepper.
Cover and shake well.

Per serving: 106 cal., 7 g total fat (1 g sat. fat), 0 mg
chol., 122 mg sodium, 11 g carbo., 4 g fiber, 2 g pro.

Fennel, Carrot, and Spinach Toss

Prep: 20 minutes   **Cook:** 15 minutes

    1½ cups packaged peeled baby carrots
    1   medium fennel bulb, trimmed and cut into
          thin wedges (about 1 pound)
    3   tablespoons olive oil
    ½   teaspoon salt
    ¼   teaspoon cracked black pepper
    1   10-ounce package fresh spinach
    ¼   cup finely shredded Parmesan cheese
          (1 ounce)

1. In a large bowl combine carrots and
fennel. Add 1 tablespoon of the oil, the salt,
and pepper; toss to coat.
2. In a large skillet heat the remaining
2 tablespoons oil over medium heat. Add
vegetable mixture; cook for 15 to 20 minutes
or until vegetables are tender, stirring
occasionally. Remove pan from heat.
Gradually add spinach to skillet, tossing until
spinach wilts.
3. Transfer vegetable mixture to a serving
plate. Sprinkle with Parmesan cheese.
MAKES 4 TO 6 SERVINGS.

Per serving: 134 cal., 11 g total fat (1 g sat. fat), 0 mg
chol., 408 mg sodium, 9 g carbo., 3 g fiber, 3 g pro.

Fennel, Carrot, and Spinach Toss

Grilled Onion Salad with Grape Tomatoes and Cabrales Cheese

Grilled Onion Salad with Grape Tomatoes and Cabrales Cheese

Prep: 20 minutes **Grill:** 10 minutes

  4 tablespoons olive oil
  1 tablespoon sherry vinegar
  ¼ teaspoon salt
  ¼ teaspoon ground cumin
  ⅛ teaspoon paprika
  ⅛ teaspoon freshly ground black pepper
  2 large red onions, sliced ¼ inch thick, or
    6 red boiling onions, quartered lengthwise
  6 cups torn watercress, arugula, or spinach
1½ cups grape or cherry tomatoes, halved
    (if desired)
  ½ cup crumbled Cabrales or other blue
    cheese (2 ounces)

1. For dressing, in a screw-top jar combine the 3 tablespoons of the olive oil, the vinegar, salt, cumin, paprika, and pepper. Cover and shake well.

2. Brush red onion pieces with the remaining 1 tablespoon oil. For a charcoal grill, place onions on the rack of an uncovered grill directly over medium coals. Grill about 10 minutes or until onions are softened and slightly charred, turning once halfway through grilling. (For a gas grill, preheat grill. Reduce heat to medium. Add onions to grill rack over heat. Cover and grill as above.) Separate onion slices into rings.

3. In a large bowl combine grilled onions, watercress, and tomatoes. Pour dressing over watercress mixture; toss gently to coat. Arrange on a large serving platter. Sprinkle with cheese. **MAKES 8 SERVINGS.**

Per serving: 115 cal., 9 g total fat (3 g sat. fat), 6 mg chol., 204 mg sodium, 6 g carbo., 1 g fiber, 4 g pro.

Spinach Salad with Strawberries

Start to Finish: 20 minutes

4 cups torn fresh spinach
1 cup watercress leaves
1 cup sliced fresh strawberries
½ of a small red onion, thinly sliced
½ cup bottled oil and vinegar salad dressing

Broccoli Slaw

1. In a large salad bowl combine spinach, watercress, strawberries, and onion. Drizzle dressing over salad; toss to coat.
MAKES 4 SERVINGS.

Per serving: 168 cal., 16 g total fat (2 g sat. fat), 0 mg chol., 468 mg sodium, 8 g carbo., 2 g fiber, 2 g pro.

Broccoli Slaw ♡

Start to Finish: 10 minutes

⅓ cup mayonnaise or salad dressing
2 tablespoons cider vinegar
1 teaspoon sugar
1 teaspoon caraway seeds
½ teaspoon salt
½ of a 16-ounce package (4 cups) broccoli
  slaw mix
½ of a 16-ounce package (4 cups) shredded
  cabbage with carrot (coleslaw mix)
2 tablespoons thinly sliced green onion (1)

1. In a very large bowl stir together mayonnaise, vinegar, sugar, caraway seeds, and salt. Add broccoli slaw mix, coleslaw mix, and green onion; toss to coat. Serve immediately or cover and chill for up to 12 hours. **MAKES 6 TO 8 SERVINGS.**

Per serving: 115 cal., 10 g total fat (1 g sat. fat), 9 mg chol., 291 mg sodium, 6 g carbo., 2 g fiber, 1 g pro.

Quick Tip The dressing in this recipe features the traditional balance of vinegar to sugar. If you like your slaw a little sweeter, increase the sugar by ½ teaspoon or so.

Creamy Lemon-Pepper Coleslaw

Prep: 10 minutes **Chill:** 2 hours

½ cup mayonnaise or salad dressing
1 teaspoon lemon-pepper seasoning
½ teaspoon dried thyme, crushed
5 cups packaged shredded cabbage with
  carrot (coleslaw mix)
¼ cup shelled sunflower seeds

1. In a large salad bowl combine mayonnaise, lemon-pepper seasoning, and thyme. Stir in shredded cabbage and sunflower seeds. Toss lightly to coat. Cover and chill for 2 to 24 hours. **MAKES 6 SERVINGS.**

Per serving: 188 cal., 18 g total fat (2 g sat. fat), 7 mg chol., 328 mg sodium, 5 g carbo., 2 g fiber, 2 g pro.

Confetti
Summer
Salad

Confetti Summer Salad ♡
Prep: 30 minutes **Chill:** 4 to 24 hours

4 medium ears fresh corn or 2 cups frozen
    whole kernel corn, thawed
4 baby zucchini, thinly sliced, or ½ of a small
    zucchini, halved lengthwise and thinly
    sliced (½ cup)
1 cup chopped, seeded tomatoes
    (2 medium)
¼ cup sliced green onions (2)
1 medium yellow bell pepper, seeded and
    chopped
¾ cup chopped red sweet pepper
    (1 medium)
½ cup bottled clear Italian salad dressing
¼ teaspoon cayenne pepper (optional)
   Fresh thyme (optional)

1. If using fresh corn, in a large covered
saucepan cook ears of corn in a small

amount of boiling water for 4 minutes. Drain;
rinse with cold water to cool. When cool
enough to handle, cut corn from cobs (you
should have about 2 cups of corn kernels).
2. In a large bowl combine corn, zucchini,
tomatoes, green onions, bell pepper, sweet
pepper, salad dressing, and, if desired,
cayenne pepper. Cover and chill for 4 to
24 hours, stirring occasionally. If desired,
garnish with fresh thyme. **MAKES 8 SERVINGS.**

Per serving: 99 cal., 5 g total fat (1 g sat. fat), 0 mg
chol., 253 mg sodium, 14 g carbo., 2 g fiber, 2 g pro.

Quick Tip To remove kernels from the cob,
begin by cutting a small portion off the tip to
make it flat. Holding the stem end, hold the
cob upright on its flat end. Set it on a plate or
cutting board and use a firm-bladed knife to
cut downward, about 3 to 4 rows at a time.

Layered Southwest Bean Salad ♡
Prep: 30 minutes **Chill:** 2 to 24 hours

4   cups shredded iceberg lettuce
2   15-ounce cans black beans, rinsed and
    drained
1   cup chopped red onion (1 large)
1   4-ounce can diced green chile peppers,
    drained
2   cups chopped red and/or green sweet
    peppers (2 large)
2   tablespoons snipped fresh cilantro
1½ cups sour cream
2   tablespoons lime juice
1   teaspoon chili powder
½   teaspoon salt
¼   teaspoon garlic powder
¾   cup chopped, seeded tomato (1 large)

1. Place the lettuce in a deep 3-quart serving
bowl. Layer drained beans, red onion,
drained chile peppers, sweet peppers, and
cilantro on top of lettuce.
2. For the dressing, in a small bowl stir
together sour cream, lime juice, chili powder,
salt, and garlic powder.
3. Cover salad and dressing; chill separately
for 2 to 24 hours.
4. Drizzle dressing over salad; gently toss
salad to coat vegetables with dressing.
Sprinkle with chopped tomato.
MAKES 8 TO 12 SERVINGS.

Per serving: 173 cal., 8 g total fat (5 g sat. fat), 16 mg
chol., 492 mg sodium, 22 g carbo., 7 g fiber, 9 g pro.

Layered
Southwest
Bean Salad

Tabbouleh with Edamame and Feta

Tabbouleh with Edamame and Feta

Start to Finish: 25 minutes

2½ cups water
1¼ cups bulgur
¼ cup lemon juice
3 tablespoons purchased basil pesto
2 cups fresh or thawed frozen shelled sweet soybeans (edamame)
2 cups cherry tomatoes, cut up
⅓ cup crumbled feta cheese
⅓ cup thinly sliced green onions
2 tablespoons snipped fresh parsley
¼ teaspoon black pepper
Fresh parsley sprigs (optional)

1. In a medium saucepan bring the water to boiling; add uncooked bulgur. Return to boiling; reduce heat. Simmer, covered, about 15 minutes or until most of the liquid is absorbed. Remove from heat. Transfer to a large bowl.
2. In a small bowl whisk together lemon juice and pesto. Add pesto mixture to bulgur; toss to coat. Add soybeans, cherry tomatoes, feta cheese, green onions, the snipped parsley, and pepper. Toss gently to combine. If desired, garnish with parsley sprigs.
MAKES 6 SERVINGS.

Per serving: 320 cal., 13 g total fat (2 g sat. fat), 8 mg chol., 175 mg sodium, 37 g carbo., 10 g fiber, 18 g pro.

Make-Ahead Directions Prepare as directed. Cover and chill for up to 4 hours.

Quick Tip When purchasing green onions (also called scallions), look for crisp, bright green tops and a firm, white base. Generally, green onions that are no larger than ½ inch in diameter taste the best. Store green onions, unwashed, in a plastic bag in the refrigerator for up to 5 days.

Quick Bread Salad

Quick Bread Salad

Start to Finish: 20 minutes

¼ cup olive oil
3 tablespoons red wine vinegar
3 tablespoons snipped fresh oregano
½ teaspoon sugar
¼ teaspoon salt
¼ teaspoon black pepper
4 ounces whole wheat sourdough or other country-style bread, cut into 1½-inch cubes
½ of a 10-ounce package Italian-style torn mixed salad greens (about 5 cups)
1 medium tomato, cut into thin wedges
¼ cup halved yellow cherry tomatoes or yellow sweet pepper cut into ½-inch pieces
½ cup Greek black olives or other olives

1. For the dressing, in a screw-top jar combine olive oil, wine vinegar, oregano, sugar, salt, and black pepper. Cover and shake well.
2. In a large salad bowl combine bread cubes, mixed greens, tomato wedges, cherry tomatoes, and olives. Add dressing; toss gently to coat. Serve immediately.
MAKES 6 SERVINGS.

Per serving: 151 cal., 11 g total fat (1 g sat. fat), 0 mg chol., 238 mg sodium, 13 g carbo., 1 g fiber, 2 g pro.

Barbecued Limas ♡

Start to Finish: 25 minutes

1	16-ounce package frozen baby lima beans
4	slices bacon, cut into ½-inch pieces
½	cup chopped onion (1 medium)
2	cloves garlic, minced
1	10.75-ounce can condensed tomato soup
2	tablespoons packed brown sugar
1	tablespoon white vinegar
1	tablespoon Worcestershire sauce
2	teaspoons yellow mustard
1	teaspoon chili powder

1. In a large saucepan cook lima beans following package directions. Drain lima beans and set aside.

2. Meanwhile, in another large saucepan cook bacon, onion, and garlic over medium heat until bacon is crisp and onion is tender. Stir in tomato soup, brown sugar, vinegar, Worcestershire sauce, mustard, and chili powder. Bring to boiling; reduce heat. Simmer, covered, for 5 minutes.

3. Stir cooked lima beans into soup mixture; heat through. **MAKES 6 SERVINGS.**

Per serving: 195 cal., 3 g total fat (1 g sat. fat), 5 mg chol., 487 mg sodium, 34 g carbo., 6 g fiber, 9 g pro.

Basil and Tomato Pasta Salad

Prep: 30 minutes **Chill:** 2 to 4 hours

1	pound dried gemelli pasta
1	pound red and/or yellow tomatoes, chopped
1	cup shredded reduced-fat mozzarella cheese (4 ounces)
½	cup thinly sliced red onion (1 medium)
½	cup quartered pitted kalamata or ripe olives
¼	cup thinly sliced fresh basil or 4 teaspoons dried basil, crushed
2	tablespoons snipped fresh oregano or 2 teaspoons dried oregano, crushed
2	tablespoons capers, rinsed and drained
2	cloves garlic, minced
¼	teaspoon salt
⅛	teaspoon black pepper
2	tablespoons olive oil

1. Cook pasta following package directions. Drain; rinse and drain again.

2. In a large bowl combine cooked pasta, tomatoes, cheese, onion, olives, basil, oregano, drained capers, garlic, salt, and pepper. Add olive oil; toss gently to mix. Cover and chill for 2 to 4 hours.

MAKES 16 SERVINGS.

Per serving: 152 cal., 4 g total fat (1 g sat. fat), 4 mg chol., 161 mg sodium, 23 g carbo., 1 g fiber, 6 g pro.

Quick Tip Capers, which are the dried flower buds of a native Mediterranean bush, range in size from the tiny nonpareil variety to giant buds that can be as large as the tip of your finger. For use in most recipes, look for the tiny variety. Store brine-packed capers, tightly sealed, in the refrigerator for up to 9 months. Before using them, be sure to thoroughly rinse off excess salt or brine.

Kale Sauté ♡

Start to Finish: 15 minutes

12	ounces kale, cut or torn into 1- to 2-inch pieces (about 12 cups)
6	teaspoons olive oil
¼	cup soft sourdough or French loaf bread crumbs
⅛	teaspoon black pepper
1	teaspoon Worcestershire-style marinade for chicken
	Lemon wedges (optional)

1. Rinse kale leaves thoroughly under cold running water. Drain well; set aside.

2. In a small skillet heat 2 teaspoons of the oil over medium heat. Add bread crumbs; cook and stir for 1 to 2 minutes or until browned. Stir in pepper; set aside.

3. In a large nonstick skillet heat the remaining 4 teaspoons oil. Add kale; cover and cook for 1 minute. Uncover. Cook and stir about 1 minute more or just until wilted.

4. Transfer kale to a serving dish. Drizzle with Worcestershire sauce. Sprinkle with the bread crumbs. If desired, squeeze lemon wedges over all. **MAKES 4 SERVINGS.**

Per serving: 89 cal., 5 g total fat (1 g sat. fat), 0 mg chol., 53 mg sodium, 9 g carbo., 4 g fiber, 3 g pro.

●●●

Whether it's a saucy simmered vegetable dish, cool pasta salad, or quick sauté, side dishes add color and interest to any meal.

Basil and
Tomato Pasta
Salad

Creamy Brussels Sprouts with Peppered Bacon

Creamy Brussels Sprouts with Peppered Bacon
Prep: 20 minutes **Cook:** 15 minutes

- 4 slices peppered bacon
- 2 pounds Brussels sprouts, trimmed and halved through stem ends
- ¾ cup reduced-sodium chicken broth
- ½ teaspoon kosher salt
- ¼ teaspoon freshly ground black pepper
- ¾ cup whipping cream
  Freshly ground black pepper

1. In a very large skillet cook bacon over medium heat until browned and crisp. Drain on paper towels, reserving 2 tablespoons drippings in skillet.
2. Add Brussels sprouts to drippings in skillet; cook and stir over medium heat for 4 minutes. Add chicken broth, salt, and the ¼ teaspoon pepper. Heat to boiling. Reduce heat. Simmer, covered, for 5 minutes. Uncover; cook for 2 to 4 minutes or until liquid is nearly evaporated. Add whipping cream. Cook about 4 minutes or until thickened.
3. Transfer sprouts to a serving dish. Sprinkle with crumbled bacon and additional pepper.
MAKES 8 SERVINGS.

Per serving: 174 cal., 14 g total fat (7 g sat. fat), 38 mg chol., 305 mg sodium, 10 g carbo., 4 g fiber, 6 g pro.

Sautéed Spinach with Bacon and Mustard

Sautéed Spinach with Bacon and Mustard
Start to Finish: 15 minutes

- 4 slices bacon, cut into 1-inch pieces
- 2 10-ounce packages fresh spinach
- 1 tablespoon butter
- 1 tablespoon Dijon mustard
- ¼ teaspoon crushed red pepper

1. In a very large skillet cook bacon over medium heat until crisp. Drain bacon on paper towels, reserving 1 tablespoon drippings in skillet.
2. Gradually add spinach to skillet, stirring frequently with metal tongs. Cook for 2 to 3 minutes or just until spinach is wilted. Remove spinach from skillet to a colander. Hold colander over sink and press lightly to drain. (If using large-leaf spinach, use kitchen scissors to snip.)
3. In the same skillet melt butter over medium heat; stir in mustard and crushed red pepper. Add drained spinach; toss to coat and, if necessary, reheat spinach. Top with cooked bacon. Serve immediately.
MAKES 4 TO 6 SERVINGS.

Per serving: 135 cal., 11 g total fat (4 g sat. fat), 18 mg chol., 340 mg sodium, 5 g carbo., 3 g fiber, 7 g pro.

Roasted
Asparagus

Roasted Asparagus

Prep: 10 minutes **Roast:** 15 minutes
Oven: 450°F

1 pound fresh asparagus, trimmed
⅛ teaspoon black pepper
1 tablespoon olive oil
3 tablespoons grated Parmesan cheese

1. Preheat oven to 450°F. Place asparagus in a 2-quart baking dish. Sprinkle with black pepper. Drizzle with olive oil. Roast, uncovered, for 15 minutes or until crisp-tender, using tongs to lightly toss twice during roasting. Transfer asparagus to a warm serving platter. Sprinkle with cheese. **MAKES 4 SERVINGS.**

Per serving: 58 cal., 5 g total fat (1 g sat. fat), 3 mg chol., 59 mg sodium, 3 g carbo., 1 g fiber, 3 g pro.

Asparagus with Almond Sauce ♡

Start to Finish: 15 minutes

1 pound fresh asparagus, trimmed
1 tablespoon butter
2 tablespoons sliced almonds
½ cup chicken broth
1 teaspoon cornstarch
2 teaspoons lemon juice
Dash black pepper

1. In a large saucepan cook asparagus, covered, in boiling lightly salted water for 3 to 5 minutes or until crisp-tender. Drain well; transfer to a serving platter. Keep warm.
2. Meanwhile, for sauce, in a large skillet melt butter over medium heat. Add almonds; cook and stir for 2 to 3 minutes or until golden. In a small bowl stir together broth, cornstarch,

lemon juice, and pepper; add to skillet. Cook and stir until thickened and bubbly. Cook and stir for 1 minute more. Spoon sauce over asparagus. **MAKES 4 SERVINGS.**

Per serving: 76 cal., 5 g total fat (2 g sat. fat), 8 mg chol., 143 mg sodium, 6 g carbo., 3 g fiber, 3 g pro.

Creamed Spinach

Start to Finish: 30 minutes

2 10-ounce packages fresh spinach (large stems removed) or two 10-ounce packages frozen chopped spinach, thawed
2 tablespoons butter
½ cup chopped onion (1 medium)
2 to 3 cloves garlic, minced
1 cup whipping cream
½ teaspoon freshly ground black pepper
¼ teaspoon salt
¼ teaspoon ground nutmeg

1. In a large pot of rapidly boiling salted water, cook fresh spinach (if using) for 1 minute. Drain well, squeezing out excess liquid. Pat dry with paper towels. Snip spinach with kitchen scissors to coarsely chop; set aside. If using frozen spinach, drain well, squeezing out excess liquid.
2. In a large skillet melt butter over medium heat. Add onion and garlic; cook about 5 minutes or until onion is tender. Stir in whipping cream, pepper, salt, and nutmeg. Bring to boiling; cook, uncovered, until cream begins to thicken. Add spinach. Simmer, uncovered, about 2 minutes or until thickened. Season with additional salt and pepper. **MAKES 4 SERVINGS.**

Per serving: 312 cal., 29 g total fat (17 g sat. fat), 98 mg chol., 347 mg sodium, 11 g carbo., 4 g fiber, 6 g pro.

Creamed
Spinach

Basil Peas and Mushrooms.

Basil Peas and Mushrooms ♡

Start to Finish: 25 minutes

- ½ cup sliced carrot (1 medium)
- 1 10-ounce package frozen peas
- 1 tablespoon butter
- 2 cups sliced fresh mushrooms
- 2 green onions, cut into ½-inch pieces
- 1 tablespoon snipped fresh basil or
  ½ teaspoon dried basil, crushed
- ¼ teaspoon salt
  Dash black pepper

1. In a medium saucepan cook carrot, covered, in a small amount of boiling lightly salted water for 3 minutes. Add peas. Return to boiling; reduce heat. Cook, covered, about 5 minutes more or until carrot and peas are tender. Drain well. Remove vegetables from saucepan; set aside.

2. In the same saucepan melt butter over medium heat. Add mushrooms and green onions; cook until tender. Stir in basil, salt, and pepper. Return carrot and peas to saucepan; stir gently to mix. Heat through.
MAKES 6 SERVINGS.

Per ⅔ cup: 69 cal., 3 g total fat (1 g sat. fat), 5 mg chol., 171 mg sodium, 9 g carbo., 3 g fiber, 4 g pro.

Farm-Style Green Beans

Farm-Style Green Beans ♡

Start to Finish: 25 minutes

- 8 ounces fresh green beans
- 2 slices bacon, cut up
- 1 medium onion, thinly sliced
- ½ cup fresh sliced mushrooms
- 1½ cups chopped fresh tomatoes or one
  14.5-ounce can diced tomatoes, drained
- ¼ teaspoon salt*

1. Trim green beans and leave whole or cut into 1-inch pieces. In a covered medium saucepan cook the beans in a small amount of boiling salted water for 10 minutes or until crisp-tender; drain.

2. Meanwhile, in a large skillet cook bacon over medium heat until crisp. Remove bacon, reserving drippings. Drain bacon on paper towels; set aside. Cook onion and mushrooms in reserved drippings over medium heat until tender. Add tomatoes and salt. Cook, uncovered, for 2 to 3 minutes or until most of the liquid evaporates.

3. Transfer beans to a serving platter or bowl. Top with onion mixture. Sprinkle bacon over the vegetables. **MAKES 4 SERVINGS.**

Per serving: 132 cal., 9 g total fat (3 g sat. fat), 13 mg chol., 312 mg sodium, 10 g carbo., 3 g fiber, 4 g pro.

*Note Omit salt if using canned tomatoes.

Honey-Glazed Carrots and Green Onions ♡
Start to Finish: 20 minutes

- 3 cups packaged sliced or crinkle-cut fresh carrots
- 4 green onions, bias-sliced into 1 inch pieces (½ cup)
- 2 tablespoons honey
- 2 tablespoons butter
- ⅛ teaspoon ground ginger
  Black pepper

1. In a covered medium saucepan cook carrots in a small amount of boiling lightly salted water for 7 to 9 minutes or until nearly tender. Drain; remove carrots from saucepan.
2. For glaze, in the same saucepan combine green onions, honey, butter, and ginger. Cook and stir over medium heat until combined. Stir in carrots. Cook, uncovered, about 2 minutes or until carrots are glazed, stirring frequently. Season with pepper.
MAKES 4 SERVINGS.

Per serving: 130 cal., 6 g total fat (4 g sat. fat), 16 mg chol., 95 mg sodium, 19 g carbo., 3 g fiber, 1 g pro.

Cinnamon-Glazed Baby Carrots ♡
Prep: 2 minutes **Cook:** 8 minutes

- 1 1-pound package peeled fresh baby carrots
- 1 tablespoon butter
- 1 tablespoon packed brown sugar
- ⅛ teaspoon ground cinnamon
- ⅛ teaspoon salt

1. In a covered medium saucepan cook carrots in a small amount of boiling salted water for 8 to 10 minutes or until carrots are crisp-tender.
2. Drain carrots. Add butter, sugar, cinnamon, and salt to carrots in saucepan; stir to coat. **MAKES 6 SERVINGS.**

Per serving: 52 cal., 2 g total fat (1 g sat. fat), 5 mg chol., 72 mg sodium, 8 g carbo., 2 g fiber, 1 g pro.

Nutty Broccoli
Start to Finish: 25 minutes

- 1 pound broccoli, trimmed and cut into 2-inch pieces
- 3 tablespoons butter
- 2 tablespoons orange juice
- ½ teaspoon finely shredded orange peel (set aside)
- ¼ teaspoon salt
- 3 tablespoons chopped walnuts or pecans, sliced almonds, or pine nuts, toasted
  Orange wedges (optional)

1. If desired, halve stem pieces of broccoli lengthwise. Place a steamer basket in a 3-quart saucepan. Add water to reach just below the bottom of the basket. Bring to boiling. Add broccoli to steamer basket. Cover and reduce heat. Steam for 8 to 10 minutes or just until stems are tender. Transfer broccoli to a serving dish.
2. Meanwhile, in a medium skillet melt butter over medium-high heat; cook and stir for 3 to 4 minutes or until medium brown in color. Add orange juice and cook for 10 seconds. Remove from heat; stir in orange peel and salt. Pour over broccoli; sprinkle with walnuts. If desired, garnish with orange wedges.
MAKES 6 SERVINGS.

Per serving: 94 cal., 8 g total fat (4 g sat. fat), 15 mg chol., 153 mg sodium, 4 g carbo., 1 g fiber, 2 g pro.

Quick Tip When shredding orange peel (or any citrus), shred only the top layer and not the white pith beneath it, which will make food taste bitter.

Even broccoli haters will embrace these tiny green trees when they're coated in a buttery orange glaze and tossed with crunchy nuts.

Nutty Broccoli

Chunky Mustard Potato Salad

Chunky Mustard Potato Salad ♡

Prep: 15 minutes

- 1 20-ounce package refrigerated new potato wedges
- ¼ teaspoon salt
- ½ cup green onions, sliced (4)
- ¼ cup coarsely chopped dill pickles
- ¼ cup chopped bottled roasted red sweet peppers
- ¼ cup chopped celery
- ¼ cup cooked bacon crumbles
- 2 tablespoons Dijon mustard
- ½ teaspoon salt
- ¼ teaspoon black pepper
- ½ cup mayonnaise or salad dressing

1. Place potatoes in a large saucepan. Add enough water to cover potatoes; add ¼ teaspoon salt. Bring to boiling; reduce heat. Simmer, covered for 5 minutes. Drain well; rinse with cold water and drain again.

2. Meanwhile, in a very large serving bowl combine green onions, pickles, roasted peppers, celery, bacon crumbles, mustard, ½ teaspoon salt, and black pepper. Stir in potatoes. Add mayonnaise and mix gently. If desired, chill up to 24 hours.

MAKES 10 SERVINGS.

Per serving: 131 cal., 9 g total fat (1 g sat. fat), 6 mg chol., 457 mg sodium, 8 g carbo., 2 g fiber, 3 g pro.

Quick Tip Different varieties of potatoes are best used for specific dishes. New potatoes or waxy white potatoes hold their shape best when boiled; they are the right choice for potato salads. Idaho or russet potatoes get mushy and fall apart in potato salad—but they make beautiful french fries and mashed potatoes.

Lemon Hollandaise on New Potatoes

Lemon Hollandaise on New Potatoes

Start to Finish: 30 minutes

- 12 ounces tiny new potatoes, halved
- 1 medium carrot, cut into thin strips
- ¼ cup sour cream
- ¼ cup mayonnaise or salad dressing
- ½ teaspoon finely shredded lemon peel
- 1 teaspoon lemon juice
  Milk
- ¼ cup thinly sliced green onions (2)
  Cherry tomatoes (optional)

1. In a covered large saucepan cook potatoes in a small amount of lightly salted boiling water for 12 minutes. Add carrot; cook for 5 to 6 minutes more or just until vegetables are tender. Drain vegetables; transfer to a serving bowl. Keep warm.

2. Meanwhile, for sauce, in a small saucepan combine sour cream, mayonnaise, lemon peel, and lemon juice. Cook and stir over low heat just until heated through; do not boil. If necessary, stir enough milk into the sour cream mixture for drizzling consistency. Drizzle sauce over cooked vegetables. Sprinkle with green onions. If desired, garnish with tomatoes. **MAKES 4 SERVINGS.**

Per serving: 197 cal., 14 g total fat (3 g sat. fat), 13 mg chol., 97 mg sodium, 17 g carbo., 2 g fiber, 3 g pro.

Oven Sweet Potato Fries

½ cup pitted kalamata olives, halved
3 cloves garlic, minced
¼ cup grated Parmesan cheese

1. Preheat oven to 450°F. Lightly grease a 15×10×1-inch baking pan; place potatoes in pan. In a small bowl combine olive oil, rosemary, salt, and pepper; drizzle over potatoes, tossing to coat.

2. Bake for 20 minutes, stirring once. Add tomatoes, olives, and garlic, tossing to combine. Bake for 5 to 10 minutes more or until potatoes are tender and brown on the edges and tomatoes are soft. Transfer to a serving dish. Sprinkle with Parmesan cheese.

MAKES 8 SERVINGS.

Per serving: 102 cal., 5 g total fat (1 g sat. fat), 2 mg chol., 208 mg sodium, 11 g carbo., 2 g fiber, 3 g pro.

Oven Sweet Potato Fries ♡

Prep: 10 minutes **Bake:** 30 minutes
Oven: 350°F

2 pounds sweet potatoes, peeled and cut into strips
2 tablespoons vegetable oil
¼ teaspoon salt
⅛ teaspoon freshly ground black pepper
   Greek-style yogurt or light sour cream (optional)

1. Preheat oven to 350°F. Place sweet potato strips in a 15×10×1-inch baking pan. Drizzle with oil and sprinkle with salt and pepper; toss to coat. Spread potatoes in a single layer.

2. Bake about 30 minutes or until tender. If desired, serve with Greek-style yogurt.

MAKES 6 SERVINGS.

Per serving: 134 cal., 5 g total fat (0 g sat. fat), 0 mg chol., 157 mg sodium, 22 g carbo., 3 g fiber, 2 g pro.

Balsamic-Roasted Potatoes and Vegetables ♡

Prep: 10 minutes **Roast:** 30 minutes
Oven: 425°F

1 pound tiny new potatoes, halved
½ pound rutabaga, peeled and cut up
½ of a 16-ounce package peeled fresh baby carrots, cut up
1 medium red onion, cut into wedges
3 tablespoons olive oil
1 tablespoon fresh snipped rosemary
¾ teaspoon salt
¼ teaspoon black pepper
3 tablespoons balsamic vinegar

1. Preheat oven to 425°F. In a lightly greased shallow baking pan combine potatoes, rutabaga, carrots, and onion. In a small bowl stir together oil, rosemary, salt, and pepper. Drizzle over vegetables; toss to coat.

2. Roast, uncovered, for 30 to 35 minutes or until potatoes and onion are tender, stirring once or twice. Drizzle with balsamic vinegar and toss to coat; serve immediately.

MAKES 6 SERVINGS.

Per serving: 179 cal., 7 g total fat (1 g sat. fat), 0 mg chol., 327 mg sodium, 27 g carbo., 3 g fiber, 3 g pro.

Rosemary-Roasted Potatoes and Tomatoes ♡

Prep: 10 minutes **Bake:** 25 minutes
Oven: 450°F

1 pound tiny new potatoes, quartered (10 to 12)
2 tablespoons olive oil
1 teaspoon snipped fresh rosemary
¼ teaspoon salt
¼ teaspoon black pepper
4 roma tomatoes, quartered lengthwise

Parsley-Herb
Rice

Parsley-Herb Rice

Prep: 15 minutes **Cook:** 15 minutes
Stand: 5 minutes

2²/₃ cups water
1¹/₃ cup uncooked long grain or regular
   brown rice
¼ cup butter
1½ teaspoons dried basil, crushed, or
   2 tablespoons snipped fresh basil
¾ teaspoon salt or 1 tablespoon instant
   chicken bouillon granules
½ cup dried cranberries
½ cup snipped fresh Italian (flat-leaf) parsley
½ cup walnut pieces

1. In a medium saucepan combine the water,
rice, butter, dried basil (if using), and salt.
Bring to boiling; reduce heat. Simmer,
covered, about 15 minutes for long grain rice
(about 40 minutes for brown rice) or until rice
is tender and liquid is absorbed. Remove
from heat. Stir in cranberries. Let stand,
covered, for 5 minutes.
2. Just before serving, stir fresh basil (if using),
parsley, and walnuts into the cooked rice.
MAKES 8 SERVINGS.

Per serving: 240 cal., 11 g total fat (4 g sat. fat), 16 mg
chol., 267 mg sodium, 32 g carbo., 2 g fiber, 4 g pro.

Chile Rice

Prep: 10 minutes **Stand:** 5 minutes

1 14.5-ounce can diced tomatoes with
   onion and garlic, undrained
1 cup water
1 4-ounce can diced green chiles,
   undrained
1 teaspoon chili powder
¼ teaspoon salt
2 cups instant white rice

1. In a medium saucepan combine undrained
tomatoes, the water, undrained chiles, chili
powder, and salt. Bring to boiling; stir in
uncooked rice.
2. Remove from heat; cover and let stand for
5 minutes. Stir before serving.
MAKES 6 SERVINGS.

Per serving: 147 cal., 1 g total fat (0 g sat. fat), 0 mg
chol., 488 mg sodium, 32 g carbo., 0 g fiber, 4 g pro.

Grits Gruyère

Prep: 15 minutes **Bake:** 20 minutes
Oven: 350°F

4 cups milk
¼ cup butter, cut up
½ teaspoon salt
1 cup quick-cooking grits
1 cup shredded Gruyère cheese or Swiss
   cheese (4 ounces)
   Several dashes bottled hot pepper sauce
   or ¼ teaspoon cayenne pepper (optional)
¼ cup grated Parmesan cheese

1. Preheat oven 350°F. Grease a 2-quart
square baking dish; set aside.
2. In a large saucepan combine milk, butter,
and salt. Cook over medium heat until almost
boiling, stirring occasionally. (Watch carefully
to prevent boiling over.) Gradually stir in grits;
cook and stir with a wooden spoon just until
boiling. Cook and stir about 2 minutes more
or until thickened. (Reduce heat if necessary.)
Remove from heat; stir in Gruyère cheese
and, if desired, hot pepper sauce. Spread
grits mixture evenly in prepared dish. Sprinkle
with Parmesan cheese.
3. Bake, uncovered, for 20 to 25 minutes or
until golden. **MAKES 8 SERVINGS.**

Per serving: 246 cal., 14 g total fat (8 g sat. fat), 43 mg
chol., 363 mg sodium, 20 g carbo., 1 g fiber, 11 g pro.

**Get your daily dose of whole grains in delicious side dishes featuring
brown rice, grits, quinoa, or barley.**

Heavenly Couscous

Spanish-Style Rice ♡

Start to Finish: 30 minutes

- 1 14.5-ounce can Mexican-style stewed tomatoes, cut up and undrained
- ½ cup water
- 1 teaspoon chili powder
- ½ cup uncooked long grain rice
- ¼ teaspoon salt
- ⅛ teaspoon black pepper
  Several dashes bottled hot pepper sauce (optional)
- ¼ cup chopped pimiento-stuffed olives or chopped pitted ripe olives
- ½ cup shredded cheddar cheese

1. In a medium saucepan combine tomatoes, the water, chili powder, rice, salt, pepper, and, if desired, hot pepper sauce. Bring to boiling; reduce heat. Simmer, covered, about 20 minutes or until rice is tender and most of the liquid is absorbed. Stir in olives. Sprinkle with cheese. **MAKES 4 SERVINGS.**

Per serving: 185 cal., 6 g total fat (3 g sat. fat), 15 mg chol., 590 mg sodium, 25 g carbo., 2 g fiber, 6 g pro.

Heavenly Couscous ♡

Start to Finish: 15 minutes

- 1 cup couscous
- ¼ teaspoon salt
- 1 cup boiling water
- 1 teaspoon butter
- ¼ cup slivered almonds
- ¼ cup snipped dried apricots
- ½ teaspoon finely shredded orange peel
  Fine orange peel curls (optional)

1. In a medium bowl mix couscous and salt. Gradually add boiling the water. Let stand about 5 minutes or until liquid is absorbed.
2. Meanwhile, in a small skillet melt butter over medium heat. Add almonds; cook until light golden brown, stirring occasionally.

Remove almonds from skillet to cool. Fluff couscous with a fork. Add apricots, orange peel, and toasted almonds to couscous. Fluff again. If desired, sprinkle with orange peel curls. Serve immediately. **MAKES 4 SERVINGS.**

Per serving: 250 cal., 5 g total fat (1 g sat. fat), 2 mg chol., 163 mg sodium, 42 g carbo., 4 g fiber, 8 g pro.

Quick Tip Most of the dried apricots you find in the supermarket are treated with sulfites to help them retain their bright color and plumpness. If you or someone you cook for has an adverse reaction to sulfites—and many people do—look for untreated dried apricots at a health food store. They will be darker in color and won't be as moist as the treated apricots, but they taste just as good.

Checkerboard Rolls

Checkerboard Rolls

Prep: 20 minutes **Chill:** 8 to 24 hours
Stand: 45 minutes **Bake:** 20 minutes
Oven: 375°F

- 2 tablespoons poppy seeds
- 2 tablespoons sesame seeds
- 1 teaspoon lemon-pepper seasoning
- 2 tablespoons yellow cornmeal
- 2 tablespoons grated or finely shredded Parmesan cheese
- 3 tablespoons butter, melted
- 16 pieces (1.3 ounces each) frozen white roll dough

1. Grease a 9×9×2-inch square baking pan; set aside. In a shallow dish combine poppy seeds, sesame seeds, and lemon-pepper seasoning. In another shallow dish combine cornmeal and Parmesan cheese. Place butter in a third dish. Working quickly, roll dough pieces in butter, then in one of the seasoning mixtures to lightly coat. (Coat half of the rolls with one seasoning mixture and the remaining rolls with the other seasoning mixture.) Alternate rolls in prepared pan. Cover rolls with greased plastic wrap. Let thaw in refrigerator for 8 to 24 hours.
2. Remove pan from refrigerator; uncover and let stand at room temperature for 45 minutes. After 35 minutes, preheat oven to 375°F.
3. Bake rolls for 20 to 25 minutes or until golden. Remove rolls from pan to wire rack. Cool slightly. **MAKES 16 ROLLS.**

Per roll: 136 cal., 5 g total fat (2 g sat. fat), 6 mg chol., 189 mg sodium, 19 g carbo., 1 g fiber, 4 g pro.

Garlic Dinner Rolls

Prep: 15 minutes **Bake:** 13 minutes
Oven: 375°F

- 1 11-ounce package (12) refrigerated breadsticks
- 2 tablespoons purchased garlic butter spread, melted
- ½ cup finely shredded or grated Asiago or Romano cheese (2 ounces)
- 1 teaspoon dried parsley flakes
- ⅛ teaspoon cayenne pepper

1. Preheat oven to 375°F. Line a large baking sheet with foil; set aside. On a lightly floured surface separate dough into 12 breadsticks. Cut each piece lengthwise into 3 strips, leaving ¾ inch uncut at one end. For each fleur-de-lis roll, coil strips from cut end toward uncut base, coiling outside strips away from center and coiling the center strip in either direction. If necessary, pinch slightly to hold shape. Transfer to prepared baking sheet.
2. Brush rolls with melted garlic butter spread. In a small bowl combine cheese, parsley flakes, and cayenne pepper; sprinkle generously on rolls.
3. Bake for 13 to 15 minutes or until golden. Serve warm. **MAKES 12 ROLLS.**

Per roll: 112 cal., 5 g total fat (2 g sat. fat), 8 mg chol., 263 mg sodium, 12 g carbo., 0 g fiber, 3 g pro.

Curried Seed Rolls ♡

Start to Finish: 17 minutes **Oven:** 375°F

- 2 tablespoons butter
- ¼ teaspoon curry powder
  Dash garlic powder
- 1 to 2 tablespoons mixed seeds (such as cumin seeds, sesame seeds, poppy seeds, and/or dill seeds)
- 8 purchased whole grain or whole wheat dinner rolls
  Butter (optional)
  Mango chutney or other fruit chutney (optional)

1. Preheat oven to 375°F. In a small shallow dish combine melted butter, curry powder, and garlic powder. Place mixed seeds in another small shallow dish or on waxed paper. Dip tops of rolls into melted butter mixture, then dip into seeds. Place rolls on an ungreased baking sheet.
2. Bake for 7 to 9 minutes or until hot. Serve warm. If desired, serve with additional butter and chutney. **MAKES 8 ROLLS.**

Per roll: 104 cal., 4 g total fat (2 g sat. fat), 8 mg chol., 158 mg sodium, 15 g carbo., 2 g fiber, 3 g pro.

Quick Tip Mango chutney may be the most familiar type of chutney, but it's not the only type. There are many kinds of fruit chutneys on the market. Some of them are made from one kind of fruit, while others are made from a blend of fruits. Fruits that are commonly cooked into chutneys include peaches, passion fruit, dates, apples, pears, and cranberries.

The wonderful smell of bread baking in the oven offers a warm welcome to anyone who walks through your door.

Easy Parmesan
Biscuits

Green Onion Parker House Biscuits

Prep: 10 minutes **Bake:** 8 minutes
Oven: 400°F

- 1 5.2-ounce container semisoft cheese with garlic and fine herbs
- ¼ cup sliced green onions (2)
- 1 12-ounce package (10) refrigerated biscuits
- 1 egg yolk
- 1 tablespoon water
- 2 tablespoons grated Parmesan cheese
    Sliced green onions

1. Preheat oven to 400°F. In a small bowl stir together semisoft cheese and the ¼ cup green onions; set aside.

2. Unwrap biscuits. Using your fingers, gently split the biscuits horizontally. Place the biscuit bottoms on a greased baking sheet. Spread about 1 tablespoon of the cheese mixture over each biscuit bottom. Replace biscuit tops.

3. In a small bowl use a fork to lightly beat together egg yolk and the water. Brush biscuit tops with yolk mixture. Sprinkle with Parmesan cheese and additional sliced green onions. Bake for 8 to 10 minutes or until golden brown. Serve warm.

MAKES 10 BISCUITS.

Per biscuit: 149 cal., 8 g total fat (5 g sat. fat), 23 mg chol., 394 mg sodium, 16 g carbo., 0 g fiber, 4 g pro.

Easy Parmesan Breadsticks

Prep: 15 minutes **Bake:** 10 minutes
Oven: 375°F

- ½ of a 12-ounce loaf baguette-style French bread (halve bread loaf crosswise)
    Nonstick cooking spray
- ¼ cup olive oil
- 6 tablespoons grated or finely shredded Parmesan cheese
    Purchased marinara sauce, warmed, and/ or flavored oils (such as lemon-, basil-, or garlic-flavor)

1. Preheat oven to 375°F. Cut bread lengthwise into quarters; cut into ¼- to ½-inch-wide strips. (Cut bread so there is crust on each strip.)

2. Line a 15×10×1-inch baking pan with foil; lightly coat foil with cooking spray. Arrange bread strips in a single layer; drizzle with oil. Using a spatula or tongs, carefully turn breadsticks to coat with oil. Sprinkle with Parmesan cheese.

3. Bake for 10 to 12 minutes or until browned and crisp. Serve with marinara sauce and/or flavored oils. **MAKES 6 SERVINGS.**

Per serving: 219 cal., 13 g total fat (3 g sat. fat), 4 mg chol., 539 mg sodium, 20 g carbo., 2 g fiber, 5 g pro.

Green Onion
Parker House
Biscuits

Corn Bread

Corn Bread

Prep: 10 minutes **Bake:** 15 minutes
Oven: 400°F

- 1 cup all-purpose flour
- ¾ cup cornmeal
- 2 to 3 tablespoons sugar
- 2½ teaspoons baking powder
- ¾ teaspoon salt
- 1 tablespoon butter
- 2 eggs
- 1 cup milk
- ¼ cup vegetable oil or melted butter

1. Preheat oven to 400°F. In a medium bowl stir together the flour, cornmeal, sugar, baking powder, and salt; set aside.
2. Add the 1 tablespoon butter to an 8×8×2-inch baking pan, a 9×1½-inch round baking pan, or a large cast-iron skillet. Place pan in the preheated oven about 3 minutes or until butter melts. Remove pan from oven; swirl butter to coat bottom and sides of pan.
3. Meanwhile, in a small bowl beat eggs with a fork; stir in milk and oil. Add egg mixture to flour mixture all at once; stir just until moistened (batter should be lumpy). Pour batter into the hot pan. Bake for 15 to 20 minutes or until a wooden toothpick inserted near the center comes out clean. Serve warm. **MAKES 8 TO 10 WEDGES.**

Per wedge: 219 cal., 10 g total fat (3 g sat. fat), 60 mg chol., 390 mg sodium, 26 g carbo., 1 g fiber, 5 g pro.

Double Corn Bread Prepare as directed, except fold ½ cup frozen whole kernel corn, thawed, into the batter.

Green Chile Corn Bread Prepare as directed, except fold 1 cup shredded cheddar cheese or Monterey Jack cheese (4 ounces) and one 4-ounce can diced green chile peppers, drained, into the batter.

Sweet Pepper Corn Bread Prepare as directed, except fold ½ cup chopped red sweet pepper into the batter.

Green Onion-Bacon Corn Bread Prepare as directed, except fold ⅓ cup crumbled cooked bacon and ¼ cup sliced green onions into the batter.

Corn Muffins Prepare as directed, except omit the 1 tablespoon butter. Spoon batter into 12 greased 2½-inch muffin cups, filling each two-thirds full. Bake in the 400°F oven about 15 minutes or until light brown and a wooden toothpick inserted in the centers comes out clean. Makes 12 muffins.

Cracked Pepper Breadsticks ♡

Prep: 25 minutes **Bake:** 10 minutes
Oven: 450°F

- 2 cups all-purpose flour
- 1 tablespoon baking powder
- 1 to 1½ teaspoons cracked black pepper
- ¼ teaspoon salt
- ⅓ cup butter
- ⅔ cup beef or chicken broth

1. Preheat oven to 450°F. In a medium bowl stir together flour, baking powder, pepper, and salt. Using a pastry blender, cut in butter until mixture resembles coarse crumbs. Make a well in the center. Add broth; stir just until dough clings together.
2. Turn dough out onto a lightly floured surface. Knead gently for 10 to 12 strokes. Divide dough in 8 equal portions; divide each portion into fourths. Roll each piece into a 10-inch-long rope. Fold each rope in half; twist two or three times. Arrange twists on an ungreased baking sheet.
3. Bake for 5 minutes; turn and bake for 5 to 6 minutes more or until brown. Serve warm or cool completely on a wire rack before serving.
MAKES 32 BREADSTICKS.

Per breadstick: 44 cal., 2 g total fat (1 g sat. fat), 5 mg chol., 54 mg sodium, 6 g carbo., 0 g fiber, 1 g pro.

With just a few basic ingredients in your pantry—flour, salt, butter, eggs, baking powder, and baking soda—homemade bread is just minutes away.

Desserts

Cakes

Cookies and Bars

Ice Cream and Pudding Desserts

Pies and Tarts

Butterscotch
Marble Cake

New Year's Champagne Cake

Butterscotch Marble Cake

Prep: 20 minutes **Bake:** 55 minutes
Cool: 2 hours **Oven:** 350°F

- 1 package 2-layer-size white cake mix
- 1 4-serving-size package instant butterscotch pudding mix
- 1 cup water
- ¼ cup vegetable oil
- 4 eggs
- ½ cup chocolate-flavor syrup
- 2 ounces sweet baking chocolate, cut up
- 2 tablespoons butter
- ¾ cup powdered sugar
- 1 tablespoon hot water

1. Preheat oven to 350°F. Grease and flour a 10-inch fluted tube pan; set aside.
2. In a large mixing bowl combine cake mix, pudding mix, the water, oil, and eggs. Beat with an electric mixer on low until combined. Beat on medium for 2 minutes, scraping sides of bowl often.
3. Transfer 1½ cups of batter to another bowl; stir in the chocolate syrup. Pour light batter into the prepared pan. Spoon chocolate batter over top. Using a knife, gently cut through batters to marble.
4. Bake for 55 to 60 minutes or until a toothpick inserted near the center comes out clean. Cool cake in pan on a wire rack for 15 minutes. Remove cake from pan; cool completely on wire rack.
5. For icing, in a medium saucepan melt chocolate and butter over low heat, stirring frequently. Remove from heat. Stir in powdered sugar and 1 tablespoon hot water. Stir in additional hot water, if needed, to reach drizzling consistency. Drizzle cake with icing.
MAKES 12 SERVINGS.

Per serving: 372 cal., 13 g total fat (4 g sat. fat), 76 mg chol., 388 mg sodium, 62 g carbo., 1 g fiber, 5 g pro.

Angel Food Cake with Peaches, Whipped Cream, and Raspberries ♡

Prep: 15 minutes

- 1 cup whipping cream
- 2 tablespoons powdered sugar
- ½ teaspoon almond extract
- 1 10-ounce package frozen red raspberries, thawed
- 12 slices angel food cake
- 1 16-ounce can peach slices in light syrup, drained
- 12 fresh mint leaves (optional)

1. In a chilled medium mixing bowl combine whipping cream, powdered sugar, and almond extract. Beat with an electric mixer on medium until soft peaks form.
2. Place raspberries in food processor or blender. Process or blend until smooth. Press puree through a sieve.
3. Arrange cake slices on 12 dessert plates. Spoon a few tablespoons seedless raspberry puree over each slice. Garnish with peach slices, whipped cream, remaining raspberry puree, and, if desired, mint.
MAKES 12 SERVINGS.

Per serving: 180 cal., 8 g total fat (5 g sat. fat), 27 mg chol., 222 mg sodium, 27 g carbo., 2 g fiber, 3 g pro.

New Year's Champagne Cake

Prep: 20 minutes **Bake:** following package directions **Cool:** 1 hour **Oven:** 350°F

- 1 package 2-layer-size white cake mix
  Champagne or sparkling wine
- 1 16-ounce can vanilla frosting
  Few drops red food coloring
  Sliced or whole strawberries (optional)

1. Preheat oven to 350°F. Grease and flour two 8×1½-inch round cake pans; set aside.
2. Prepare cake mix following package directions, except replace water with an equal amount of Champagne or sparkling wine. Divide batter evenly among the prepared pans. Bake following package directions. Cool layers in pans on wire racks for 10 minutes. Remove layers from pans and cool completely on wire racks.
3. Place frosting in a medium bowl. Stir in a few drops of red food coloring to make light pink. Fill and frost cake with tinted frosting. If desired, garnish with strawberries.
MAKES 10 SERVINGS.

Per serving: 465 cal., 17 g total fat (4 g sat. fat), 0 mg chol., 423 mg sodium, 72 g carbo., 1 g fiber, 3 g pro.

Cinnamon
Toasted Pound
Cake and
Strawberries

Cinnamon Toasted Pound Cake and Strawberries

Start to Finish: 15 minutes

- ½ teaspoon ground cinnamon
- 1 tablespoon sugar
- 3 cups strawberries, washed and quartered
- ¼ cup strawberry jam
- 1 tablespoon lemon juice
- 1 10.75-ounce frozen pound cake, thawed and cut into 12 slices
- 2 tablespoons butter, softened
  Frozen whipped dessert topping, thawed
  Cinnamon (optional)

1. In a small bowl stir together cinnamon and sugar. In a large bowl toss together strawberries, jam, lemon juice, and 1 teaspoon of the cinnamon-sugar mixture until berries are well coated.

2. Toast cake slices. Spread 1 side of each slice with butter. Sprinkle with remaining cinnamon-sugar mixture. To serve, place 2 cake slices on each of 6 plates. Top with strawberries and whipped topping. Sprinkle toppings with a little cinnamon if desired. **MAKES 6 SERVINGS.**

Per serving: 875 cal., 56 g total fat (31 g sat. fat), 378 mg chol., 540 mg sodium, 135 g carbo., 5 g fiber, 13 g pro.

Quick Tip When strawberries are at peak season in May and early June, look for a pick-your-own patch nearby. You can often buy pints of berries that were already picked. There is nothing equal to the taste of perfectly ripe strawberries. You know they're good when they're red all the way through.

Mocha Pound Cake

Start to Finish: 20 minutes

- ½ of a 10.75-ounce frozen pound cake, thawed
- 3 tablespoons sugar
- 2 tablespoons unsweetened cocoa powder
- 1 teaspoon instant coffee crystals
- ⅓ cup milk
- 1 3-ounce package cream cheese, softened
- 1 medium orange
  Orange slices, cut into eighths, or orange peel curls (optional)

1. Preheat broiler. Cut pound cake into 8 thin slices; place on a baking sheet. Broil 3 to 4 inches from heat for 1 to 2 minutes per side or until toasted. In a small bowl whisk together sugar, cocoa powder, and coffee crystals. Gradually whisk in milk until smooth.

2. In a medium mixing bowl beat cream cheese with an electric mixer on medium until smooth. Gradually beat in the milk mixture until smooth, scraping sides of bowl as needed.

3. Peel orange and cut crosswise into 4 slices. Place a pound cake slice on each of 4 dessert plates. Top each with an orange slice and the cream cheese mixture. Add remaining pound cake slices. If desired, garnish with additional orange slice pieces. **MAKES 4 SERVINGS.**

Per serving: 291 cal., 16 g total fat (10 g sat. fat), 109 mg chol., 224 mg sodium, 35 g carbo., 2 g fiber, 5 g pro.

Quick Tip To make an orange peel curl garnish, use a zester with a large hole or a vegetable peeler to make long, thin strips of orange peel. Wrap the peel tightly around a pencil or chopstick and let stand at room temperature for 30 minutes or until curl holds its shape. Remove curl from the pencil or chopstick.

Crispy Chocolate Chewies

Prep: 20 minutes **Bake:** 10 minutes per batch
Oven: 350°F

- 1 package 2-layer-size German chocolate cake mix
- ½ cup butter, melted
- 1 egg
- ¼ cup milk
- ¾ cup crisp rice cereal
- ¼ cup flaked coconut
- 1 cup canned coconut-pecan frosting
  Flaked coconut, toasted* (optional)

1. Preheat oven to 350°F. In a large mixing bowl combine cake mix, melted butter, egg, and milk. Beat with an electric mixer on low until smooth. Stir in cereal and the ¼ cup coconut. Drop dough by rounded teaspoons 2 inches apart onto an ungreased cookie sheet.
2. Bake for 10 to 12 minutes or until bottoms are light brown. Let stand for 1 minute on cookie sheet. Transfer to a wire rack and let cool. Spread cookies with coconut-pecan frosting. If desired, sprinkle with toasted coconut. **MAKES 40 COOKIES.**

Per cookie: 108 cal., 5 g total fat (5 g sat. fat), 11 mg chol.,132 mg sodium, 15 g carbo., 0 g fiber, 1 g pro.

*Note To toast coconut, spread flaked or shredded coconut in a shallow baking pan. Bake in a 350°F oven about 5 minutes or just until a light golden brown, stirring once or twice. Check frequently to make sure they aren't becoming too brown.

Easy 'Mallow Cookies

Easy 'Mallow Cookies

Start to Finish: 30 minutes

- 16 maraschino cherries with stems
- ⅓ cup marshmallow creme
- 1 tablespoon finely chopped maraschino cherries
- 32 vanilla wafers
- 4 ounces vanilla-flavor candy coating, coarsely chopped

1. Place cherries with stems on paper towels; drain well. Line a cookie sheet with waxed paper; set aside. In a small bowl stir together marshmallow creme and chopped cherries. Spread 1 level teaspoon of the marshmallow mixture on bottoms of half of the vanilla wafers. Top with the remaining wafers, bottom sides down. Place on the prepared cookie sheet.
2. Place candy coating in a small saucepan. Cook and stir over low heat until melted. Cool slightly.
3. Dip half of each cookie into melted coating; let excess drip back into pan. Return dipped cookie to the cookie sheet. Holding each cherry by the stem, dip bottom of cherry into melted coating. Place on the dipped portion of a cookie; hold for several seconds or until set. Let stand until coating is completely set. **MAKES 16 COOKIES.**

Per cookie: 126 cal., 5 g total fat (3 g sat. fat), 0 mg chol., 37 mg sodium, 20 g carbo., 0 g fiber, 1 g pro.

Sour Cream-Blueberry Pie

Sour Cream-Blueberry Pie

Prep: 15 minutes **Bake:** 40 minutes
Chill: 4 hours **Oven:** 400°F

- 1 egg, lightly beaten
- 1 8-ounce carton sour cream
- ¾ cup sugar
- 2 tablespoons all-purpose flour
- 1 teaspoon vanilla
- ¼ teaspoon salt
- 2½ cups fresh blueberries
- ½ of a 15-ounce package rolled refrigerated unbaked piecrust (1 crust)
- ¼ cup all-purpose flour
- ¼ cup butter, softened
- ¼ cup chopped pecans or walnuts

1. Preheat oven to 400°F. Bring piecrust to room temperature following package directions.
2. In a large bowl combine egg, sour cream, sugar, the 2 tablespoons flour, the vanilla, and salt, stirring until smooth. Fold in blueberries. Unroll piecrust and ease into a 9-inch pie plate. Pour filling into piecrust.
3. Bake for 25 minutes. Meanwhile, in a small bowl thoroughly combine the ¼ cup flour, the butter, and nuts. Pinch off small bits of flour mixture and sprinkle on top of pie. Bake pie for 15 minutes more. Cool on a wire rack. Chill pie for at least 4 hours before serving. **MAKES 8 SERVINGS.**

Per serving: 397 cal., 24 g total fat (10 g sat. fat), 54 mg chol., 211 mg sodium, 42 g carbo., 3 g fiber, 5 g pro.

Quick Tip Look for blueberries that are plump, firm, uniform in size, and a silver-frosted indigo blue color. To store blueberries, refrigerate them, tightly covered, for up to 10 days. Before use, discard any shriveled or moldy blueberries and remove any stems.

Little Lemon Snowbites

Prep: 25 minutes **Bake:** 7 minutes per batch
Oven: 375°F

- 1 17.5-ounce package sugar cookie mix
- ¼ cup crushed hard lemon candies
- ⅔ cup purchased lemon curd
- ⅔ cup frozen whipped dessert topping, thawed
- 2 tablespoons powdered sugar

1. Preheat oven to 375°F. Line a cookie sheet with foil or parchment paper; set aside. Prepare cookie mix following package directions. Stir in the crushed candies. If necessary, cover and chill dough about 1 hour or until easy to handle. Roll dough into 1-inch balls. Place balls 2 inches apart on prepared cookie sheet.
2. Bake for 7 to 9 minutes or until edges are firm and cookies are light brown on bottoms. Cool on cookie sheet for 1 minute. Transfer to a wire rack and let cool.
3. For filling, in a small bowl stir together lemon curd and whipped topping; set aside. To assemble cookies, place a rounded teaspoon of filling on the bottom side of a cookie; top with another cookie, top side up. Repeat with remaining cookies and filling. Sprinkle tops of cookies with powdered sugar. Store filled cookies in the refrigerator for up to 3 days or freeze for up to 1 month. **MAKES 24 SANDWICH COOKIES.**

Per sandwich cookie: 169 cal., 7 g total fat (3 g sat. fat), 26 mg chol., 87 mg sodium, 25 g carbo., 1 g fiber, 1 g pro.

Little Lemon
Snowbites

Ultimate
Chocolate
Sundaes

Ultimate Chocolate Sundaes

Start to Finish: 30 minutes

　8　ounces semisweet or bittersweet
　　　chocolate, coarsely chopped
　⅓　cup water
　¼　cup sugar
　¼　cup pear liqueur or pear nectar
　4　small Forelle or Bosc pears (1 pound)
　3　tablespoons butter
　2　tablespoons sugar
　1　quart vanilla ice cream

1. For the chocolate sauce, in a small saucepan combine chocolate, the water, and the ¼ cup sugar. Cook over low heat until chocolate is melted, stirring constantly. Stir in pear liqueur. Set aside to cool slightly.

2. If desired, peel pears cut into halves and remove cores.* If desired, leave stem on 1 portion. In a large skillet melt butter. Add pear halves; cook over medium heat about 12 minutes or until brown and tender, turning once. Add the 2 tablespoons sugar. Cook and stir gently until sugar is dissolved and pears are glazed.

3. To assemble, place scoops of ice cream in 8 dessert bowls. Spoon a pear half and some butter mixture around the ice cream in each bowl. Top with the chocolate sauce.

MAKES 8 SERVINGS.

Per serving: 538 cal., 33 g total fat (20 g sat. fat), 132 mg chol., 119 mg sodium, 56 g carbo., 3 g fiber, 7 g pro.

*Note If pears are larger, cut into sixths or eighths (should have about 16 pieces).

Raspberry-Pecan Bars

Prep: 15 minutes **Bake:** 45 minutes
Oven: 350°F

　1　cup butter, softened
　1　cup sugar
　1　egg
2¼　cups all-purpose flour
　1　cup chopped pecans
　1　10-ounce jar raspberry preserves

1. Preheat oven to 350°F. In a large mixing bowl beat butter with an electric mixer on medium to high for 30 seconds. Add sugar; beat until combined. Add the egg; beat until combined. Beat in flour until crumbly. Stir in pecans. Measure 1½ cups of the mixture. Set aside.

2. Press the remaining flour mixture into the bottom of an ungreased 8×8×2-inch baking pan. Spread preserves evenly over crust, leaving a ½-inch border around sides. Crumble reserved mixture over the top.

3. Bake cookies for 45 to 50 minutes until top is golden brown. Cool in pan on a wire rack. Cut into bars. **MAKES 16 BARS.**

Per bar: 308 cal., 17 g total fat (8 g sat. fat), 44 mg chol., 92 mg sodium, 38 g carbo., 1 g fiber, 3 g pro.

Raspberry-Pecan Bars

Blueberry-
Lemon Tarts

Praline Crunch Bars

Prep: 10 minutes **Bake:** 12 minutes
Stand: 5 minutes **Chill:** 10 minutes
Oven: 350°F

  1 18-ounce roll refrigerated sugar cookie
     dough
  ½ cup toffee pieces
  ½ cup finely chopped pecans
  1 12-ounce package miniature semisweet
     chocolate pieces
  ⅓ cup toffee pieces

1. Preheat oven to 350°F. In a large resealable plastic bag place cookie dough, the ½ cup toffee pieces, and the pecans; knead to combine. Press dough evenly over the bottom of an ungreased 13×9×2-inch baking pan.
2. Bake for 12 to 15 minutes or until golden brown. Sprinkle with chocolate pieces immediately after baking. Let stand for 5 to 10 minutes or until softened, then spread evenly over the bars. Sprinkle with the ⅓ cup toffee pieces.
3. Chill for 10 to 15 minutes or until chocolate is set. Cut into bars.

MAKES 28 BARS.

Per bar: 191 cal., 11 g total fat (4 g sat. fat), 8 mg chol., 105 mg sodium, 19 g carbo., 2 g fiber, 1 g pro.

To Store Cover and chill for up to 3 days or freeze for up to 1 month.

Blueberry-Lemon Tarts

Start to Finish: 10 minutes

  ⅓ cup sour cream
  ⅓ cup purchased lemon curd or orange curd
  1 2.1-ounce package miniature phyllo dough
     shells (15)
  ¼ cup fresh blueberries
     Sifted powdered sugar (optional)

1. In a small bowl stir together sour cream and lemon curd. Divide sour cream mixture among phyllo dough shells. Top with blueberries. If desired, sprinkle with powdered sugar. **MAKES 15 TARTS.**

Per tart: 56 cal., 2 g total fat (1 g sat. fat), 7 mg chol., 18 mg sodium, 8 g carbo., 1 g fiber, 1 g pro.

Praline
Crunch Bars

Lemon Cream Tart

Prep: 30 minutes **Bake:** 35 minutes
Cool: 1 hour **Chill:** 2 hours **Oven:** 350°F

  1 16.5-ounce package lemon bar mix
  ½ cup finely chopped macadamia nuts
  1 8-ounce package cream cheese, softened
  1 teaspoon vanilla
  1 teaspoon finely shredded lemon peel
  1 8-ounce carton sour cream
  1 tablespoon sugar
  1½ to 2 cups fresh berries (blueberries,
       raspberries, and/or blackberries)
       Fresh mint leaves, cut into long, thin strips
       (optional)

1. Preheat oven to 350°F. Prepare lemon filling mixture according to package directions for lemon bar mix; set aside. Press packaged lemon bar crust mixture into the bottom of a 10-inch springform pan or a 9×9×2-inch baking pan. Sprinkle macadamia nuts evenly over crust; press gently into crust. Bake about 10 minutes or until light brown. Cool on a wire rack.
2. Meanwhile, in a medium mixing bowl combine cream cheese and ½ teaspoon of the vanilla; beat with an electric mixer on medium to high until smooth. Add lemon filling mixture; beat until combined. Stir in lemon peel. Pour cream cheese mixture evenly over the crust in the pan.
3. Bake about 25 minutes or until filling is set. Cool on wire rack for 1 hour. Cover and chill for 2 to 24 hours.
4. Just before serving, in a small bowl stir together sour cream, sugar, and the remaining ½ teaspoon vanilla. Spread sour cream mixture over tart. Sprinkle fresh berries and, if desired, mint leaf strips evenly over tart.

MAKES 12 TO 16 SERVINGS.

Per serving: 190 cal., 16 g total fat (8 g sat. fat), 82 mg chol., 109 mg sodium, 7 g carbo., 5 g fiber, 4 g pro.

Quick Tip When purchasing shelled nuts, such as macadamia nuts, look for nuts that are plump, crisp-looking, and uniform in color and size. Avoid those that are shriveled or discolored. Store nuts in an airtight container in a cool place. Refrigerate shelled nuts for up to 4 months or freeze them for up to 8 months.

Raspberry
Cheesecake
Shake

Cranberry-Pumpkin Bread Pudding with Brandy-Butter Sauce

Prep: 20 minutes **Bake:** 55 minutes
Stand: 15 minutes **Oven:** 350°F

     4 eggs, lightly beaten
     2 egg yolks, lightly beaten
     4 cups milk
     1 cup sugar
     1 15-ounce can pumpkin
    ¼ cup brandy
 1½ teaspoons pumpkin pie spice
     9 slices whole wheat bread, cut into
          ½-inch cubes (about 8 cups)
     1 cup dried cranberries
     1 recipe Brandy-Butter Sauce

1. Preheat oven to 350°F. In a very large
bowl combine eggs, egg yolks, milk, sugar,
pumpkin, brandy, and pumpkin pie spice.
Add bread cubes and cranberries; mix well.
Let stand for 15 minutes. Transfer to a lightly
greased 3-quart rectangular baking dish.
2. Bake, uncovered, about 55 minutes or until
a knife inserted in the center comes out
clean. Cool slightly. Serve warm with
Brandy-Butter Sauce. **MAKES 15 SERVINGS.**

Brandy-Butter Sauce In a small saucepan
melt ½ cup butter over medium heat. Stir in
1½ cups powdered sugar until mixture is
smooth. Stir in 2 egg yolks; cook and stir just
until bubbly. Remove from heat. Stir in 1 to
2 tablespoons brandy. Serve warm.

Per serving: 338 cal., 12 g total fat (6 g sat. fat), 136 mg
chol., 216 mg sodium, 49 g carbo., 3 g fiber, 7 g pro.

Raspberry Cheesecake Shake

Start to Finish: 10 minutes

     1 12-ounce package frozen unsweetened
          red raspberries, thawed
     1 3-ounce package cream cheese, softened
    ¼ teaspoon almond extract
     1 quart vanilla ice cream, softened
     2 12-ounce cans or bottles cream soda
          Fresh raspberries (optional)

1. In a blender combine raspberries, cream
cheese, and almond extract; add half of the
ice cream and ½ cup of the cream soda.
Cover and blend until smooth.
2. Pour into six 16-ounce glasses. Add a
scoop of the remaining ice cream to each
glass. Top with the remaining cream soda.
3. If desired, garnish with fresh raspberries.
Serve immediately. **MAKES 6 SERVINGS.**

Per serving: 305 cal., 15 g total fat (9 g sat. fat), 54 mg
chol., 130 mg sodium, 36 g carbo., 2 g fiber, 4 g pro.

Cranberry-
Pumpkin
Bread Pudding
with Brandy-
Butter Sauce

Easy, Pleasing Peppermint Stick Pie

Easy, Pleasing Peppermint-Stick Pie

Prep: 10 minutes **Freeze:** 4 hours
Stand: 5 minutes

1 half-gallon peppermint ice cream, softened
1 chocolate-flavor crumb pie shell
1 12-ounce jar fudge ice cream topping
Crushed peppermint candies (optional)

1. In a chilled large bowl stir the ice cream until softened.

2. Spoon ice cream into pie shell, spreading evenly. Return to freezer; freeze at least 4 hours or until serving time.

3. To serve, let pie stand at room temperature for 5 minutes before cutting. Meanwhile, warm the fudge topping following microwave directions on jar. Serve pie with warmed topping and, if desired, peppermint candies. **MAKES 8 SERVINGS.**

Per serving: 554 cal., 24 g total fat (13 g sat. fat), 63 mg chol., 474 mg sodium, 72 g carbo., 1 g fiber, 8 g pro.

Today's French Silk Pie

Prep: 35 minutes **Bake:** 13 minutes
Chill: 5 hours **Oven:** 450°F

1 recipe Baked Pastry Shell
¾ cup butter, softened
¾ cup sugar
1 cup semisweet chocolate pieces, melted and cooled
1 teaspoon vanilla
¾ cup refrigerated or frozen egg product, thawed
Whipped cream (optional)
Chocolate curls (optional)

1. Prepare Baked Pastry Shell; set aside.

2. For filling, in a large mixing bowl beat butter and sugar with an electric mixer on medium about 4 minutes or until fluffy. Stir in chocolate and vanilla. Gradually add egg product, beating on high and scraping sides of bowl constantly until light and fluffy.

3. Pour the filling into Baked Pastry Shell. Cover and chill for at least 5 hours. If desired, serve with whipped cream and chocolate curls. **MAKES 10 SERVINGS.**

Baked Pastry Shell Preheat oven to 450°F. In a large bowl stir together 1¼ cups all-purpose flour and ¼ teaspoon salt. Using a pastry blender, cut in ⅓ cup shortening until pieces are pea size. Sprinkle 1 tablespoon cold water over part of the mixture; gently toss with a fork. Push moistened dough to the sides of the bowl. Repeat moistening dough, using 1 tablespoon cold water at a time, until all the dough is moistened (4 to 5 tablespoons cold water total). Form dough into a ball. On a lightly floured surface use your hands to slightly flatten dough. Roll dough from center to edge into a circle about 12 inches in diameter. To transfer pastry, wrap it around the rolling pin. Unroll pastry into a 9-inch pie plate. Ease into pie plate, being careful not to stretch pastry. Trim pastry to ½ inch beyond edge of pie plate. Fold under extra pastry. Crimp edge as desired. Generously prick bottom and all around where bottom and side meet in pie plate with a fork. Line pastry with a double

thickness of foil. Bake for 8 minutes. Remove foil. Bake for 5 to 6 minutes more or until golden. Cool on a wire rack. Makes one 9-inch pie shell.

Per serving: 378 cal., 24 g total fat (10 g sat. fat), 37 mg chol., 229 mg sodium, 38 g carbo., 0 g fiber, 4 g pro.

Cherry and Chocolate Pastry Hearts

Prep: 15 minutes **Bake:** 15 minutes
Cool: 1 hour **Oven:** 375°F

½ of a 17.25-ounce package frozen puff pastry sheets (1 sheet), thawed
¾ cup canned cherry pie filling
8 teaspoons fudge ice cream topping
2 tablespoons chopped nuts

1. Preheat oven to 375°F. On a lightly floured surface unfold pastry sheet. Using a 3½- to 4-inch heart-shape cookie cutter, cut out pastry, discarding scraps or reserving for another use. Place pastry hearts on an ungreased baking sheet.

2. Bake for 15 to 18 minutes or until puffed and golden. Cool completely on a wire rack. Split pastry hearts horizontally; fill with pie filling. Drizzle with fudge topping; sprinkle with nuts. **MAKES 8 SERVINGS.**

Per serving: 193 cal., 11 g total fat (0 g sat. fat), 0 mg chol., 144 mg sodium, 22 g carbo., 0 g fiber, 2 g pro.

Quick Tip Serve these filled pastry hearts immediately so they stay crisp. If they sit too long, they get soggy.

There's hardly a soul who doesn't love a slice of cool and creamy peppermint-chocolate pie—for the holidays or on a hot summer day.

Index

In-a-Pinch Substitutions

It can happen to the best of cooks: Halfway through a recipe, you find you're completely out of a key ingredient. Here's what to do:

Recipe Calls For:	You May Substitute:
1 square unsweetened chocolate	3 Tbsp. unsweetened cocoa powder + 1 Tbsp. butter/margarine
1 cup cake flour	1 cup less 2 Tbsp. all-purpose flour
2 Tbsp. flour (for thickening)	1 Tbsp. cornstarch
1 tsp. baking powder	¼ tsp. baking soda + ½ tsp. cream of tartar + ¼ tsp. cornstarch
1 cup corn syrup	1 cup sugar + ¼ cup additional liquid used in recipe
1 cup milk	½ cup evaporated milk + ½ cup water
1 cup buttermilk or sour milk	1 Tbsp. vinegar or lemon juice + enough milk to make 1 cup
1 cup sour cream (for baking)	1 cup plain yogurt
1 cup firmly packed brown sugar	1 cup sugar + 2 Tbsp. molasses
1 tsp. lemon juice	¼ tsp. vinegar (not balsamic)
¼ cup chopped onion	1 Tbsp. instant minced
1 clove garlic	¼ tsp. garlic powder
2 cups tomato sauce	¾ cup tomato paste + 1 cup water
1 Tbsp. prepared mustard	1 tsp. dry mustard + 1 Tbsp. water

How to Know What You Need

Making a shopping list based on a recipe can be tricky if you don't know how many tomatoes yields 3 cups chopped. Here are some handy translations:

When the Recipe Calls For:	You Need:
4 cups shredded cabbage	1 small cabbage
1 cup grated raw carrot	1 large carrot
2½ cups sliced carrots	1 pound raw carrots
4 cups cooked cut fresh green beans	1 pound beans
1 cup chopped onion	1 large onion
4 cups sliced raw potatoes	4 medium-size potatoes
1 cup chopped sweet pepper	1 large pepper
1 cup chopped tomato	1 large tomato
2 cups canned tomatoes	16-oz. can
4 cups sliced apples	4 medium-size apples
1 cup mashed banana	3 medium-size bananas
1 tsp. grated lemon rind	1 medium-size lemon
2 Tbsp. lemon juice	1 medium-size lemon
4 tsp. grated orange rind	1 medium-size orange
1 cup orange juice	3 medium-size oranges
4 cups sliced peaches	8 medium-size peaches
2 cups sliced strawberries	1 pint
1 cup soft bread crumbs	2 slices fresh bread
1 cup bread cubes	2 slices fresh bread
2 cups shredded Swiss or cheddar cheese	8 oz. cheese
1 cup egg whites	6 or 7 large eggs
1 egg white	2 tsp. egg white powder + 2 Tbsp. water
4 cups chopped walnuts or pecans	1 pound shelled